THE WORKS OF SHAKESPEARE

EDITED FOR THE SYNDICS OF THE
CAMBRIDGE UNIVERSITY PRESS
BY
JOHN DOVER WILSON

CYMBELINE

EDITED BY
J C. MAXWELL

CYMBELINE

CAMBRIDGE

AT THE UNIVERSITY PRESS

1968

PUBLISHED BY
THE SYNDICS OF THE CAMBRIDGE UNIVERSITY PRESS
Bentley House, P.O. Box 92, 200 Euston Road, London, N.W.1
American Branch: 32 East 57th Street, New York, N.Y. 10022

First edition 1960
First paperback edition 1968

First printed in Great Britain at the University Press, Cambridge
Reprinted in Great Britain by Hazell Watson & Viney Ltd,
Aylesbury, Bucks.

CONTENTS

PREFATORY NOTE

With some Observations on the Vision
in the last Act

By undertaking full responsibility for the ensuing volume Mr J. C. Maxwell once again places me very much in his debt. And subscribers will be glad to learn that he is already busily engaged upon *Henry VIII*; that *King Lear* for which Professor Duthie and I are jointly responsible and *Coriolanus* which I am tackling single-handed are both now in the press; and that when these three are published, some time in 1960, it is hoped, or earlier, they will complete the tale of thirty-seven plays belonging to the accepted canon. After that will follow the *Poems* and the *Sonnets*, which Mr Maxwell and I plan to share between us, while Mr Peter Ure has kindly consented to edit for me the un-canonical *Two Noble Kinsmen* which many consider to be by Shakespeare and Fletcher working in collaboration, and which thus has probably as much right as *Pericles* to be included in the Works. It begins to look therefore as if this edition, hopefully launched as a ten-year project in 1921, under the sporting title of *The New Shakespeare*, may reach its conclusion some forty years later.

Unlike most previous editors, Mr Maxwell can find, he tells us, no grounds for believing that Shakespeare was not the sole author of *Cymbeline*. He is even ready to accept as genuine the Vision at 5. 4. 30 ff. which critics as eminent and as diverse as Pope and Johnson, Edmund Chambers and Granville-Barker dismiss as 'a spectacular theatrical interpolation'. I quote Chambers's words, and must confess that I find myself subscribing to them.

It cannot be denied that the Vision had become an integral part of the play before the text left Shakespeare's hands, and must therefore be held to carry his imprimatur, since the references to it in the following scene (5. 5. 426 ff.) are indisputably his. The case too for its authenticity seems to have been much strengthened of late through the discovery by Mr Wilson Knight and others of parallels between it and other plays written by Shakespeare at the same period. Yet such parallels, I suggest, might have occurred in works by another dramatist familiar with the plays in question, and though I am not proposing Marston as a candidate, the well-known echoes of Shakespeare in *The Malcontent* illustrate the sort of thing I have in mind. The most striking of the parallels in the Vision is for example that in the opening lines:

> No more, thou thunder-master, show
> Thy spite to mortal flies,

which is an obvious reflexion of Gloucester's cry in *King Lear*:

> As flies to wanton boys are we to the gods;
> They kill us for their sport.

But though Shakespeare often repeats himself, does he ever do so after this crude fashion elsewhere? To my mind the passage is not repetition but imitation, and a bad one at that.

Further, when the circumstances in which he and the company stood at the time *Cymbeline* was first produced are considered, it is not difficult to see how he might have agreed to a spectacular interpolation by another writer. By 1609–10 he was probably often at Stratford, and the text of *Cymbeline* like that of other late plays contains some of those long and detailed stage-directions which suggest that he could not feel certain of being present to supervise rehearsal.[1] It was a time of change for the company too; this being the year when they began playing at the Blackfriars Theatre as well as at the Globe. Now the Blackfriars, an indoor candle-lighted playhouse, was much more suitable for the creation of theatrical illusion than an open-air one and served a more sophisticated and more fashionable audience. And though it would be going too far to claim these conditions as responsible for the episodic structure and fairyland atmosphere of Shakespeare's last plays, those plays assuredly ministered to the taste of a public nourished on the court masques which, especially after the advent of Inigo Jones in 1607, became the rage of Jacobean London.[2] The Vision in *Cymbeline* was clearly designed in response to this taste, and it is even possible that Inigo Jones was called in to produce it, inasmuch as a Jupiter riding astride an eagle and grasping thunderbolts in one hand is the subject of one of his designs, now at Chatsworth, for the masque of *Tempe Restored* which he produced in 1632.[3] In any case in 1610 such a flight was a new and thrilling development of the theatrical machines and was probably the play's chief attraction for most of the audience.[4]

Let us then imagine Shakespeare at Stratford with his hands full of local and domestic affairs, suddenly receiving word from London that his company wished

[1] See W. W. Greg, *The Shakespeare First Folio* (1955), pp. 398, 404, 412.

[2] See G. E. Bentley, *Shakespeare Survey*, I (1948), 38–50.

[3] The design is reproduced as Fig. 45 in Allardyce Nicoll's *Stuart Masques* (1937).

[4] See J. C. Adams, *The Globe Playhouse* (1942), pp. 336–41.

INTRODUCTION

I. *Date and Authenticity*

The first recorded mention of *Cymbeline* is by Simon Forman.[1] The performance he describes is not likely to have been the first, but we cannot be sure how much earlier the play is. The commonly accepted dates for Shakespeare's 'romances' are still those proposed by Chambers: *Cymbeline*, 1609–10; *The Winter's Tale*, 1610–11; *The Tempest*, 1611–12;[2] but *The Tempest* is the only one that is at all securely dated, in 1611. Even the relative dating of the other two is uncertain, though it is reasonable to associate the greater artistic assurance of *The Winter's Tale* with a later date, which is also supported by the fact that Shakespeare undoubtedly knew the Boccaccio source of *Cymbeline* when he wrote *The Winter's Tale*.[3] I think Chambers's date for *The Winter's Tale* may well be a year too late. There is a fairly close verbal parallel between *The Winter's Tale*, 4. 4. 129–32 and *Philaster*, 4. 4. 2–6,[4] which seems to me most easily explained as an echo of the former by the latter; and *Philaster* is not later than 8 October 1610.[5] (Parallels which Nosworthy[6] cites between *Philaster*

---

[1] See Stage-history, p. xliii.

[2] E. K. Chambers, *William Shakespeare* (1930), I, 271; the dating is in terms of theatrical seasons.

[3] See *The Winter's Tale*, Herford cited in note on 4. 4. 778–85 in this edition.

[4] Noted by E. M. W. Tillyard, *Shakespeare's Last Plays* (1938), p. 9. The Shakespeare passage is reminiscent also of *Pericles*, 5. 3. 44–5, as Malone noted.

[5] E. K. Chambers, *The Elizabethan Stage* (1923), III, 223.

[6] Arden edition of *Cymbeline* (1955), p. xxxix; cf. below, 5. 2. 2–6 n.

and *Cymbeline* are less persuasive, though the mention
in *Philaster*, 4. 5. 115 of 'Augustus Caesar', who has
nothing to do with the subject, may, as he suggests, be
due to a recollection of *Cymbeline*.) If *The Winter's
Tale* is 1609–10,[1] then perhaps *Cymbeline* is 1608–9.[2]
This is the season to which Chambers attributes
Pericles, but an earlier date seems more probable.[3] It
may well be that, as Nosworthy suggests, the composi-
tion of *Cymbeline* and *The Winter's Tale* 'was more or
less simultaneous or, at any rate, that both had been
written, revised and prepared for the stage before either
was actually performed, with consequent cross-fertilisa-
tion';[4] if the first performance of *Cymbeline* was a public
one, it cannot have been earlier than December 1609,
when the theatres reopened for the first time since
August 1608.

The exclusively Shakespearian authorship of *Cymbeline* has not been as radically challenged as has that of
Pericles or of *Henry VIII*, but the play lies under more
suspicion than either *The Winter's Tale* or *The Tempest*. The Variorum edition, left in an unsatisfactory
state by H. H. Furness at his death and published in
1913, contains a number of arbitrary assertions in
Introduction and Notes which, taken together, would
deny a good deal of the play to Shakespeare; and H.
Granville-Barker in 1930 was still sufficiently under the
influence of this sort of criticism to hold that 'a fair

---

[1] Thorndike's claim (see *The Winter's Tale* in this
edition, pp. x–xi) that the dance in *The Winter's Tale*, 4. 4,
is a borrowing from Jonson's masque *Oberon* (1 January
1611), does not strike me as plausible.

[2] There were private performances in London during this
season, though the plague prevented public ones (Chambers,
The Elizabethan Stage, IV, 351).

[3] See *Pericles* in this edition, pp. 88–9.

[4] Arden *Cymbeline*, p. xvi.

amount of the play—both of its design and execution—
is pretty certainly not Shakespeare's'.[1] Granville-
Barker's own positive contribution to the criticism of
the play goes a long way towards undermining the
foundations of this view, and the play's substantial
integrity is generally accepted today. But there is one
part that has more often than not been denied to Shakespeare from Pope onwards: the Vision of 5. 4, which
even such a conservative critic as Sir Edmund Chambers
rejects as 'a spectacular theatrical interpolation'.[2]
Certainly the central part of this is a passage which few
would be sorry to attribute to another hand, but I cannot feel that the evidence for denying it to Shakespeare
is at all strong.[3]

The first question to be asked is: if there is an interpolation, how extensive is it? Pope rejected the whole
of 5. 4 after line 29, and also 5. 5. 425–57. Chambers,
against Dowden who 'would limit the extent of [the
interpolation] to 30–92, leaving the dumb-show, with
97–126, and possibly 93–6 as genuine', held that 'the
whole passage [that is, presumably, lines 30–150, with
the introductory dumb-show] must stand or fall together. And with it must of course go the reference to
the vision in 5. 5. 425–59 [=57]'.[4] It is certainly
difficult to limit the interpolation as strictly as Dowden
does, but it is equally difficult to regard 5. 4. 114–50 as
wholly non-Shakespearian. And if there is some Shakespearian verse in the episode, the onus of proof is on
those who claim to detect any alien material at all. On
stylistic grounds Posthumus's speech on waking is
surely unassailable, and with it must go the inscription
on the tablet and, of course (as Chambers recognizes),

[1] *Prefaces to Shakespeare, Second Series* (1930), p. 243.
[2] *William Shakespeare* (1930), I, 486.
[3] For the opposite view, see Prefatory Note.
[4] *William Shakespeare* (1930), I, 486.

the explanation of it in the final scene, where, again, it
would be hard to attribute to anyone but Shakespeare
such lines as

> whose containing
> Is so from sense in hardness that I can
> Make no collection of it.

Even before Posthumus wakes, Sicilius's speech at
ll. 114–19 has a Shakespearian ring. It seems clear,
then, that there was a vision, and an enigmatic tablet,
in Shakespeare's text of the play. The solution which
some scholars, such as Fleay, have sought is to accept
the stage-directions but reject the dialogue; and indeed
it is only the fourteeners of ll. 30–92 that have caused
real offence—ll. 93–113 pretty clearly stand or fall with
them, but I do not think that they would in isolation
have aroused any misgivings. The lines are certainly
crude, but then this is on any showing a scene in which
speech is subordinate to spectacle. The question as I see
it resolves itself into this: is there any positive reason to
suppose that Shakespeare would have presented this
Vision entirely in dumb-show, or alternatively, that he
would have assigned the task of writing about sixty[1]
lines of verse in a deliberately old-fashioned style[2] for a
special purpose to some playhouse hack, rather than
undertake it himself?[3] I can see none, and accept the
whole scene as Shakespeare's. I do so with no particular
enthusiasm; but I think the more thoroughgoing defence by G. Wilson Knight[4] deserves attention. His
elaborate discussion would probably not convince a

----

[1] According to the traditional lineation; in reality, thirty
fourteeners with three short lines.

[2] Cf. Hardin Craig, *Shakespeare Survey*, 1 (1948), 55.

[3] Nosworthy, p. xxxvi of his edition, is probably right in
tracing this passage to the introductory theophany in *Love
and Fortune*.

[4] *The Crown of Life* (1947), pp. 168–202.

hardened sceptic that the Vision is authentic, but it
shows that the author, whoever he was, knew the rest
of the play well. And against Chambers's rejection of
the whole episode, I regard as weighty Wilson Knight's
contention that, without it 'Cymbeline is left, alone
in this group, without any striking transcendental
moment',[1] though I think the phrase inflates the
significance of what the scene in fact offers.

II. Sources

The chronicle material which is used in Cymbeline
consists of scattered fragments in and about the reign of
'Kymbeline or Cimbeline the sonne of Theomantius',
whom Holinshed dates 33 B.C. to A.D. 2. (The historical Cunobellinus, whose dates are somewhat later,
need not detain us.)[2] These are collected in W. G.
Boswell-Stone's Shakespere's Holinshed (1896), and
present no features of special interest. All that Shakespeare takes for his main plot is the account of the
temporary refusal of tribute (either by Cymbeline or by
his son).[3] The battle, completely fictitious in this historical context, represents Shakespeare's closest borrowing from Holinshed in the play, but it is from the
History of Scotland, the account of the battle of
Luncarty (near Perth) in A.D. 976, where 'an husband-
man...named Haie' and his two sons play the parts of
Belarius and the princes. In the Appendix A (d) which

---

[1] Ibid. p. 191. A convenient conspectus of earlier views
is given in Appendix D of A. J. Wyatt's Warwick edition
[1897].

[2] There is a recent sketch by C. M. Matthews, 'The True
Cymbeline' (History Today, VII (1957), 755–9).

[3] The son, Guiderius, in Holinshed (Boswell-Stone,
p. 10). Shakespeare, as Dowden notes (p. xix of his
edition), agrees with Spenser, Faerie Queene, II. x. 50.

he has contributed to J. M. Nosworthy's Arden edition (1955), H. F. Brooks cites parallels which establish a reasonable probability that Shakespeare also consulted Blenerhasset's 'Complaint of Guidericus' in the *Second Part of the Mirrour for Magistrates* (1578), and some of the 'tragedies' in Higgins's *Mirrour for Magistrates* (1587; some already in earlier editions). What is of more interest than the details of Shakespeare's selection of historical material is its combination with the other elements in the play, and this will be discussed in a later section.

The non-chronicle material raises more complicated problems. The main source for the Italianate element in the story, in particular the wager plot, is, as has always been recognized, Boccaccio's *novella*, 'Bernabò da Genova e la moglie Zinevra' (*Decamerone*, II. 9). The central theme of this is familiar to students of folklore, but it is doubtful if any earlier versions are relevant to Shakespeare. One closely similar version of the story has certainly had some influence on *Cymbeline*: the late fifteenth-century German *Historie von vier Kaufmännern*, translated into English, through a Dutch intermediary, as *Frederick of Jennen*,[1] first published at Antwerp in 1518, and reprinted *c.* 1520 and *c.* 1560.[2]

Boccaccio's story opens with the laying of the wager, after Ambruogiuolo of Piacenza, at a gathering of Italian merchants in Paris, has challenged the claims made by Bernabò of Genoa on behalf of his wife's chastity. Ambruogiuolo goes to Genoa, and, having

---

[1] This is the name assumed by the heroine in masculine disguise.

[2] *Shakespeare Quarterly*, IX (1958), 262, records an article by Margaret Schlauch, *Kwartalnik Neofilologiczny*, IV (1957), 95–120, which argues that the translator may be Lawrence Andrewe (on whom see *Dictionary of National Biography*).

heard of the reputation borne by Bernabò's wife Zinevra, decides that his enterprise is hopeless. However, by bribing a woman who frequents Zinevra's house, he obtains access to her bedchamber concealed in a chest, notes the details of the room and a distinguishing mark on Zinevra's body, and steals a purse and other articles. When he returns to Paris, he finally convinces Bernabò, whom the other tokens have left sceptical, by telling him that Zinevra has a mole under her left breast, surrounded by about six golden hairs. Bernabò, on his return, stops twenty miles from Genoa and sends a servant with a letter summoning Zinevra to come to him. At the same time he instructs the servant to take her to a suitable place and kill her. When the moment comes, she pleads successfully for her life, and persuades the servant to return with some of her clothes as evidence that he has killed her. From this point, the story has no close resemblance to that of *Cymbeline*. Zinevra assumes masculine disguise and, after various adventures, finds herself in the service of the sultan at Alexandria; and after meeting Ambruogiuolo at Acre, in possession of some of the tokens stolen from her, she finally extracts a confession from him at Alexandria, in the presence of Bernabò, who has been summoned thither. Ambruogiuolo is anointed with honey and tied to a stake, where he is stripped to the bones by flies, wasps and gadflies, while Zinevra returns to live happily with Bernabò at Genoa.

It is evident that Boccaccio, whether in the original or in the French translation of Antoine le Maçon (1545, often reprinted),[1] is Shakespeare's main source. Most of his modifications are intelligible in the light of other elements in the plot, or from their dramatic effective-

---

[1] H. G. Wright, *Modern Language Review*, L (1955), 45–8, argues that Shakespeare probably used this translation for *All's Well that Ends Well*.

ness. There is, however, one detail that makes it clear that the *Frederick of Jennen* version was familiar to him in some form: the Frenchman, Dutchman and Spaniard who appear in the Folio stage-direction at the head of Act 1, scene 4, though the last two do not figure in the dialogue, correspond to the 'Courant of Spayne' and 'Borcharde of Fraunce' of that version, whose paragraph-heading notes that the four merchants involved 'were of foure diuers londes'.[1] Though this is the only completely convincing piece of evidence for Shakespeare's use of this form of the story, it is reasonable, once the case has been established, to attribute to it certain variations from Boccaccio which might otherwise be considered Shakespeare's own invention. *Frederick of Jennen*, unlike Boccaccio, has the wager proposed by the villain and not by the hero. Nosworthy notes also that the wager itself, five thousand 'gyldens' on each side, corresponds to Posthumus's offer (1. 4. 131) to wager 'gold' to Jachimo's ten thousand ducats, whereas in Boccaccio the wager eventually agreed on is five thousand florins on Bernabò's side and a thousand on Ambruogiuolo's. On the other hand there is no dispute about the terms in *Frederick*, whereas *Cymbeline*, like Boccaccio, has a more dramatic sequence: in Boccaccio, Bernabò first offers to stake his head, and the five thousand florins is Ambruogiuolo's substitute for this. Though the attempted seduction by Jachimo is Shakespeare's addition, the villain in *Frederick* does at least speak with the wife, and it is this—not, as in Boccaccio, what he hears of her reputation—that makes him give up hope. The hero is 'more sorier then he was before' when he receives the news of his wife's death, and, as in *Cymbeline*, the tokens which the servant

[1] All quotations from the Appendix to Nosworthy's edition, reproducing the reprint of the 1560 edition in J. Raith's *Historie von den vier Kaufleuten* (1936).

offers are stained with blood, from a pet lamb which the wife had conveniently brought with her.[1] At the end, the villain confesses that he deserves death, whereas in Boccaccio he is struck dumb with shame. In the bed-chamber scene the heroine is sleeping alone, as in *Cymbeline*, whereas in Boccaccio she has a little girl with her. But in general Shakespeare's agreements with Boccaccio against *Frederick* are more striking:[2] notably the light burning in the heroine's bedchamber (2. 2. 19), and the mole (2. 2. 38), for which *Frederick* has a black wart on the left arm. The presence of Philario in Act 2, scene 4 is of doubtful force. It contrasts with the stress on complete privacy in *Frederick*, but it is natural—though not, as Nosworthy thinks, necessary—to have Philario present as stake-holder, and Shakespeare de-parts from what is central to the story in Boccaccio: the presence of all the merchants who were there when the wager was made.

There is certainly not much in this part of *Cymbeline* which cannot be accounted for by Boccaccio and *Frederick* between them. But the possibility of a lost intermediate source, though regarded with healthy scepticism by recent scholars,[3] cannot be entirely dis-missed. W. F. Thrall, to whom we owe the most careful

[1] Nosworthy seems fanciful in thinking that this detail may be echoed in 3. 4. 97.

[2] W. F. Thrall, *Studies in Philology*, XXVIII (1931), 646–7, notes these and some less important agreements.

[3] For example, Nosworthy, p. xx of his edition; F. P. Wilson, *Shakespeare Survey*, 3 (1950), 16; for a *commedia dell'arte* derivative of Boccaccio that is in some respects closer to *Cymbeline* than is either Boccaccio or *Frederick*, see the *scenario* of *La Innocencia Rivenuta* printed by K. M. Lea, *Italian Popular Comedy* (1934), II, 568–72, and discussed by F. D. Hoeniger, *Shakespeare Quarterly*, VIII (1957), 133.

survey of coincidences between the play and *Frederick*, was not himself convinced that either the latter or Boccaccio was a direct source, and was inclined, with Gaston Paris,[1] to believe in a lost English source. At this point, another analogue, the anonymous *Westward for Smelts*, becomes relevant. This was formerly put forward as a source, on the strength of Steevens's assertion that he had seen a 1603 edition; but the only surviving edition is dated 1620, and follows a Stationers' Register entry of January in that year.[2] The parallels with *Cymbeline* that are not present in Boccaccio and *Frederick* are rather more impressive in Thrall's summary than in the story itself, which is much farther from the other three versions than they are from each other. The whole scene is transferred to England in the Wars of the Roses, which leads Thrall to talk of an 'English historical background, with enveloping war action';[3] but the way in which the Boccaccian and the historical elements are related in *Cymbeline* makes it quite unlike *Westward for Smelts*, in which the historical setting is a mere backcloth and does not involve new plot-material. It is very hard to imagine a common source for *Cymbeline* and *Westward for Smelts* which would account for the slender resemblances between them and would at the same time be close enough to Boccaccio to account for the Boccaccian material in Shakespeare which *Westward for Smelts* completely lacks. That the 'actors [are] not merchants but of the gentry' is also a slender parallelism. In *Cymbeline*, the

---

[1] *Romania*, XXXII (1903), 481–551. H. G. Wright, *Boccaccio in England from Chaucer to Tennyson* (1957), p. 220, n. 3, writes that in *Miscellanea di studi critici edita in onore di Arturo Graf* (1903), which I have not seen, Paris 'had already modified his views'.

[2] Nosworthy, p. xix, n. 1, by an oversight, has 1619.

[3] Dowden, p. xxix of his edition, had also noted this.

rank of the characters is determined by the historical plot; in *Westward for Smelts*, it is a mere matter of the use of the words 'gentleman' and 'gentlewoman'. The villain does, indeed, become acquainted with the heroine on terms of more familiarity than in *Frederick* (it will be recalled that they do not meet at all in Boccaccio), but the specific Shakespearian development is wholly lacking, and whereas the absence of an accomplice in *Cymbeline* arises from what is new in Shakespeare, in *Westward for Smelts* it is merely part of the general simplification the story undergoes: there is, for instance, no bodily token, and the hero is convinced solely by a stolen crucifix.[1] The resemblances detected between *Westward for Smelts* and the later part of the play are slight, and, such as they are, they may be the result of the author's recollections of *Cymbeline* on the stage. Thrall's final remark about 'the presence of most of these traits in *Miracle* or other versions of the "French" type' is not elaborated, and is not borne out by my reading of the *Miracle*. But a couple of rather striking resemblances between it and *Cymbeline*, which can scarcely be other than accidental, were pointed out long ago by Collier.[2] The villain boasts that he can overcome any woman if he can speak to her twice: 'Que je ne sçay femme vivant | Mais que deux foiz a li parlasse | Que la tierce avoir n'en cuidasse | Tout mon delit'[3] (cf. 1. 4. 127–30); and in his interview with the heroine, he accuses the hero of unfaithfulness to her at Rome: 'De Romme vien ou j'ay

---

[1] On some of these divergences, see W. W. Lawrence, *PMLA*, xxxv (1920), 398, n. 14 (on p. 400).

[2] *Shakespeare's Library* [1843], II, Introduction to section on *Cymbeline*, pp. xi–xii.

[3] 'Miracle de Oton, Roy d'Espaigne' in *Miracles de Nostre Dame*, ed. G. Paris and U. Robert, IV (1879), ll. 654–7.

laissié | Vostre seigneur, qui ne vous prise | Pas la queue
d'une serise.; | D'une garce s'est acointié | Qu'il a en si
grant amistié | Qu'il ne scet d'elle departir'[1] (cf. 1. 6.
98–138). If this represents parallel but independent
developments of the possibilities of the story—and
there seems no reason to doubt it—it is easy to accept
any slighter resemblances between different versions as
coincidental. They are only to be expected in a wide-
spread story with many variants. Thus in the Middle
English romance, *The Earl of Toulouse*, there is an
analogue to Jachimo's pretence at 1. 6. 155 ff. The
would-be seducer claims that he has not been in
earnest, 'Y did nothyng but you to afray'.[2]

The analogue that most readily comes to our minds
for Imogen and her stepmother is the story of *Snow
White*, and the parallel was drawn in 1864 by K.
Schenkl;[3] but no evidence has been found that this tale
was known in England in Shakespeare's day. Another
stepmother who has been pressed into service is the one
who seeks to procure the death of her stepson by poison
in Apuleius, *Metamorphoses*, x, 1–12.[4] There are some
resemblances between the stories, and there is no reason
why Shakespeare should not have read Apuleius; but,

---

[1] Ll. 728–33.

[2] In *Middle English Metrical Romances* (1930), ed. W. H.
French and C. B. Hale, l. 581. E. Greenlaw, who pointed
out the parallel in *PMLA*, XXI (1906), 617–18, exaggerated
the resemblance by calling it a claim 'that his purpose was
merely to prove her virtue'; what he says is, however, true
of another version he mentions (p. 620), *Sir Tryamoure*,
where the temptation is claimed to be 'But for a fondynge'
(ed. A. J. E. Schmidt (1937), l. 111). On the analogues of
The Earl of Toulouse, see P. Christophersen, *The Ballad of
Sir Aldingar* (1952), pp. 127–42.

[3] *Germania*, IX, 458 ff.

[4] See H. Reich, *Shakespeare Jahrbuch*, XLI (1905),
177–81.

as F. Brie has pointed out,[1] almost all the parallels, in a context closer to *Cymbeline*, also occur in Richard Johnson's *Tom a Lincolne* (Stationers' Register, 1599), Part I, ch. 5.

There is a good deal in *Cymbeline* that cannot be traced either to Holinshed or to Boccaccio (plus *Frederick of Jennen*). Is it all of Shakespeare's own invention? The view put forward by A. H. Thorndike[2] that he was indebted to Beaumont and Fletcher tragicomedy, and in particular to *Philaster*, is now generally rejected. There was never any good reason to believe that *Philaster* was earlier than *Cymbeline*, and there is nothing in *Cymbeline* itself to suggest such a debt. But the case is different with at least one, and probably two, earlier romantic comedies. In 1887 R. W. Boodle[3] argued that Shakespeare was indebted, especially in the Belarius part of the play, to the anonymous *Rare Triumphs of Love and Fortune* (performed 1582 and printed 1589). This claim is accepted by Nosworthy, and is fairly plausible. It turns chiefly on the role of Bomelio, who has lived in a cave as a hermit, after being banished from court by the father of the present king Phizantius[4] because of the false accusation of a treacherous friend. His son Hermione, whose parentage is at first unknown, is in love with Phizantius's daughter Fidelia, and is banished when her boorish brother Armenio reveals the affair to his father. The whole play is introduced by a dispute among the gods about the relative power of Venus and Fortune, pre-

[1] *Shakespeare Jahrbuch*, XLIV (1908), 167–70.
[2] *The Influence of Beaumont and Fletcher on Shakespeare* (1901); *contra*, C. M. Gayley, *Francis Beaumont: Dramatist* (1914), pp. 386–95.
[3] *Notes and Queries*, 7th series, IV (1887), 405.
[4] Nosworthy, p. xxv, makes Phizantius himself responsible for the banishment.

sided over by Jupiter. Nosworthy is probably right in regarding as beyond coincidence the fact that 'both plays present the banished lover as a pauper brought up at Court, both include a boorish brother,[1] and both introduce Jupiter and use him, flagrantly, as a *deus ex machina*'.[2] There is also the coincidence of names between Fidelia and Fidele, and the identity of the hero's name, Hermione, with that of the Queen in *The Winter's Tale*. Bomelio is also presented, in a rather inconsequential way, as a magician, and there is some crude stuff about the destruction of his books that may be faintly echoed in *The Tempest*.

Nosworthy suggests that *Love and Fortune* came to Shakespeare's notice among old romantic plays which the King's Men may have been thinking of reviving, as the title-page of the 1610 Quarto tells us that they did in fact revive *Mucedorus*.[3] This is very speculative, but if we admit that Shakespeare did by some means or other come to read this crude old play, the probability ought in consistency to be admitted that he also read a similar play, *Sir Clyomon and Sir Clamydes*. This play, 'sundry times Acted by her Maiesties Players',[4] was published in 1599, but probably belongs to the 1580's at the latest. Dyce, on the slenderest of evidence, attributed it to Peele, and Bullen retained it in his edition of Peele, though rejecting the attribution, in agreement with all modern scholars. In 1925, R. S.

---

[1] In *Cymbeline*, of course, only a stepbrother.

[2] P. xxvi.

[3] L. Kirschbaum, *Modern Language Review*, L (1955), 5, is 'loath to posit a revival by the King's Men on the basis of Jones's title-page alone'. Nosworthy, on no evidence that I know of, dates the revival 1607; for various possible dates, see E. K. Chambers, *The Elizabethan Stage* (1923), IV, 35.

[4] Was it still in the repertory when Shakespeare was a Queen's Man—if he ever was?

Forsythe[1] pointed out some fairly close parallels between it and *Cymbeline*, but his note has since been overlooked. In a way, it is less surprising that Shakespeare should have read this than *Love and Fortune*, for it has an engaging absurdity about it, and would have furnished him with good specimens of King Cambyses' vein. G. L. Kittredge[2] in fact attributed it to Thomas Preston, the author of *Cambyses*. Forsythe cited the train of events in scenes 11, 12, 15, 16 and 18 of *Clyomon and Clamydes*, in which Neronis, in love with Clyomon, is abducted by Thrasellus, King of Norway. She escapes in man's attire, and takes service with an old shepherd Corin. Clyomon sets out to rescue her, and meets and slays Thrasellus, and, with the help of Corin, buries him, hanging up his own golden shield and sword over the grave, with an inscription. Neronis enters, assumes from the shield that her beloved lies in the grave, and is dissuaded from suicide only by the personal intervention of Providence in visible shape. There is clearly a general resemblance to the circumstances of Imogen's discovery of the body of Cloten, but I doubt whether the evidence Forsythe cites is quite enough to prove his conclusion. But he weakens his case by stopping his comparison at scene 18, and so missing strong corroborative evidence in the succeeding scenes.[3] Neronis leaves the shepherd, and enters the

---

[1] *Modern Language Notes,* XL (1925), 313–14.

[2] *Journal of Germanic Philology,* II (1899), 8–9. It may be noted that the trick of appending a personal pronoun, as in 'Phœbus, he, "that wandering knight so fair"' (*1 Henry IV,* 1. 2. 15–16), usually to a proper name, is common in this play: ll. 22, 761, 765, 778, 827, 878, 886, 1020, 1041, 1201, 1506, 1615, 1800, 1897 (all references to Malone Society Reprint, 1913).

[3] Forsythe's concentration on Neronis at the grave is probably the result of his desire to modify a suggestion he

service of her beloved, Clyomon, as his page, though, as he is also in disguise, she does not know him. She assumes the name 'Cur Daceer', i.e. Cœur d'acier (l. 1639), and Clyomon comments on its meaning, 'heart of Steele' (l. 1640). It is surely more than a coincidence that Imogen gives a French name to her alleged former master (4. 2. 377), and that Lucius comments on the meaning of her own assumed name 'Fidele' (4. 2. 382–3). The final discovery bears no close resemblance to that in *Cymbeline*, though Neronis asks permission to talk in private with the Queen of Denmark (ll. 1948–50), as Imogen with Cymbeline (5. 5. 115–16).

Most other suggested sources are either improbable, or unimportant, or both. But there is some similarity between Imogen's adventures in Wales and those of Erminia in Tasso's *Gerusalemme Liberata*, cantos VII and XIX.[1]

There is, perhaps, more profit in noticing places where Shakespeare seems to have recalled his own earlier work,[2] and reminiscences of *King Lear* in particular are interesting. The speeches of Guiderius and Arviragus in 3. 3. 27–44 recall *Lear*, 2. 4. 211–15[3] (cf. also 2. 4. 270, 'Man's life's as cheap as beast's'), and there is a

had made earlier (*Modern Language Notes*, XXVII (1912), 110) that the scene in *Cymbeline* was indebted to *The First Part of Jeronimo*, 2. 4.

[1] W. J. Craig, in Dowden's edition (1903), p. xxxvii, and also in Craig's own 'Little Quarto' edition (1905), p. xxiii; and E. Greenlaw, *Studies in Philology*, XIII (1916), 142–4.

[2] See also K. Muir, *Shakespeare's Sources*, I (1957), p. 239.

[3] Furness noted the link between 'our pinching care' and *Lear*, 2. 4. 214, 'Necessity's sharp pinch'. A wider set of associations with 'pinch' is discussed by E. A. Armstrong, *Shakespeare's Imagination* (1946), chs. 5–6 (for *Cymbeline*, see p. 50).

more specific resemblance between *Cymbeline*, 3. 3. 42–4 and *Lear*, 5. 3. 8 ff. Professor G. Melchiori, who has called my attention to these parallels, notes that the scenes are linked 'by analogy of theme, i.e. lack of, and necessity of "experience"'; he also points out that the *Cymbeline* scene is a link between *Lear* and *The Tempest*: the 'cell of ignorance' (3. 3. 33) recalls 'the prison in which Lear wanted to seek refuge and liberation from the world, but at the same time looks forward to Prospero's cell'.

III. *The Play*

There is no need for a comprehensive survey of the fortunes of *Cymbeline* at the hands of critics. This has been given by Nosworthy in the Introduction to his Arden edition of 1955 (pp. xl–xlviii: with incidental comments at other points), and still more recently Philip Edwards has published an excellent study of the criticism of the Last Plays as a group in the present century,[1] which usefully balances Nosworthy's more specialized account. But an editor is bound to say where he stands on a number of central issues, and I shall confine my attention to these. It is probably impossible to avoid being accused either of blindness and insensitivity by critics who detect profound symbolism in the play, or of fantastication by their opponents. As far as *Cymbeline* is concerned (it might be different with *The Winter's Tale*), I prefer to run the former risk.

[1] *Shakespeare Survey*, 11 (1958), 1–18. Edwards apologizes for his emphasis on 'prevailing critical attitudes', which has not allowed him 'to discuss many important studies of individual plays' (p. 1). I confess to thinking that he pushes his method rather far when he makes no mention at all of Granville-Barker on *Cymbeline*.

Cymbeline was rather a popular play in the nineteenth century. Tennyson's fondness for it is well known,[1] and Swinburne made a point of ending his *Study of Shakespeare* (1880) 'upon the name of the woman best beloved in all the world of song and all the tide of time; upon the name of Shakespeare's Imogen'. But there was an older and more hard-headed tradition, whose classic expression is Johnson's comment at the end of the play:

This Play has many just sentiments, some natural dialogues, and some pleasing scenes, but they are obtained at the expence of much incongruity.

To remark the folly of the fiction, the absurdity of the conduct, the confusion of the names and manners of different times, and the impossibility of the events in any system of life, were to waste criticism upon unresisting imbecillity, upon faults too evident for detection, and too gross for aggravation.

Is it enough to say that most of these 'faults' are of the essence of romance and that Johnson did not understand romance? That would be too easy a way out: it is hard to deny an 'incongruity' that goes beyond the mere factual anachronisms and confusions that Johnson refers to; and it is perfectly possible to combine an enthusiastic admiration for others among the Last Plays with strong misgivings about *Cymbeline*. Certainly, hostile voices have not been silenced. Hazelton Spencer holds that 'of all the completed plays of Shakespeare's unaided authorship, this seems to me the poorest'.[2] Others have implicitly acquiesced in a belittling judgment on the play as a whole by continuing the nineteenth-century

---

[1] A copy was buried with him (*Alfred, Lord Tennyson: A Memoir by his Son* (1897), II, 429).

[2] *The Art and Life of William Shakespeare* (1940), p. 361. Contrast this with his judgment on *Pericles* a few lines earlier: 'a noble play'.

custom of lavishing all their praise on the single character of Imogen. Thus M. R. Ridley, after writing that 'four competent, and sometimes excellent, acts' are followed by 'a fifth act that...might put forward a reasonable claim to be the very worst last act in the world's drama', consoles himself with the thought that 'it is not the technique that we worry about, or ought to worry about. This play is Imogen, almost as much as *Hamlet* is Hamlet [an odd comment on the latter play as well!]. To all readers who read with attention she is, I suppose, of all Shakespeare's heroines, in either tragedy or comedy, the rarest, the most perfect piece of womanhood.'[1]

Yet the theatre gives the lie to such sweeping judgments. *Cymbeline*, with all its faults, can be relied upon—to put it no higher—for a good evening's entertainment;[2] nor does the spectator—whatever may be the case with the over-romantic reader, day-dreaming by his fireside—so 'anchor upon Imogen' as to be merely impatient with the scenes in which she does not appear. The play has somewhat the air of a cumbrous and over-elaborate mechanism that one feels ought not to work and that none the less does work. But it is perfectly possible for an effective stage play to be deficient in dramatic unity and coherence, and it will be well to approach *Cymbeline* without any prior determination to prove it a masterpiece. Our evaluation of it will have to proceed by way of a candid recognition of its odd combination of incongruous elements, and must not

[1] *William Shakespeare: A Commentary* (1936), pp. 109–10.
[2] Spencer, *The Art and Life of William Shakespeare*, p. 363, confesses that he has never seen it acted; and oddly conjectures that 'the right sort of dreamy performance could create a romantic haze through which the vicissitudes of its plot might prove alluring'. I can think of no surer recipe for killing the play.

attempt to deny or minimize such incongruities as we find.

It may be best to start with a few words on its probable place in Shakespeare's development. We have already seen[1] that its exact date is not certain, but there is no good reason to reject the general belief that it follows *Antony and Cleopatra* and *Coriolanus* but precedes *The Winter's Tale* and *The Tempest*. It is, then— if we hold that *Pericles* is a partly rewritten version of an originally non-Shakespearian play[2]—Shakespeare's first independent experiment in a new type of drama; and certainly some of the difficulties it presents can be plausibly linked with its experimental character.[3] To recognize this does not make the task of the critic particularly easy: he has simultaneously to decide what sort of effect Shakespeare was aiming at and to assess the degree of success he achieves; and the two kinds of judgment must constantly influence each other.

On the face of it, the problem of definition goes right back to the Folio, which classifies the play as a tragedy. I think it is rash to dismiss this as a mere blunder,[4] or to lay too much weight on such conjectures as that offered by Greg, that the arrival of the copy was delayed.[5] This may have been what happened, but it may also illuminate certain things about the play to look at it from the point of view of editors who were working with only the three categories, Comedies, Histories and Tragedies, and to ask whether the correct decision for them to make was self-evident. It is at least conceivable that they should have felt it the lesser of two evils to put this

[1] Pp. xi–xii.

[2] See pp. xvi–xxiii of the Introduction to *Pericles* in this edition.

[3] See Nosworthy's Introduction, pp. xlviii–lxii.

[4] See Note on the Copy, p. 125.

[5] *The Shakespeare First Folio* (1955), p. 414.

play, with its prominent public and national themes, along with *King Lear* rather than *The Winter's Tale*. Indeed, a purely external description of the materials used—partly British history[1] freely handled and partly romance—could make *Cymbeline* sound very like *King Lear*. The treatment, as well as the outcome, is of course about as different as it could be from the same author, but the potentially tragic elements, if less profound than, say, in *Measure for Measure*, are more obtrusive than in any of the earlier comedies. This is, in fact, the one play in the canon that seems to cry out for the description 'tragi-comedy' in order to avoid giving a false impression. (It is worth noting that another play that raises difficulties of classification for modern critics, and that had been treated as a comedy by its first publisher, *Troilus and Cressida*,[2] was a tragedy for Heminge and Condell.)

The term 'tragi-comedy' has, in fact, been found useful by a number of writers on *Cymbeline*. The theory propounded more than fifty years ago by A. H. Thorndike that in *Cymbeline*, *The Winter's Tale* and *The Tempest* Shakespeare was imitating the new Beaumont and Fletcher tragi-comedy, especially *Philaster*, is justly in disfavour nowadays. There is no evidence in its favour, and, as noted on p. xi, there is some reason to suppose that *Philaster* is later than *The*

[1] We do not always realize how exceptional *King Lear* and *Cymbeline* are in their choice of historical material. The earlier extant plays drawing on the pre-English period of British history are an unimpressive lot: *Gorboduc*, *The Misfortunes of Arthur*, *Leir*, *Locrine*, *Nobody and Somebody*, of which only the last is later than the early 1590's. After *Cymbeline* too there are only *Bonduca*, *Fuimus Troes*, *The Valiant Welshman*, *The Mayor of Queenborough*, and *The Birth of Merlin*, the last two perhaps revisions of pre-1600 plays.   [2] See p. ix of the edition in this series.

Winter's Tale. But it is significant that *Cymbeline* is the
only play of the three for which the theory has any
plausibility at all, though the differences between it and
Philaster remain much more important than the
resemblances;[1] and there are advantages in looking at
the play as an early example of a type of drama that was
entering upon a period of popularity. It is probably
correct to associate certain things in the *genre* with the
regular use of the Blackfriars Theatre by the King's
Men from 1609 (as the result of arrangements made in
1608), though the uncertainty of the exact date of
Cymbeline (see pp. xi–xii) should make us cautious of
seeing it as a play specifically written for those new
conditions,[2] and though we know that it was also
performed at the Globe.

The most helpful exploration of Shakespeare's tragi-
comic methods in *Cymbeline* is that offered by Granville-Barker in the second series of his *Prefaces to
Shakespeare* (1930), and his account is worth quoting
at some length. He begins by pointing out a number of
structural clumsinesses and other instances of artlessness
such as the naïvely informative soliloquies (e.g. 3. 3.
79–107), and he concedes, in my view, too much to
theories of composite authorship. But then he goes on:

> Allowing, then, for some collaboration, and some in-
> certitude besides, at what, are we to suppose, is he aiming,
> what sort of play is he setting out to write? And if the
> sophisticated artlessness is his, what end is this meant to
> serve? These are the practical questions to be answered here.

[1] See H. S. Wilson's essay in *English Institute Essays 1951*
(1952).
[2] See H. Granville-Barker, *Prefaces to Shakespeare,
Second Series* (1930), pp. 247–50 (accepting *Cymbeline* as
'about 1610'); F. P. Wilson, *Elizabethan and Jacobean*
(1945), p. 126; G. E. Bentley, *Shakespeare Survey*, 1 (1948),
38–50.

He has an unlikely story to tell, and in its unlikelihood lies not only its charm, but largely its very being; reduce it to reason, you would wreck it altogether. Now in the theatre there are two ways of dealing with the inexplicable. If the audience are to take it seriously, leave it unexplained. They will be anxious—pathetically anxious—to believe you; with faith in the dose, they will swallow a lot. The other plan is to show one's hand, saying in effect: Ladies and gentlemen, this is an exhibition of tricks, and what I want you to enjoy among other things is the skill with which I hope to perform them. This art, which deliberately displays its art, is very suited to a tragi-comedy, to the telling of a serious story that must yet not be taken too seriously, lest its comedy be swamped by its tragedy and a happy ending become too incongruous. Illusion must by no means be given the go-by; if this does not have its due in the theatre, our emotions will not be stirred. Nor should the audience be overwhelmed by the cleverness of the display; arrogance in an artist antagonises us. This is where the seeming artlessness comes in; it puts us at our ease, it is the equivalent of 'You see there is no deception.' But very nice steering will be needed between the make-believe in earnest and in jest.

Shakespeare sets his course (as his habit is, and here we may safely assume that it is he) in his very first scene. We have the immediately necessary tale of Posthumus and Imogen, and the more extraordinary one of the abduction of the princes is added. And when the First Gentleman brings the Second Gentleman's raised eyebrows down with

> How soe'er 'tis strange...

Yet it is true, sir.

we of the audience are asked to concur in the acquiescent

> I do well believe you.

For 'this', Shakespeare and the First Gentleman are telling us, 'is the play you are about to hear; and not only these facts, but their rather leisurely amplifying, and that supererogatory tale of Posthumus' birth, should show you the sort of play it is. There is trouble in the air, but you are not to be too strung up about it. Moreover, the way you are being told it all, the easy fall of this verse, with its light endings and spun-out sentences, should be wooing you into the right mood. And this talk about Cassibelan is to help you back into a fabulous past in which these romantic things may legitimately happen. So now submit yourselves, please, to the illusion of them'.

The beginning, then—quite properly—inclines to make-believe in earnest, rendering to the theatre its normal due. And the play's story will follow its course, nor may any doubt of its likelihood be hinted; that is a point of dramatic honour. But in half a hundred ways, without actually destroying the illusion, Shakespeare can contrive to prevent us taking it too seriously.[1]

I think this conveys a great deal of the truth about the play, and it makes it easier to understand why it comes over on the stage as well as it does. By taking us into his confidence, the playwright counteracts any tendency to look for a depth of dramatic illusion that he has no intention of offering. But it may still be felt that this 'sophisticated artlessness' is wasteful of some of the richer potentialities of the material. To say that, on one side, the play belongs to the world of fairy-tale is true enough. Yet the best type of fairy-tale, accepted on its own terms, has a kind of seriousness, a kind of imaginative integrity, that *Cymbeline* lacks. This is perhaps most notably so with regard to the Queen, who does not have the bold simplicity of a fairy-tale figure of evil. We learn at an early stage that her plotting is to be ineffective—Cornelius comes forward to tell us so (1. 5. 33 ff.)—and there is surely a deliberate touch of deflating comedy in the announcement of her death. Cornelius's words might, in isolation, link her, if only momentarily, with Goneril and Lady Macbeth:

> With horror, madly dying, like her life,
> Which, being cruel to the world, concluded
> Most cruel to herself. (5. 5. 31–3)

[1] *Prefaces to Shakespeare, Second Series* (1930), pp. 244–6.

But they have been neutralized in advance by the ludicrous words with which Cymbeline has greeted the bare announcement of her death:

> Who worse than a physician
> Would this report become? But I consider
> By medicine life may be prolonged, yet death
> Will seize the doctor too.   (5. 5. 27–30)

This is not the work of a dramatist who wants his individual themes to have their full emotional effect.

Some have been offended when the same comic techniques are applied to Imogen, but there seems little doubt that, whether successful or not, they are deliberate. The best example is the scene in which Imogen awakes beside the headless body of Cloten, clad in Posthumus's garments. That she should think it is her husband is in the nature of things, but need Shakespeare have made her claim such positive recognition?—

> I know the shape of's leg; this is his hand;
> His foot Mercurial; his Martial thigh;
> The brawns of Hercules; but his Jovial face—
> Murder in heaven? How? 'Tis gone.
>
>   (4. 2. 309–12)

This is, for Granville-Barker,

from one point of view at least, dramatically inexcusable. It is a fraud on Imogen; and we are accomplices in it.... Imogen herself is put, quite needlessly, quite heartlessly, on exhibition. How shall we sympathise with such futile suffering? And surely it is a vicious art that can so make sport of its creatures.

All this is true. But tragi-comedy—in this phase of its development, at least—is a bastard form of art; better not judge it by too strict aesthetic law.[1]

It is doubtful critical method to put the blame on 'tragi-comedy' as an abstract category, but certainly

[1] *Ibid.* pp. 340–1.

what is equivocal about this scene is related to the things about the play that encourage us to introduce the category. What is questionable is whether Shakespeare, as Granville-Barker goes on to say, 'veils [the] crudity [of his trick] in beauty'.[1] Here as elsewhere, I think his technique is rather more like a deliberate pushing of the convention to extremes, with a strong encouragement to savour the comic implications. And when one thinks of the pasteboard pseudo-seriousness of *Philaster*, there is a great deal to be said for Shakespeare's choice.

This neutralization of strong emotional effects by means of comedy can be traced in other parts of the play as well. The historical and political side is an interesting example of this. The failure of the most solemn and sustained attempt to take this seriously—that of Wilson Knight—is instructive. For him, the play is 'concerned to blend Shakespeare's two primary historical interests, the Roman and the British, which meet here for the first time',[2] and at the end, 'Shakespeare's two national faiths are here married, his creative faith in ancient Rome, felt in the Roman dramas from *Titus Andronicus* to *Coriolanus*, and his faith in England';[3] he quotes in support the concluding six and a half lines. I do not think the whole play can make this impression on an unprepossessed reader or spectator. Any seriousness the war may have had is simply cancelled out by the perfunctory attribution of the refusal of tribute to the machinations of the Queen (5. 5. 458–64). It takes the eye of faith to see in this 'a strangely paradoxical harmony of war-negating peace, wherein the victor in fine humility acknowledges the loser's right'.[4]

This is not to say that the historical setting is mere back-cloth. As J. P. Brockbank has recently pointed

[1] *Prefaces to Shakespeare, Second Series* (1930), p. 341.
[2] *The Crown of Life* (1947), p. 130.
[3] *Ibid.* p. 166. [4] *Ibid.* p. 166.

out,[1] the whole body of Brutan historical material in Holinshed has a certain consonance with the romantic world of the play, and the broad contrast between British ingenuousness and Italian sophistication is probably more than a mere literary device.[2] But perhaps it is principally the absence of any strongly marked qualities in the 'historical' material that allows Shakespeare to treat it in as cavalier a fashion as he does. And it is because Roman material puts up more resistance to this de-actualizing than British that this side of the play is least satisfactory when it brings us into contact with the realities of the Roman empire. As Nosworthy writes, 'romance can carry a Cymbeline but not a Caesar; it can encompass a half-civilized Britain but not the ordered state of Rome'.[3]

The pastoral or arcadian element in the play is again something that Shakespeare seems to handle with humorous detachment. It is no accident that its first introduction is accompanied by an obtrusive example of the conventionally informative soliloquy (3. 3. 79–107), which prompted one of Johnson's bluntest comments, 'the latter part of this soliloquy is very inartificial, there being no particular reason why Belarius should now tell to himself what he could not know better by telling it'. Nosworthy sees a special difficulty in this part of the play about the relation of character to symbol, 'Arviragus and Guiderius, for instance, are successful as

[1] *Shakespeare Survey*, 11 (1958), 42–9.

[2] Brockbank, p. 45, quotes Harrison's *Description of Britaine*, ch. XX, 'we that dwell northward...are commonly taken to be men of great strength and little policie', and his favourable comparison of the English with 'Comineus and his countrimen'.

[3] Arden edition (1955), Introduction, p. l. Lytton Strachey's comments on 3. 1. 16–33 are also relevant here (*Literary Essays* (1948), p. 10).

symbols. There is no damaging reality about them, they
live in romantic surroundings, they speak beautiful
verse and intone exquisite lyrics. Yet, on the stage they
are unconvincing, an embarrassment to actor, producer
and audience';[1] and he adds a footnote, 'Perhaps I
exaggerate. In the performances which I have seen the
Princes have been sadly unconvincing.' I wonder
whether this is not part of a tendency to play down the
comedy. There are certainly fluctuations of tone, but I
find a good deal of stage vitality in the princes, and in
all the productions I have seen, the nonchalance of
Guiderius's 'I cut off's head' (5. 5. 295) has roused
genuine (and unembarrassed) laughter—'young prince
and young savage in a sentence', as Granville-Barker[2]
remarks on the slightly earlier lines, 'Let me end the
story: | I slew him there' (5. 5. 286–7). Shakespeare
leaves us with no excuse for being too solemn about the
'royal blood will out' business. His mocking treatment
is compatible with a genuine naïve charm about these
scenes, but we have only to think of *As You Like It* to
see the difference between what Shakespeare offers in
Cymbeline and the complex ironic exploration of
pastoral attitudes in the earlier play.

So far I have not explicitly considered the central
theme of the plot—the wager story. Part of the
difficulty is that it is not possible to describe it as
'central' with absolute confidence. Its place in the
economy of the play is an odd one. As far as Posthumus
is concerned, the main intrigue is played out as early as
the end of the second act—and what a feeble exit he is
given! When he reappears at the beginning of the last
act, his opening soliloquy makes a perfunctory link
between the earlier part of the play and the dénouement. But these facts do not in themselves prevent us

[1] P. li.

[2] *Prefaces to Shakespeare, Second Series* (1930), p. 284.

from treating the wager story as the main plot: it is certainly, as we have seen,[1] the part of the play for which Shakespeare has most purposefully combined his source-material. Yet here, too, we are conscious of a reluctance on Shakespeare's part to commit himself wholly to the claims of his material. Is there not some deliberate exaggeration in the picture of Posthumus drawn by the First Gentleman in the opening scene— a sense of 'too good to be true'? Certainly the context of 'sophisticated artlessness' should prevent us from becoming too deeply involved.

Does Jachimo introduce an inappropriate kind of dramatic reality into the world of the play? Shakespeare has certainly done something even here to discourage too complete seriousness. As Granville-Barker remarks, 'no tragically-potent scoundrel, we should be sure, will ever come out of a trunk'.[2] But there is a vigour and tenseness about the scenes in which he appears that makes them more of isolated set-pieces than any individual scenes are in Shakespeare's greatest plays, or even in the best of the plays not quite among the greatest. Jachimo remains the clearest example of Nosworthy's contention that 'there is, at times, a destructive reality about the main personages of the play'.[3]

I have not tried to do much more than follow out, in relation to various themes of the play, Granville-Barker's notion of 'sophisticated artlessness', with some suggestion that deliberate incongruity and comic exploitation of conventions is carried even further than he indicates. I think it is some confirmation of the general soundness of this viewpoint that theatrical critics have felt that *Cymbeline* on the stage calls for description in

[1] Pp. xvi–xix.
[2] *Prefaces to Shakespeare, Second Series* (1930), pp. 305–6.
[3] Arden edition (1955), Introduction, p. li.

paradoxical terms. Thus we find Henry James writing
of the Henry Irving production of 1896,[1]

The thing is a florid fairy-tale, of a construction so loose
and unpropped that it can scarce be said to stand upright at
all, and of a psychological sketchiness that never touches
firm ground, but plays, at its better times, with an indifferent
shake of golden locks, in the high, sunny air of delightful
poetry.

And Kenneth Tynan of the Stratford production of
1957,[2]

What [the producer] has done is to weld all the play's
manifold facets—its jokes and beheadings, its Roman
armies and Renaissance villainies—into the same experience:
and he has achieved this by throwing over the whole production a sinister veil of faery, so that it resembles a Grimm
fable transmuted by the Cocteau of 'La Belle et la Bête'.

There is, however, a little more to be said. I mentioned earlier the ecstatic praise given by some critics to
Imogen, whom they have felt to make up for, or to
render unimportant, many defects in the rest of the
play. A good deal of nonsense has been talked about
her, from Swinburne downwards. This is partly because she conforms so well to one of the favourite male
stereotypes of female character: as Hazlitt (a favourable
example of this type of critic) writes, 'No one ever hit
the true perfection of the female character, the sense of
weakness leaning on the strength of its affections for
support, so well as Shakespear'.[3] But the very possibility of concentrating thus on a single character shows
the lack of the finest kind of dramatic integration in the

---

[1] *The Scenic Art* (New Brunswick, 1948; London, 1949),
p. 282; the review is reprinted from *Harper's Weekly*,
21 November 1896.
[2] *The Observer*, 7 July 1957, p. 13.
[3] *Works*, ed. P. P. Howe (1930), IV, 180.

play as a whole. Certain immediately attractive qualities of freshness and spontaneity may be more prominent
in Imogen than in Perdita or Miranda—and perhaps a
representative of 'Nature' is specially welcome in this
play with its excess of a certain kind of 'Art'—but she
means much less for her play than they do for theirs:
largely because there is so much less for her to mean.

Finally, there is the side of the play that is normally
given more prominence in accounts which stress its
relation to the other 'Last Plays': themes of loss and
recovery, reconciliation, rebirth, with a sense of the
deeper rhythms of life reflected in the stage action.
Cymbeline has less of this than (pre-eminently) *The
Winter's Tale, The Tempest,* or even *Pericles.*[1] But
what there is lies in an odd and rather fascinating way
behind the surface action, and the occasional glimpses
of it have a special power and charm. The best example
of this playing off of intrigue against underlying theme
is in the interchange between Guiderius and Arviragus
over the body of the supposedly dead Fidele. Arviragus's lines are among the most subtly evocative passages in the play, and carry overtones of the cyclical
processes of death and renewal:[2]

> With fairest flowers,
> Whilst summer lasts, and I live here, Fidele,
> I'll sweeten thy sad grave. Thou shalt not lack
> The flower that's like thy face, pale primrose, nor
> The azured harebell, like thy veins; no, nor
> The leaf of eglantine, whom not to slander,

[1] F. R. Leavis makes the point in his very judicious 'The
Criticism of Shakespeare's Last Plays: A Caveat' (*Scrutiny*,
X (1941–2), 339–45; reprinted in *The Common Pursuit*
(1952)).

[2] For emphasis on these themes in recent criticism, together with a salutary warning against letting it go too far,
see Philip Edwards in *Shakespeare Survey*, 11 (1958), 7–8.

> Out-sweet'ned not thy breath. The ruddock would
> With charitable bill—O bill sore shaming
> Those rich-left heirs that let their fathers lie
> Without a monument!—bring thee all this;
> Yea, and furred moss besides, when flowers are none,
> To winter-ground thy corse.   (4. 2. 218–29)

From the point of view of plot, Guiderius has some justification for breaking in with

> Prithee have done,
> And do not play in wench-like words with that
> Which is so serious.   (4. 2. 229–31)

Yet we know that 'that which is so serious' is mere make-believe, and it is the 'wench-like words', in spite of some degree of mere fancifulness about them, that touch, however fleetingly, on what is of more truly serious import. There is a similar contrast in the final scene between the surface virtuosity of the dénouement, 'a recognition scene to end all recognition scenes', as Mark Van Doren puts it,[1] and the rich poetry of the occasional phrase—

> Hang there like fruit, my soul,
> Till the tree die!   (5. 5. 263–4)

We may still feel that some of the more ecstatic accounts of the play go far beyond the truth, but there is something about it to which such general descriptions as 'tragi-comedy', 'melodrama' and 'romance' do less than justice.

J. C. M.

July 1958

[1] *Shakespeare* (1939), p. 305.

THE STAGE-HISTORY OF
CYMBELINE

Simon Forman saw the play, presumably at the Globe, on some date before 12 September 1611, when he died. In his *Bocke* [*sic* in MS.] *of Plaies* he tells the plot and names the characters as in Shakespeare, except that he writes 'Innogen'.[1] Our only other record of a pre-Restoration performance is in the office-book of Sir Henry Herbert, who was Master of the Revels from 1622 to 1673. It states that the play was acted 'at court by the Kings players' on 1 January '1633' (i.e. 1634), 'well likte by the kinge'.[2]

Our next information is of an adaptation which displaced Shakespeare's play on the stage for over sixty years. This was Thomas D'Urfey's *The Injured Princess*, or *The Fatal Wager*, published in 1682, and first performed that year at Theatre Royal—probably by the King's Company before the union with the Duke's in November.[3] Again staged at Lincoln's Inn Fields in 1702, and each year, 1717–20, with seventeen showings in all, it was last given at Covent Garden on

[1] See the whole passage printed in E. K. Chambers, *William Shakespeare* (1930), II, 338–9.

[2] See J. Q. Adams, *Dramatic Records of Sir Henry Herbert* (1917), p. 53; Chambers, *op. cit.* II, 352.

[3] See John Genest, *Some Account of the English Stage* (1832), I, 331–4. Allardyce Nicoll dates it '*c.* March' in his *History of the Restoration Drama, 1600–1700* (1923), p. 190 (4th ed. as vol. I of *A History of English Drama, 1660–1900* (1952), p. 408). G. C. D. Odell thinks that the production followed the union (*Shakespeare from Betterton to Irving* (1921), I, 67–9); Hazelton Spencer (*Shakespeare Improved* (1927), pp. 103–4) discusses, but rejects, this view.

four nights of 1737, and on 20 March 1738. There is
little to commend in D'Urfey's alteration, which
Genest thought 'vile'. He cut and rewrote freely.
Act 5, scenes 3 and 4, are omitted; Act 4, scene 2, is a
bad instance of his abridgements, with its sacrifice of the
lovely dirge. *Per contra* a sub-plot is added, of the
kidnapping of 'Clarinna', Pisanio's daughter, an
attendant of the princess. One major change affects
Pisanio's character. On getting his master's letter, he
believes in the princess's guilt and prepares to kill her,
but relents and merely deserts her. Later, after saving
Clarinna from violation, he is disarmed and blinded by
Cloten. The would-be ravisher, a drunken friend of
Cloten, is called Jachimo and Shakespeare's villain is
given the mongrel-French name of Shattillion; for the
wager is made in France as in Boccaccio's story.[1]
Similarly, but for no obvious reason, Leonatus Posthumus becomes Ursaces, and Imogen Eugenia. Before
the final scene, Ursaces meets and kills Shattillion, who
clears Eugenia's name before he dies. The dénouement
D'Urfey is then able to reduce to half its length.[2] Of
the three earliest productions we possess no casts. In
1718, Christopher Bullock was Shattillion to Keene's
Ursaces; their Eugenia was Mrs Thurmond. In 1720,
Ryan was Ursaces; in 1737 and 1738, he was the king,
and Delane took Ursaces. Boheme was Pisanio in
1720; in the two latest revivals this was Bridgwater's

---

[1] On D'Urfey's knowledge of the *Decameron*, see H. G.
Wright, *Boccaccio in England from Chaucer to Tennyson*
(1957), pp. 253, 277–84.

[2] Cf. Genest, *ibid.*; H. H. Furness, variorum ed. (1913),
pp. 481–9; Odell, *op. cit.* I, 69–70; Spencer, *op. cit.* pp. 313–
18. C. B. Hogan in his *Shakespeare in the Theatre: London,
1701–50* (1952), p. 102, analyses the play scene by scene,
noting its agreement with, and divergence from,
Shakespeare.

part. In all the latest three, in precisely the same way,
Bullock was followed by Walker as Shattillion and
Mrs Bullock by Mrs Templer as Eugenia.

The original play replaced D'Urfey from 1744 on-
wards, when, on 8 November, it was shown at the
Haymarket. Genest thinks that the Posthumus was
Theophilus Cibber, who himself tells us that Miss
Cibber played Imogen.[1] In April 1746, at Covent
Garden, the cast included Ryan (Posthumus), Hale
(Jachimo), Bridgwater (Pisanio), and Mrs Pritchard
(Imogen). Another alteration, by William Hawkins,
ex-Professor of Poetry at Oxford, was acted in the
Garden on 15 February 1759. He aimed at restoring
the unities; all the action was either in the King's
palace or in or near a Welsh forest; there is no wager
and no 'Jachimo'. Instead, Imogen has been traduced
by 'Pisanio', friend of Cloten, and is already disin-
herited and imprisoned when the play opens. She
escapes, disguised as a boy, with the aid of 'Philario'
(=Pisanio), friend of 'Leonatus'. Thereafter, with
added details and omissions, Hawkins works out the
story to the same final upshot; but rewrites most of
Shakespeare's own dialogue. The play thus mangled
was acted seven times, but was described as 'entirely
ruined by unpoetical additions and injudicious altera-
tions', though the *Dramatic Censor* deemed it of
'considerable merit'.[2] Ryan took Cymbeline, Ross was
Leonatus, and Mrs Vincent Imogen, after Mrs Bel-
lamy had declined the part. On 28 November 1761,
Garrick put on a *Cymbeline*, in essence Shakespeare's,
at Drury Lane, and acted Posthumus, with Holland as

[1] See Genest, IV, 172; Hogan, p. 104.
[2] See also Genest, IV, 561–4; Odell, I, 367–71; Hogan,
Shakespeare in the Theatre: London, 1751–1800 (1957),
p. 166; [Francis Gentleman], *Dramatic Censor* (1770),
p. 95.

Jachimo, Packer as Pisanio, and the actor-bookseller, Thomas Davies, as the King;[1] a Miss Bride was Imogen. Garrick's version, 'most judicious' in Genest's eyes, cut out the prison-scene with the masque, conflated some of the prose scenes with Cloten, and transposed several scenes or parts of scenes. He restored many lines omitted by Hawkins (too many, thought Gentleman),[2] and added few lines of his own.[3] There were sixteen performances till 28 April 1762. Garrick was well suited for Posthumus, and the part proved one of his best. Production followed production year by year; but in December 1763, when Garrick was away on the Continent, Powell took his place, and, though very inferior to him, retained it even after his return. The Imogens till 1767 included Mrs Yates, Miss Plym, and Mrs Palmer. In October 1768, Elizabeth Younge (later Mrs Pope) was the Drury Lane Imogen; it was her first appearance on the stage, and secured for her instant approbation. After the summer of 1767, Powell and Mrs Yates transferred to Covent Garden, acting their old parts there in December, with 'Gentleman Smith'[4] as Jachimo. (He had been 'Palador' [=Arvi-

---

[1] Churchill in his *Rosciad*, published March 1761, wrote of Davies (l. 322): 'he mouths a sentence as curs mouth a bone', a line which Dr Johnson believed led him to forsake the stage, but this he did only the next year.

[2] *Dramatic Censor*, II, 80, 84, 96. He deplored, for instance, the retention of the coarser lines in Posthumus' soliloquy (2. 5) and the 'violent trespass upon decorum' in letting Imogen speak, as in Shakespeare's 1. 6, of 'a Romish stew'.

[3] On Garrick's *Cymbeline*, cf. *op. cit.* II, 76–102; Genest, IV, 635; Hogan, *op. cit.* p. 167.

[4] For Smith, see Miss M. St C. Byrne's note in the Catalogue of the 1947 Arts Council's Exhibition in London, No. 37 (*A History of Shakespearean Production*, 1947, p. 14).

ragus] in Hawkins's adaptation in 1759.) At Drury
Lane Reddish and Mrs Baddeley carried on the play in
October. In December 1770, he, Palmer and Mrs
Spranger Berry (the former Mrs Dancer) were the trio.
Reddish's last appearance was in the Garden's production on 5 May 1779, when he was already showing
signs of imbecility. While dressing, and again whenever
he was 'off', the firm delusion possessed him that he was
there to act Romeo; yet the moment he stepped on to
the stage, his mind 'cleared and he acted Posthumus as
well as he had ever done.[1] At Covent Garden on
18 October 1784, the Posthumus was John Henderson,
regarded at the time as next in merit to the great
Garrick himself; in 1780 he had played the part in
Liverpool.

A little over a year before this London production,
Kemble had arrived from Dublin, and rapidly put
Henderson in the shade. His first Posthumus was at
Drury Lane on 21 November 1785, Smith and Mrs
Jordan being the other principals. Mrs Siddons—'the
only perfect Imogen I have ever seen', writes Boaden[2]
—joined her brother and Smith in the next revival
there on 29 January 1787 and acted the part five more
times in the next two months. She had previously been
Imogen four times in Bath and Bristol, 1779–81. With
her and Kemble at Drury Lane, the Garden productions were somewhat overshadowed, though from 1787
to 1800 the leads in them were Holman (first in 1786)
and Pope, with Mrs Pope as Imogen at the outset. In
March 1797, Palmer was Jachimo to Kemble's Posthumus, and Mrs Siddons was absent, but in the 1801
revival (12–19 February) she was back. The next year

[1] See James Boaden, *Memoirs of John Philip Kemble*
(1825), I, xvi–xvii; and *Samuel Reddish* (in the *Dictionary
of National Biography*), by Joseph Knight.
[2] James Boaden, *Memoirs of Mrs Siddons* (1827), II, 220.

on 29 January she gave her last London Imogen.[1] The 1801 production was remarkable for Kemble's elaborate setting with scenery by William Capon and Thomas Greenwood,[2] but it was not a financial success.[3] His brother Charles was Guiderius in it, a part he also played in some of Kemble's five remaining revivals, 1806–17. These were at Covent Garden, of which he was now the manager; with lesser Imogens than Mrs Siddons, they had a more qualified success. Cooke and Pope were the Jachimos to Kemble's Posthumus in 1806 and 1807; C. M. Young replaced them in 1812 and 1816. Kemble's last appearance in the part was on 30 May 1817; on 15 March, J. B. Booth had been in his place. On 20 March the Imogen was Miss Foote, later the Countess of Harrington; she had taken the part first in July 1816, when Conway was Posthumus.

On 30 June 1818, Macready gave his first London Posthumus at Covent Garden with Sarah Booth as Imogen; he had once before taken the part in Newcastle in 1812, when under nineteen. In October 1820, he was Jachimo to Charles Kemble's Posthumus, new roles for both of them; Miss Foote was again Imogen. Macready resumed Posthumus to Young's Jachimo in June 1822, still at Covent Garden; Miss Ann Maria Tree was Imogen. The next year Edmund Kean's one and only performance of Posthumus, to Young's Jachimo, was seen on 22 January at Drury Lane; but it was not one of his great successes. In 1825 Young was back at Covent Garden with Charles Kemble and Miss Foote. On 10 May 1826 she was at Drury Lane with Macready as Posthumus and George Bennett as

[1] Her absolute last was a year later in Dublin.

[2] See p. 120 of Sybil Rosenfeld's 'Scene Designs of William Capon' (*Theatre Notebook*, X (1955–6), 118–22).

[3] Herschel Baker, *John Philip Kemble* (1942), p. 242.

Jachimo. Exactly a year later Kemble and Young were together again at Covent Garden; on 23 May 1828, the Lane saw Macready and Miss Foote together for the last time, when Cooper, the Guiderius in Kean's *Cymbeline*, who had played Posthumus at Drury Lane in November 1826, was now Jachimo. On 9 February 1828, this theatre saw Young's last Posthumus, Cooper again Jachimo. Macready performed Posthumus twice more, but at Covent Garden: in October 1833 (Cooper, Jachimo; Miss Ellen Tree, afterwards Mrs Charles Kean, Imogen); and on 18 May 1837, with Elton as Jachimo, and the young Helen Faucit, most of her triumphs still in the future, as Imogen. Macready had not yet done with the play, however. When Samuel Phelps arrived in London he engaged him to act at Covent Garden, where, on 26 September 1838,[1] he staged the play, giving Posthumus to Phelps, Jachimo to Vandenhoff, and having Helen Faucit again as Imogen. Bennett acted Pisanio, and Elton and J. R. Anderson Guiderius and Arviragus; the play was acted twice.[2] In Macready's last *Cymbeline* (first night, 21 January 1847) he reverted to Jachimo and gave to J. R. Anderson Posthumus, to Elton Pisanio, to Phelps Belarius; Helen Faucit inevitably kept Imogen. This production, not so elaborate as some of Macready's previous, was commended for its 'taste and art'; it was shown four times.[3] Phelps opened his fourth season as manager at Sadler's Wells with *Cymbeline* on 23 August

[1] See John Coleman (*Memoirs of Samuel Phelps* (1886), p. 295). W. May Phelps and J. Forbes Robertson, *Life and Lifework of Samuel Phelps* (1886), p. 48, wrongly date it the 24th, when *Coriolanus* was actually the play.

[2] See William Archer, *William Charles Macready* (1890), pp. 148, 149.

[3] See May Phelps and Forbes Robertson, *op. cit.* pp. 55, 256; and William Archer, *op. cit.* pp. 135, 157.

1847; it was acted twenty-three times in about two months. He and Marston were Posthumus and Jachimo and Laura Addison Imogen; Bennett played Belarius and Mrs Marston the Queen. He received letters of high praise from Charles Dickens and John Forster for this production. His second revival was in October 1850, repeated in January; the third in September 1854. In the autumn and winter of 1857 he staged the play three times; his last production as manager was on 6 and 17 October 1860. But after retiring from Sadler's Wells he figured as Posthumus once more, on 15 October 1864 at Drury Lane, when Helen Faucit, now Mrs Theodore Martin, reappeared; Creswick was Jachimo, Marston's part till 1860. Phelps's Imogens from 1850 to 1857 were successively Miss Lyons, Miss Cooper and Mrs Charles Young (later Mrs Hermann Vezin). On 3 March 1865, Mrs Martin acted Imogen once more; but now with Walter Montgomery and J. R. Anderson in place of Phelps and Creswick.[1]

There followed some years of few productions, so that when Irving staged the play in 1896, *The Times* critique described it as 'practically new to the playgoing public'. There had been a revival in 1872 at the Queen's Theatre with George Rignold, John Ryder and Henrietta Hodson; in two later ones Miss Wallis was the Imogen: at Drury Lane with Edward Compton and John Ryder at the end of 1878, and at the Gaiety with J. R. Barnes and E. S. Willard early in 1883.

[1] For Helen Faucit's Imogens, see Henry Morley's account of her 1865 performance in his *Journal of a London Playgoer* (1866), pp. 346–8; and for her own conception of the part, her book, *On Some of Shakespeare's Female Characters* (1887), pp. 157–226. She thought Imogen 'Shakespeare's masterpiece of characterisation' (pp. 159–60).

present there have been nine revivals there, four of them on the birthday. Already in the lean years before Irving there had been two. In 1884 Charles Bernard had brought his company down from London for a one-week Festival; his leading lady, Miss Alleyn, whom he married during the week, took Imogen to Felix Pitt's Posthumus and J. G. Bayley's Jachimo; Robert Ayrton was the King. The next year he put it on again for one day. In 1909 F. R. Benson chose it for the birthday, himself acting Posthumus to Cyril Keightley's Jachimo and Margaret Halstan's Imogen; Murray Carrington was Pisanio. Bridges-Adams did the same in 1920, with Edmund Willard, Murray Carrington and Phyllis Relph as the leading characters. He also staged it in the Summer Festival that year, and once more in 1922. This time William Stack and Baliol Holloway played Posthumus and Jachimo to Ethel Carrington's Imogen; Stanley Lathbury was Cloten, Maurice Colbourne Guiderius and Dorothy Green the Queen. Before this a noteworthy London production had been Ben Greet's for the Old Vic on 4 March 1918, when Sybil Thorndike played Imogen to Mark Stanley's Posthumus and Russell Thorndike's Jachimo; Florence Saunders the Queen, and Mary Sumner Arviragus. In September 1923 at the Kew Theatre Miss Thorndike, once again Imogen, was partnered by Charles Carson and Robert Farquharson; Lewis Casson produced, also acting Philario and Arviragus, and G. R. Foss took the King. This same year Nugent Monck with his Norwich players produced the play at their Maddermarket Theatre. A second Old Vic revival, produced by Harcourt Williams, was given in November 1932, with Peggy Ashcroft as Imogen, George Devine as Posthumus and Malcolm Keen as Jachimo; Anthony Quayle (Caius Lucius), Roger Livesey (Pisanio), Alastair Sim (the King) and Marius Goring (Second

Lord and Gaoler), were other future 'stars' in the cast.
There were two revivals in 1937, one in Stratford and
one in London. Iden Payne produced in Stratford, and
the three principals were Godfrey Kenton, Donald
Wolfit, and Joyce Bland; Baliol Holloway was Cloten,
and Clement McCallin the King. There was a perma-
nent setting with insets to show changes of location.[1]
The London production at the Embassy Theatre sub-
stituted for the last act George Bernard Shaw's alteration (*Cymbeline Refinished*). Cuts and abridgements
reduce this to a single scene of some 280 lines where
Shakespeare's last scene alone runs to over 480. The
gaol scenes and vision are omitted; scene 1, with a single
line altered to put the battle in the past, follows a new
opening in which a Roman captain tells Philario of
their defeat; this merges into a short encounter of Posthumus with Jachimo, and then the final dénouement.
The remodelling certainly achieved a neater, less
drawn-out ending; but it involved a violent change of
tone from the fairy-tale and romantic atmosphere of the
earlier acts to the Shavian wit, with a touch of cynicism,
of the end. Shaw's reputation and the unfamiliarity of
theatre audiences with the original doubtless carried off
the incongruity. The *Times* reviewer, seeing it on its
first night, declared that the leading actors were
'visibly thrilled' by the 'new challenge' of a modern
note in the final act. These were Geoffrey Toone,
George Hayes, and Joyce Bland. In 1946 Donald
Wolfit produced the play at the Winter Garden,
partnered as in 1937 at Stratford by Godfrey Kenton,
with Rosalind Iden as Imogen. The same year it was
once again the Birthday Play at Stratford, produced by
Nugent Monck; Miles Eason, David King-Wood, and

[1] See Arts Council Exhibition Catalogue No. 99, p. 26,
and T. C. Kemp in Kemp and Trewin's *The Stratford
Festival* (1953), pp. 235–6.

Valerie Taylor took the leading parts, and Paul Scofield
was Cloten. In 1949 Stratford offered it once more and
included part of the masque, Michael Benthall pro-
ducing; McCallin and John Slater were Posthumus and
Jachimo, Leon Quartermaine was the King; Harry
Andrews and Kathleen Michael took Pisanio and
Imogen.[1] During the 1951 Festival of Britain the
Oxford University Festival Committee also included
the masque in its staging in the Great Quadrangle of
All Souls, with Nevill Coghill as Jupiter. The next year
there was an open-air production by Robert Atkins in
Regent's Park, and another in Sloane School, Chelsea,
with the boys as the actors, by the headmaster, Mr Guy
Boas, who again used Shaw's ending.[2] In 1953, a pro-
duction by Mr Willard Stoker was given in the Liver-
pool Playhouse. In September 1956 the third Old Vic
revival took place in pursuance of their plan to present
all Shakespeare's plays within five years. Michael
Benthall was the producer; Barbara Jefford and Leon
Gluckman played the wronged lovers, and Derek
Godfrey was Jachimo. The latest Stratford revival
(July 1957) was produced by Peter Hall, with Peggy
Ashcroft as Imogen, and Richard Johnson, Geoffrey
Keen and Mark Dignam as Posthumus, Jachimo and
Pisanio.

In the United States the play has not had the same
vogue. The first performance was at Southwark Theatre,
Philadelphia, by Lewis Hallam and David Douglass,
25 May 1767;[3] they took it to their New York, John

---

[1] See T. C. Kemp in *op. cit.* pp. 235-6; and a comment
by A. C. Sprague in his *Shakespearian Players and Performances*, 1953 (British ed. 1954), p. 162.

[2] See Guy Boas, *Shakespeare and the Young Actor* (1955),
pp. 67-72.

[3] This record, as well as much else in this paragraph, I
owe to the kindness of Mr C. B. Hogan of Yale.

Street, Theatre in December. William Winter (*Shakespeare on the Stage*, 3rd ser., p. 126) records fifteen performances between 1767 and 1797. Professor Odell notes just over a dozen in New York in the nineteenth century. J. B. Booth was Posthumus in 1823–4, William Conway in 1825 and 1827, and Edward Eddy in 1853. In May 1877, the genius of Adelaide Neilson ('the ideal Imogen...captivating all hearts', wrote Winter in the New York *Tribune*)[1] awakened interest in *Cymbeline*. Her four more appearances in April 1880, followed Fanny Davenport's the same month; Helena Modjeska[2] (1882, 1892), Margaret Mather (1890–91), and Julia Marlowe (later Mrs E. H. Sothern) from 1891 succeeded them. Viola Allen was another Imogen in 1906. The play has not been seen in New York since 1923, when there was a brief run at the 59th Street Theatre; the cast included E. H. Sothern (Posthumus), Frederick Lewis (Jachimo), V. L. Granville (Cymbeline), Julia Marlowe (Imogen). In 1936 *Cymbeline* was given at the Pasadena Playhouse, California.

C. B. YOUNG

August 1957

[1] See G. C. D. Odell, *Annals of the New York Stage* (1909– , still in progress), X, 190.
[2] On whom see Odell, XIII, 449, 559.

TO THE READER

A bracket at the beginning of a speech signifies an 'aside'.

CYMBELINE

The scene: Britain and Rome

CHARACTERS IN THE PLAY

CYMBELINE, *king of Britain*
CLOTEN, *son to the Queen by a former husband*
POSTHUMUS LEONATUS, *a gentleman, husband to Imogen*
BELARIUS, *a banished lord, disguised under the name of Morgan*
GUIDERIUS ⎱ *sons to Cymbeline, disguised under the*
ARVIRAGUS ⎰ *names of Polydore and Cadwal, supposed sons to Morgan*
PHILARIO, *friend to Posthumus* ⎱ *Italians*
JACHIMO, *friend to Philario* ⎰
CAIUS LUCIUS, *general of the Roman forces*
PISANIO, *servant to Posthumus*
CORNELIUS, *a physician*
A Roman Captain
Two British Captains
A Frenchman, friend to Philario
Two Lords of Cymbeline's court
Two Gentlemen of the same
Two Gaolers

Queen, *wife to Cymbeline*
IMOGEN, *daughter to Cymbeline by a former queen*
HELEN, *a lady attending on Imogen*

Lords, Ladies, Roman Senators, Tribunes, a Soothsayer, a Dutchman, a Spaniard, Musicians, Officers, Captains, Soldiers, Messengers, and other Attendants, Apparitions

CYMBELINE

[1. 1.] *Britain. The garden of*
Cymbeline's palace

Enter two Gentlemen

1 *Gentleman.* You do not meet a man but frowns.
   Our bloods
No more obey the heavens than our courtiers
Still seem as does the king.

2 *Gentleman.*   But what's the matter?

1 *Gentleman.* His daughter, and the heir of's
      kingdom, whom
He purposed to his wife's sole son—a widow
That late he married—hath referred herself
Unto a poor but worthy gentleman. She's wedded;
Her husband banished; she imprisoned. All
Is outward sorrow, though I think the king
Be touched at very heart.

2 *Gentleman.*   None but the king?   10

1 *Gentleman.* He that hath lost her too. So is
      the queen,
That most desired the match. But not a courtier,
Although they wear their faces to the bent
Of the king's looks, hath a heart that is not
Glad of the thing they scowl at.

2 *Gentleman.*   And why so?

1 *Gentleman.* He that hath missed the princess
   is a thing
Too bad for bad report; and he that hath her—
I mean, that married her, alack, good man!
And therefore banished—is a creature such

20 As, to seek through the regions of the earth
For one his like, there would be something failing
In him that should compare. I do not think
So fair an outward and such stuff within
Endows a man but he.

    2 *Gentleman*.   You speak him far.

    1 *Gentleman*. I do extend him, sir, within himself,
Crush him together, rather than unfold
His measure duly.

    2 *Gentleman*.   What's his name and birth?

    1 *Gentleman*. I cannot delve him to the root.
      His father
Was called Sicilius, who did join his honour
30 Against the Romans with Cassibelan,
But had his titles by Tenantius, whom
He served with glory and admired success,
So gained the sur-addition Leonatus;
And had, besides this gentleman in question,
Two other sons, who in the wars o'th'time
Died with their swords in hand; for which their father,
Then old and fond of issue, took such sorrow
That he quit being; and his gentle lady,
Big of this gentleman, our theme, deceased
40 As he was born. The king he takes the babe
To his protection, calls him Posthumus Leonatus,
Breeds him and makes him of his bed-chamber,
Puts to him all the learnings that his time
Could make him the receiver of, which he took
As we do air, fast as 'twas minist'red,
And in's spring became a harvest; lived in court—
Which rare it is to do—most praised, most loved;
A sample to the youngest, to th'more mature
A glass that feated them, and to the graver
50 A child that guided dotards. To his mistress,

For whom he now is banished, her own price
Proclaims how she esteemed him; and his virtue
By her election may be truly read,
What kind of man he is.

  2 *Gentleman*.   I honour him
Even out of your report. But pray you tell me,
Is she sole child to th'king?

  1 *Gentleman*.   His only child.
He had two sons—if this be worth your hearing,
Mark it—the eldest of them at three years old,
I'th'swathing clothes the other, from their nursery
Were stol'n, and to this hour no guess in knowledge   60
Which way they went.

  2 *Gentleman*.   How long is this ago?

  1 *Gentleman*. Some twenty years.

  2 *Gentleman*. That a king's children should be
      so conveyed,
So slackly guarded, and the search so slow
That could not trace them!

  1 *Gentleman*.   Howsoe'er 'tis strange,
Or that the negligence may well be laughed at,
Yet is it true, sir.

  2 *Gentleman*.   I do well believe you.

  1 *Gentleman*. We must forbear. Here comes
      the gentleman,
The queen and princess.   [*they go*

Enter the Queen, POSTHUMUS *and* IMOGEN

Queen. No, be assured you shall not find me, daughter, 70
After the slander of most stepmothers,
Evil-eyed unto you. You're my prisoner, but
Your gaoler shall deliver you the keys
That lock up your restraint. For you, Posthumus,
So soon as I can win th'offended king,

I will be known your advocate. Marry, yet
The fire of rage is in him, and 'twere good
You leaned unto his sentence with what patience
Your wisdom may inform you.
    Posthumus.   Please your highness,
80 I will from hence to-day.
    Queen.   You know the peril.
I'll fetch a turn about the garden, pitying
The pangs of barred affections, though the king
Hath charged you should not speak together. [*she goes*
    Imogen.   O
Dissembling courtesy! How fine this tyrant
Can tickle where she wounds! My dearest husband,
I something fear my father's wrath, but nothing—
Always reserved my holy duty—what
His rage can do on me. You must be gone,
And I shall here abide the hourly shot
90 Of angry eyes, not comforted to live,
But that there is this jewel in the world
That I may see again.
    Posthumus.   My queen, my mistress:
O lady, weep no more, lest I give cause
To be suspected of more tenderness
Than doth become a man. I will remain
The loyal'st husband that did e'er plight troth.
My residence in Rome at one Philario's,
Who to my father was a friend, to me
Known but by letter; thither write, my queen,
100 And with mine eyes I'll drink the words you send,
Though ink be made of gall.

Re-enter Queen

    Queen.   Be brief, I pray you.
If the king come, I shall incur I know not

How much of his displeasure. [*aside*] Yet I'll
    move him
To walk this way. I never do him wrong
But he does buy my injuries, to be friends;
Pays dear for my offences.   [*she goes*
   Posthumus.   Should we be taking leave
As long a term as yet we have to live,
The loathness to depart would grow. Adieu!
   Imogen. Nay, stay a little.
Were you but riding forth to air yourself,   110
Such parting were too petty. Look here, love:
This diamond was my mother's; take it, heart;
But keep it till you woo another wife,
When Imogen is dead.
   Posthumus.   How, how? another?
You gentle gods, give me but this I have,
And cere up my embracements from a next
With bonds of death. [*putting on the ring.*] Remain,
    remain thou here
While sense can keep it on. And, sweetest, fairest,
As I my poor self did exchange for you
To your so infinite loss, so in our trifles   120
I still win of you. For my sake wear this;
It is a manacle of love; I'll place it
Upon this fairest prisoner.
               [*putting a bracelet on her arm*
   Imogen.   O the gods!
When shall we see again?

       Enter CYMBELINE *and Lords*

   Posthumus.   Alack, the king!
   Cymbeline. Thou basest thing, avoid hence, from
    my sight!
If after this command thou fraught the court

With thy unworthiness, thou diest. Away!
Thou'rt poison to my blood.

    Posthumus.   The gods protect you,
And bless the good remainders of the court.
130 I am gone.   [*he goes*

    Imogen.   There cannot be a pinch in death
More sharp than this is.

    Cymbeline.   O disloyal thing,
That shouldst repair my youth, thou heap'st
A year's age on me.

    Imogen.   I beseech you, sir,
Harm not yourself with your vexation.
I am senseless of your wrath; a touch more rare
Subdues all pangs, all fears.

    Cymbeline.   Past grace? obedience?

    Imogen.   Past hope, and in despair; that way
         past grace.

    Cymbeline.   That mightst have had the sole son of
         my queen!

    Imogen.   O blessèd, that I might not; I chose
         an eagle,
140 And did avoid a puttock.

    Cymbeline.   Thou took'st a beggar, wouldst have
         made my throne
A seat for baseness.

    Imogen.   No, I rather added
A lustre to it.

    Cymbeline.   O thou vile one!

    Imogen.   Sir,
It is your fault that I have loved Posthumus:
You bred him as my playfellow, and he is
A man worth any woman; overbuys me
Almost the sum he pays.

    Cymbeline.   What, art thou mad?

Imogen. Almost, sir. Heaven restore me! Would
　　I were
A neat-herd's daughter, and my Leonatus
Our neighbour shepherd's son!

Re-enter Queen

Cymbeline.　　　　　　Thou foolish thing!　　150
[*to the Queen*] They were again together; you have done
Not after our command. Away with her,
And pen her up.
　　Queen.　　　　Beseech your patience. Peace,
Dear lady daughter, peace! Sweet sovereign,
Leave us to ourselves, and make yourself some comfort
Out of your best advice.
　　Cymbeline.　　　　Nay, let her languish
A drop of blood a day; and, being aged,
Die of this folly.　　　　[*Cymbeline and lords go*

Enter PISANIO

　　Queen.　　　　Fie, you must give way.
Here is your servant. How now, sir? What news?
　　Pisanio. My lord your son drew on my master.
　　Queen.　　　　　　　　Ha?　160
No harm, I trust, is done?
　　Pisanio.　　　　　There might have been,
But that my master rather played than fought,
And had no help of anger; they were parted
By gentlemen at hand.
　　Queen.　　　　I am very glad on't.
　　Imogen. Your son's my father's friend; he takes his part
To draw upon an exile. O brave sir!
I would they were in Afric both together;
Myself by with a needle, that I might prick
The goer-back. Why came you from your master?

170 *Pisanio.* On his command. He would not suffer me
To bring him to the haven; left these notes
Of what commands I should be subject to
When't pleased you to employ me.
      Queen.   This hath been
Your faithful servant. I dare lay mine honour
He will remain so.
      Pisanio.   I humbly thank your highness.
      Queen. Pray walk awhile.
      Imogen. About some half-hour hence, pray you
            speak with me.
You shall at least go see my lord aboard.
For this time leave me.   [*they go*

[1. 2.]   *The same. A public place*

Enter CLOTEN *and two Lords*

1 *Lord.* Sir, I would advise you to shift a shirt; the
violence of action hath made you reek as a sacrifice.
Where air comes out, air comes in; there's none abroad
so wholesome as that you vent.

Cloten. If my shirt were bloody, then to shift it.
Have I hurt him?

(2 *Lord.* No, faith; not so much as his patience.

1 *Lord.* Hurt him? his body's a passable carcass, if
he be not hurt. It is a throughfare for steel, if it be
10 not hurt.

(2 *Lord.* His steel was in debt; it went o'th'backside
the town.

Cloten. The villain would not stand me.

(2 *Lord.* No, but he fled forward still, toward your
face.

1 *Lord.* Stand you? You have land enough of your own; but he added to your having, gave you some ground.

(2 *Lord.* As many inches as you have oceans. Puppies!

Cloten. I would they had not come between us.　　20

(2 *Lord.* So would I, till you had measured how long a fool you were upon the ground.

Cloten. And that she should love this fellow, and refuse me!

(2 *Lord.* If it be a sin to make a true election, she is damned.

1 *Lord.* Sir, as I told you always, her beauty and her brain go not together. She's a good sign, but I have seen small reflection of her wit.

(2 *Lord.* She shines not upon fools, lest the reflection 30 should hurt her.

Cloten. Come, I'll to my chamber. Would there had been some hurt done!

(2 *Lord.* I wish not so; unless it had been the fall of an ass, which is no great hurt.

Cloten. You'll go with us?

1 *Lord.* I'll attend your lordship.

Cloten. Nay, come, let's go together.

2 *Lord.* Well, my lord.　　　　　　　　　　　*[they go*

[1. 3.]　　　*A room in Cymbeline's palace*

Enter IMOGEN *and* PISANIO

Imogen. I would thou grew'st unto the shores
　　　o'th'haven,
And questionedst every sail; if he should write
And I not have it, 'twere a paper lost

As offered mercy is. What was the last
That he spake to thee?

Pisanio.　　　　　It was his queen, his queen!

Imogen.　Then waved his handkerchief?

Pisanio.　　　　　And kissed it, madam.

Imogen.　Senseless linen, happier therein than I!
And that was all?

Pisanio.　　No, madam; for so long
As he could make me with this eye or ear

10　Distinguish him from the others, he did keep
The deck, with glove, or hat, or handkerchief,
Still waving, as the fits and stirs of's mind
Could best express how slow his soul sailed on,
How swift his ship.

Imogen.　　　　Thou shouldst have made him
As little as a crow, or less, ere left
To after-eye him.

Pisanio.　　Madam, so I did.

Imogen.　I would have broke mine eye-strings,
　　cracked them but
To look upon him, till the diminution
Of space had pointed him sharp as my needle;

20　Nay, followed him till he had melted from
The smallness of a gnat to air; and then
Have turned mine eye, and wept. But, good Pisanio,
When shall we hear from him?

Pisanio.　　　　　Be assured, madam,
With his next vantage.

Imogen.　I did not take my leave of him, but had
Most pretty things to say. Ere I could tell him
How I would think on him at certain hours
Such thoughts and such; or I could make him swear
The shes of Italy should not betray

30　Mine interest and his honour; or have charged him,

At the sixth hour of morn, at noon, at midnight,
T'encounter me with orisons, for then
I am in heaven for him; or ere I could
Give him that parting kiss which I had set
Betwixt two charming words, comes in my father,
And like the tyrannous breathing of the north
Shakes all our buds from growing.

Enter a Lady

Lady.   The queen, madam,
Desires your highness' company.
Imogen. Those things I bid you do, get
    them dispatched.
I will attend the queen.
    Pisanio.   Madam, I shall.   [*they go* 40

[I. 4.]   *Rome. Philario's house*

Enter PHILARIO, JACHIMO, *a Frenchman, a Dutchman,
and a Spaniard*

Jachimo. Believe it, sir, I have seen him in Britain;
he was then of a crescent note, expected to prove so
worthy as since he hath been allowed the name of.
But I could then have looked on him without the help
of admiration, though the catalogue of his endowments
had been tabled by his side, and I to peruse him by
items.
    Philario. You speak of him when he was less furnished
than now he is with that which makes him both without and within.   10
    Frenchman. I have seen him in France; we had very
many there could behold the sun with as firm eyes as he.

Jachimo. This matter of marrying his king's daughter, wherein he must be weighed rather by her value than his own, words him, I doubt not, a great deal from the matter.

Frenchman. And then his banishment.

Jachimo. Ay, and the approbation of those that weep this lamentable divorce under her colours are wonder-
20 fully to extend him, be it but to fortify her judgement, which else an easy battery might lay flat, for taking a beggar without less quality. But how comes it he is to sojourn with you? how creeps acquaintance?

Philario. His father and I were soldiers together, to whom I have been often bound for no less than my life.

Enter POSTHUMUS

Here comes the Briton. Let him be so entertained amongst you as suits with gentlemen of your knowing to a stranger of his quality. I beseech you all be better known to this gentleman, whom I commend to you as
30 a noble friend of mine. How worthy he is I will leave to appear hereafter, rather than story him in his own hearing.

Frenchman. Sir, we have known together in Orleans.

Posthumus. Since when I have been debtor to you for courtesies which I will be ever to pay and yet pay still.

Frenchman. Sir, you o'er-rate my poor kindness; I was glad I did atone my countryman and you; it had been pity you should have been put together, with so mortal a purpose as then each bore, upon importance of so
40 slight and trivial a nature.

Posthumus. By your pardon, sir, I was then a young traveller; rather shunned to go even with what I heard than in my every action to be guided by others' experiences; but upon my mended judgement—if I offend

not to say it is mended—my quarrel was not altogether
slight.

Frenchman. Faith, yes, to be put to the arbitrement
of swords, and by such two that would by all likelihood
have confounded one the other, or have fall'n both.

Jachimo. Can we with manners ask what was the 50
difference?

Frenchman. Safely, I think; 'twas a contention in
public, which may without contradiction suffer the
report. It was much like an argument that fell out last
night, where each of us fell in praise of our country
mistresses; this gentleman at that time vouching—and
upon warrant of bloody affirmation—his to be more
fair, virtuous, wise, chaste, constant, qualified, and less
attemptable than any the rarest of our ladies in France.

Jachimo. That lady is not now living; or this gentle- 60
man's opinion, by this, worn out.

Posthumus. She holds her virtue still, and I my mind.

Jachimo. You must not so far prefer her 'fore ours of
Italy.

Posthumus. Being so far provoked as I was in France,
I would abate her nothing, though I profess myself her
adorer, not her friend.

Jachimo. As fair and as good—a kind of hand-in-hand
comparison—had been something too fair and too good
for any lady in Britain. If she went before others I have 70
seen, as that diamond of yours outlustres many I have
beheld, I could not but believe she excelled many; but
I have not seen the most precious diamond that is, nor
you the lady.

Posthumus. I praised her as I rated her: so do I my
stone.

Jachimo. What do you esteem it at?

Posthumus. More than the world enjoys.

Jachimo. Either your unparagoned mistress is dead,
80 or she's outprized by a trifle.

Posthumus. You are mistaken: the one may be sold or
given, or if there were wealth enough for the purchase,
or merit for the gift; the other is not a thing for sale,
and only the gift of the gods.

Jachimo. Which the gods have given you?

Posthumus. Which by their graces I will keep.

Jachimo. You may wear her in title yours; but you
know strange fowl light upon neighbouring ponds.
Your ring may be stol'n too, so your brace of unprizable
90 estimations, the one is but frail and the other casual; a
cunning thief, or a that way accomplished courtier,
would hazard the winning both of first and last.

Posthumus. Your Italy contains none so accomplished
a courtier to convince the honour of my mistress, if in
the holding or loss of that you term her frail. I do
nothing doubt you have store of thieves; notwithstand-
ing, I fear not my ring.

Philario. Let us leave here, gentlemen.

Posthumus. Sir, with all my heart. This worthy signior,
100 I thank him, makes no stranger of me; we are familiar
at first.

Jachimo. With five times so much conversation, I
should get ground of your fair mistress; make her go
back even to the yielding, had I admittance, and opportunity to friend.

Posthumus. No, no.

Jachimo. I dare thereupon pawn the moiety of my
estate to your ring, which in my opinion o'ervalues it
something. But I make my wager rather against your
110 confidence than her reputation; and to bar your offence
herein too, I durst attempt it against any lady in the
world.

Posthumus. You are a great deal abused in too bold a persuasion, and I doubt not you sustain what you're worthy of by your attempt.

Jachimo. What's that?

Posthumus. A repulse; though your attempt, as you call it, deserve more—a punishment too.

Philario. Gentlemen, enough of this. It came in too suddenly; let it die as it was born, and I pray you be better acquainted. 120

Jachimo. Would I had put my estate and my neighbour's on th'approbation of what I have spoke—

Posthumus. What lady would you choose to assail?

Jachimo. Yours, whom in constancy you think stands so safe. I will lay you ten thousand ducats to your ring that, commend me to the court where your lady is, with no more advantage than the opportunity of a second conference, and I will bring from thence that honour of hers which you imagine so reserved. 130

Posthumus. I will wage against your gold, gold to it. My ring I hold dear as my finger; 'tis part of it.

Jachimo. You are a friend, and therein the wiser. If you buy lady's flesh at a million a dram, you cannot preserve it from tainting; but I see you have some religion in you, that you fear.

Posthumus. This is but a custom in your tongue; you bear a graver purpose, I hope.

Jachimo. I am the master of my speeches, and would undergo what's spoken, I swear. 140

Posthumus. Will you? I shall but lend my diamond till your return. Let there be covenants drawn between's. My mistress exceeds in goodness the hugeness of your unworthy thinking. I dare you to this match: here's my ring.

Philario. I will have it no lay.

Jachimo. By the gods, it is one. If I bring you no
sufficient testimony that I have enjoyed the dearest
bodily part of your mistress, my ten thousand ducats
150 are yours; so is your diamond too. If I come off, and
leave her in such honour as you have trust in, she your
jewel, this your jewel, and my gold are yours—provided
I have your commendation for my more free entertainment.

Posthumus. I embrace these conditions; let us have
articles betwixt us. Only, thus far you shall answer: if
you make your voyage upon her, and give me directly
to understand you have prevailed, I am no further your
enemy; she is not worth our debate. If she remain
160 unseduced, you not making it appear otherwise, for
your ill opinion and th'assault you have made to her
chastity, you shall answer me with your sword.

Jachimo. Your hand—a covenant. We will have these
things set down by lawful counsel, and straight away
for Britain, lest the bargain should catch cold and starve.
I will fetch my gold, and have our two wagers recorded.

Posthumus. Agreed.   [*Posthumus and Jachimo go*
Frenchman. Will this hold, think you?

Philario. Signior Jachimo will not from it. Pray let
170 us follow 'em.   [*they go*

[1. 5.]   *Britain. A room in*
                     Cymbeline's palace

             Enter Queen, Ladies, and CORNELIUS

Queen. Whiles yet the dew's on ground, gather
        those flowers;
Make haste. Who has the note of them?
   1 *Lady.*   I, madam.

Queen. Dispatch.   [*ladies go*
Now, master doctor, have you brought those drugs?
  Cornelius. Pleaseth your highness, ay. Here they
          are, madam.   [*presenting a small box*
But I beseech your grace, without offence—
My conscience bids me ask—wherefore you have
Commanded of me these most poisonous compounds,
Which are the movers of a languishing death,
But though slow, deadly.
  Queen.   I wonder, doctor,   10
Thou ask'st me such a question. Have I not been
Thy pupil long? Hast thou not learned me how
To make perfumes? distil? preserve? yea, so
That our great king himself doth woo me oft
For my confections? Having thus far proceeded—
Unless thou think'st me devilish—is't not meet
That I did amplify my judgement in
Other conclusions? I will try the forces
Of these thy compounds on such creatures as
We count not worth the hanging—but none human— 20
To try the vigour of them and apply
Allayments to their act, and by them gather
Their several virtues and effects.
  Cornelius.   Your highness
Shall from this practice but make hard your heart;
Besides, the seeing these effects will be
Both noisome and infectious.
  Queen.   O, content thee.

Enter PISANIO

[*aside*] Here comes a flattering rascal; upon him
Will I first work. He's factor for his master,
And enemy to my son. [*aloud*] How now, Pisanio?
Doctor, your service for this time is ended;   30

Take your own way.

(*Cornelius.*   I do suspect you, madam;
But you shall do no harm.

    Queen. [*to Pisanio*]   Hark thee, a word.

    (*Cornelius.* I do not like her. She doth think she has
Strange ling'ring poisons. I do know her spirit,
And will not trust one of her malice with
A drug of such damned nature. Those she has
Will stupefy and dull the sense awhile,
Which first perchance she'll prove on cats and dogs,
Then afterward up higher; but there is
40 No danger in what show of death it makes,
More than the locking up the spirits a time,
To be more fresh, reviving. She is fooled
With a most false effect; and I the truer
So to be false with her.

    Queen.   No further service, doctor,
Until I send for thee.

    Cornelius.   I humbly take my leave.   [*goes*

    Queen. Weeps she still, say'st thou? Dost thou
        think in time
She will not quench, and let instructions enter
Where folly now possesses? Do thou work.
When thou shalt bring me word she loves my son,
50 I'll tell thee on the instant thou art then
As great as is thy master; greater, for
His fortunes all lie speechless, and his name
Is at last gasp. Return he cannot, nor
Continue where he is. To shift his being
Is to exchange one misery with another,
And every day that comes comes to decay
A day's work in him. What shalt thou expect
To be depender on a thing that leans,
Who cannot be new built, nor has no friends

So much as but to prop him? [*the Queen drops the box:*
  Pisanio takes it up] Thou tak'st up   60
Thou know'st not what; but take it for thy labour:
It is a thing I made, which hath the king
Five times redeemed from death. I do not know
What is more cordial. Nay, I prithee take it;
It is an earnest of a further good
That I mean to thee. Tell thy mistress how
The case stands with her; do't as from thyself.
Think what a chance thou changest on; but think
Thou hast thy mistress still; to boot, my son,
Who shall take notice of thee. I'll move the king   70
To any shape of thy preferment, such
As thou'lt desire; and then myself, I chiefly,
That set thee on to this desert, am bound
To load thy merit richly. Call my women.
Think on my words.   [*Pisanio goes*
          A sly and constant knave;
Not to be shaked; the agent for his master,
And the remembrancer of her to hold
The hand-fast to her lord. I have given him that
Which, if he take, shall quite unpeople her
Of liegers for her sweet; and which she after,   80
Except she bend her humour, shall be assured
To taste of too.

        Re-enter PISANIO with Ladies

      So, so; well done, well done.
The violets, cowslips, and the primroses,
Bear to my closet. Fare thee well, Pisanio;
Think on my words.   [*Queen and ladies go*
  Pisanio.   And shall do.
But when to my good lord I prove untrue,
I'll choke myself—there's all I'll do for you.   [*goes*

[1. 6.] *The same. Another room in the palace*

Enter IMOGEN *alone*

Imogen. A father cruel and a step-dame false,
A foolish suitor to a wedded lady
That hath her husband banished. O, that husband,
My supreme crown of grief, and those repeated
Vexations of it! Had I been thief-stol'n,
As my two brothers, happy; but most miserable
Is the desire that's glorious. Blest be those,
How mean soe'er, that have their honest wills,
Which seasons comfort. Who may this be? Fie!

Enter PISANIO *and* JACHIMO

10 *Pisanio.* Madam, a noble gentleman of Rome,
Comes from my lord with letters.
    Jachimo.   Change you, madam?
The worthy Leonatus is in safety,
And greets your highness dearly.   [*presents a letter*
    Imogen.   Thanks, good sir;
You're kindly welcome.
    (*Jachimo.* All of her that is out of door most rich!
If she be furnished with a mind so rare,
She is alone th'Arabian bird, and I
Have lost the wager. Boldness be my friend;
Arm me audacity from head to foot;
20 Or, like the Parthian, I shall flying fight;
Rather, directly fly.
    Imogen. [*reads*] 'He is one of the noblest note, to
whose kindnesses I am most infinitely tied. Reflect
upon him accordingly, as you value your trust—
                                        LEONATUS.'
So far I read aloud.

But even the very middle of my heart
Is warmed by th'rest, and takes it thankfully.
You are as welcome, worthy sir, as I
Have words to bid you, and shall find it so
In all that I can do.

   Jachimo.   Thanks, fairest lady.   30
What, are men mad? Hath nature given them eyes
To see this vaulted arch and the rich crop
Of sea and land, which can distinguish 'twixt
The fiery orbs above and the twinned stones
Upon the numbered beach, and can we not
Partition make with spectacles so precious
'Twixt fair and foul?

   Imogen.   What makes your admiration?

   Jachimo. It cannot be i'th'eye—for apes
      and monkeys,
'Twixt two such shes, would chatter this way and
Contemn with mows the other; nor i'th'judgement— 40
For idiots in this case of favour would
Be wisely definite; nor i'th'appetite—
Sluttery, to such neat excellence opposed,
Should make desire vomit emptiness,
Not so allured to feed.

   Imogen. What is the matter, trow?

   Jachimo.   The cloyéd will,
That satiate yet unsatisfied desire, that tub
Both filled and running, ravening first the lamb,
Longs after for the garbage.

   Imogen.   What, dear sir,
Thus raps you? Are you well?

   Jachimo.   Thanks, madam, well. 50
[*to Pisanio*] Beseech you sir,
Desire my man's abode where I did leave him:
He's strange and peevish.

Pisanio.   I was going, sir,
To give him welcome.   [*goes*

Imogen. Continues well my lord? His health,
     beseech you?

Jachimo. Well, madam.

Imogen. Is he disposed to mirth? I hope he is.

Jachimo. Exceeding pleasant; none a stranger there
So merry and so gamesome: he is called
60 The Briton reveller.

Imogen.   When he was here
He did incline to sadness, and oft-times
Not knowing why.

Jachimo.   I never saw him sad.
There is a Frenchman his companion, one
An eminent monsieur, that, it seems, much loves
A Gallian girl at home. He furnaces
The thick sighs from him; whiles the jolly Briton—
Your lord, I mean—laughs from's free lungs, cries, 'O,
Can my sides hold, to think that man, who knows
By history, report, or his own proof,
70 What woman is, yea, what she cannot choose
But must be, will's free hours languish for
Assuréd bondage?'

Imogen.   Will my lord say so?

Jachimo. Ay, madam; with his eyes in flood
     with laughter.
It is a recreation to be by
And hear him mock the Frenchman. But heavens know
Some men are much to blame.

Imogen.   Not he, I hope.

Jachimo. Not he; but yet heaven's bounty towards
     him might
Be used more thankfully. In himself 'tis much;
In you, which I account his, beyond all talents.

Whilst I am bound to wonder, I am bound   80
To pity too.
  Imogen.   What do you pity, sir?
  Jachimo. Two creatures heartily.
  Imogen.   Am I one, sir?
You look on me: what wreck discern you in me
Deserves your pity?
  Jachimo.   Lamentable! What,
To hide me from the radiant sun, and solace
I'th'dungeon by a snuff?
  Imogen.   I pray you, sir,
Deliver with more openness your answers
To my demands. Why do you pity me?
  Jachimo. That others do,
I was about to say, enjoy your——But   90
It is an office of the gods to venge it,
Not mine to speak on't.
  Imogen.   You seem to know
Something of me, or what concerns me; pray you
Since doubting things go ill often hurts more
Than to be sure they do; for certainties
Either are past remedies, or, timely knowing,
The remedy then born—discover to me
What both you spur and stop.
  Jachimo.   Had I this cheek
To bathe my lips upon; this hand, whose touch,
Whose every touch, would force the feeler's soul   100
To th'oath of loyalty; this object, which
Takes prisoner the wild motion of mine eye,
Fixing it only here; should I, damned then,
Slaver with lips as common as the stairs
That mount the Capitol; join gripes with hands
Made hard with hourly falsehood—falsehood as
With labour; then by-peeping in an eye

Base and illustrous as the smoky light
That's fed with stinking tallow—it were fit
110 That all the plagues of hell should at one time
Encounter such revolt.

   Imogen.   My lord, I fear,
Has forgot Britain.

   Jachimo.   And himself. Not I
Inclined to this intelligence pronounce
The beggary of his change, but 'tis your graces
That from my mutest conscience to my tongue
Charms this report out.

   Imogen.   Let me hear no more.

   Jachimo. O dearest soul, your cause doth strike
     my heart
With pity that doth make me sick. A lady
So fair, and fastened to an empery
120 Would make the great'st king double, to be partnered
With tomboys hired with that self exhibition
Which your own coffers yield; with diseased ventures
That play with all infirmities for gold
Which rottenness can lend nature; such boiled stuff
As well might poison poison. Be revenged,
Or she that bore you was no queen, and you
Recoil from your great stock.

   Imogen.   Revenged?
How should I be revenged? If this be true—
As I have such a heart that both mine ears
130 Must not in haste abuse—if it be true,
How should I be revenged?

   Jachimo.   Should he make me
Live like Diana's priest betwixt cold sheets,
Whiles he is vaulting variable ramps,
In your despite, upon your purse—revenge it.
I dedicate myself to your sweet pleasure,

More noble than that runagate to your bed,
And will continue fast to your affection,
Still close as sure.
   Imogen.   What ho, Pisanio!
   Jachimo. Let me my service tender on your lips.
   Imogen. Away, I do condemn mine ears that have   140
So long attended thee. If thou wert honourable,
Thou wouldst have told this tale for virtue, not
For such an end thou seek'st, as base as strange.
Thou wrong'st a gentleman who is as far
From thy report as thou from honour, and
Solicits here a lady that disdains
Thee and the devil alike. What ho, Pisanio!
The king my father shall be made acquainted
Of thy assault. If he shall think it fit
A saucy stranger in his court to mart   150
As in a Romish stew, and to expound
His beastly mind to us, he hath a court
He little cares for and a daughter who
He not respects at all. What ho, Pisanio!
   Jachimo. O happy Leonatus! I may say,
The credit that thy lady hath of thee
Deserves thy trust, and thy most perfect goodness
Her assured credit. Blesséd live you long,
A lady to the worthiest sir that ever
Country called his; and you his mistress, only   160
For the most worthiest fit. Give me your pardon.
I have spoke this to know if your affiance
Were deeply rooted, and shall make your lord
That which he is new o'er; and he is one
The truest mannered, such a holy witch
That he enchants societies into him;
Half all men's hearts are his.
   Imogen.   You make amends.

Jachimo. He sits 'mongst men like a descended god;
He hath a kind of honour sets him off,
170 More than a mortal seeming. Be not angry,
Most mighty princess, that I have adventured
To try your taking of a false report, which hath
Honoured with confirmation your great judgement
In the election of a sir so rare,
Which you know cannot err. The love I bear him
Made me to fan you thus, but the gods made you,
Unlike all others, chaffless. Pray your pardon.
  Imogen. All's well, sir: take my power i'th'court
    for yours.
  Jachimo. My humble thanks. I had almost forgot
180 T'entreat your grace but in a small request,
And yet of moment too, for it concerns
Your lord; myself and other noble friends
Are partners in the business.
  Imogen.   Pray what is't?
  Jachimo. Some dozen Romans of us, and
    your lord—
The best feather of our wing—have mingled sums
To buy a present for the emperor;
Which I, the factor for the rest, have done
In France. 'Tis plate of rare device, and jewels
Of rich and exquisite form, their values great;
190 And I am something curious, being strange,
To have them in safe stowage. May it please you
To take them in protection?
  Imogen.   Willingly;
And pawn mine honour for their safety; since
My lord hath interest in them, I will keep them
In my bedchamber.
  Jachimo.   They are in a trunk,
Attended by my men. I will make bold

To send them to you, only for this night;
I must aboard to-morrow.

Imogen.   O, no, no.

Jachimo. Yes, I beseech; or I shall short my word
By length'ning my return. From Gallia   200
I crossed the seas on purpose and on promise
To see your grace.

Imogen.   I thank you for your pains;
But not away to-morrow!

Jachimo.   O, I must, madam.
Therefore I shall beseech you, if you please
To greet your lord with writing, do't to-night.
I have outstood my time, which is material
To th'tender of our present.

Imogen.   I will write.
Send your trunk to me; it shall safe be kept
And truly yielded you. You're very welcome. [*they go*

[2. 1.]   *Britain. Before Cymbeline's palace*

Enter CLOTEN *and two Lords*

Cloten. Was there ever man had such luck? when I
kissed the jack upon an upcast, to be hit away! I had
a hundred pound on't; and then a whoreson jackanapes
must take me up for swearing, as if I borrowed mine
oaths of him, and might not spend them at my pleasure.

1 *Lord.* What got he by that? You have broke his pate
with your bowl.

(2 *Lord.* If his wit had been like him that broke it, it
would have run all out.

Cloten. When a gentleman is disposed to swear, it is 10
not for any standers-by to curtail his oaths, ha?

2 Lord. No, my lord; [*aside*] nor crop the ears of them.

Cloten. Whoreson dog! I give him satisfaction? Would he had been one of my rank!

(*2 Lord.* To have smelt like a fool.

Cloten. I am not vexed more at any thing in th'earth. A pox on't! I had rather not be so noble as I am; they dare not fight with me, because of the queen my mother. Every jack-slave hath his bellyful of fighting, and I must
20 go up and down like a cock that nobody can match.

(*2 Lord.* You are cock and capon too; and you crow cock with your comb on.

Cloten. Sayest thou?

2 Lord. It is not fit your lordship should undertake every companion that you give offence to.

Cloten. No, I know that; but it is fit I should commit offence to my inferiors.

2 Lord. Ay, it is fit for your lordship only.

Cloten. Why, so I say.
30 *1 Lord.* Did you hear of a stranger that's come to court to-night?

Cloten. A stranger, and I not know on't?

(*2 Lord.* He's a strange fellow himself, and knows it not.

1 Lord. There's an Italian come, and, 'tis thought, one of Leonatus' friends.

Cloten. Leonatus? a banished rascal; and he's another, whatsoever he be. Who told you of this stranger?

1 Lord. One of your lordship's pages.
40 *Cloten.* Is it fit I went to look upon him? is there no derogation in't?

2 Lord. You cannot derogate, my lord.

Cloten. Not easily, I think.

(*2 Lord.* You are a fool granted; therefore your issues, being foolish, do not derogate.

Cloten. Come, I'll go see this Italian. What I have
lost to-day at bowls I'll win to-night of him. Come, go.
   2 Lord. I'll attend your lordship.
                            [*Cloten and* 1 *Lord go*
That such a crafty devil as is his mother
Should yield the world this ass! a woman that   50
Bears all down with her brain; and this her son
Cannot take two from twenty, for his heart,
And leave eighteen. Alas, poor princess,
Thou divine Imogen, what thou endur'st,
Betwixt a father by thy step-dame governed,
A mother hourly coining plots, a wooer
More hateful than the foul expulsion is
Of thy dear husband, than that horrid act
Of the divorce he'ld make. The heavens hold firm
The walls of thy dear honour; keep unshaked   60
That temple, thy fair mind, that thou mayst stand
T'enjoy thy banished lord and this great land!   [*goes*

[2. 2.]   *Imogen's bedchamber in Cymbeline's
palace: a trunk in one corner of it*

IMOGEN *in bed, reading; a Lady attending*

   Imogen. Who's there? my woman Helen?
   Lady.   Please you, madam.
   Imogen. What hour is it?
   Lady.   Almost midnight, madam.
   Imogen. I have read three hours then. Mine eyes
     are weak;
Fold down the leaf where I have left; to bed.
Take not away the taper, leave it burning;
And if thou canst awake by four o'th'clock,

I prithee call me. Sleep hath seized me wholly.

[*lady goes*

To your protection I commend me, gods.
From fairies and the tempters of the night
10 Guard me, beseech ye.

[*sleeps. Jachimo comes from the trunk*

Jachimo. The crickets sing, and man's o'er-
    laboured sense
Repairs itself by rest. Our Tarquin thus
Did softly press the rushes ere he wakened
The chastity he wounded. Cytherea,
How bravely thou becomest thy bed! fresh lily,
And whiter than the sheets! That I might touch,
But kiss, one kiss! Rubies unparagoned,
How dearly they do't! 'Tis her breathing that
Perfumes the chamber thus. The flame o'th'taper
20 Bows toward her and would under-peep her lids
To see th'enclosèd lights, now canopied
Under these windows, white and azure-laced
With blue of heaven's own tinct. But my design—
To note the chamber. I will write all down:
Such and such pictures; there the window; such
Th'adornment of her bed; the arras, figures,
Why, such and such; and the contents o'th'story.
Ah, but some natural notes about her body
Above ten thousand meaner movables
30 Would testify, t'enrich mine inventory.
O sleep, thou ape of death, lie dull upon her,
And be her sense but as a monument,
Thus in a chapel lying. Come off, come off;

[*taking off her bracelet*

As slippery as the Gordian knot was hard.
'Tis mine; and this will witness outwardly,
As strongly as the conscience does within,

To th'madding of her lord. On her left breast
A mole cinque-spotted, like the crimson drops
I'th'bottom of a cowslip. Here's a voucher,
Stronger than ever law could make; this secret   40
Will force him think I have picked the lock and ta'en
The treasure of her honour. No more. To what end?
Why should I write this down that's riveted,
Screwed to my memory? She hath been reading late
The tale of Tereus; here the leaf's turned down
Where Philomel gave up. I have enough;
To th'trunk again, and shut the spring of it.
Swift, swift, you dragons of the night, that dawning
May bare the raven's eye! I lodge in fear;
Though this a heavenly angel, hell is here.   50
                              [*clock strikes*

One, two, three. Time, time!
                    [*goes into the trunk; the scene closes*

[2. 3.]   *An ante-chamber adjoining Imogen's*
              apartments

              Enter CLOTEN *and Lords*

1 *Lord*. Your lordship is the most patient man in loss,
the most coldest that ever turned up ace.

Cloten. It would make any man cold to lose.

1 *Lord*. But not every man patient after the noble
temper of your lordship. You are most hot and furious
when you win.

Cloten. Winning will put any man into courage. If I
could get this foolish Imogen, I should have gold
enough. It's almost morning, is't not?

10   1 *Lord.* Day, my lord.

Cloten. I would this music would come. I am advised
to give her music o' mornings; they say it will penetrate.

Enter Musicians

Come on, tune. If you can penetrate her with your
fingering, so; we'll try with tongue too. If none will do,
let her remain; but I'll never give o'er. First, a very
excellent good-conceited thing; after, a wonderful sweet
air, with admirable rich words to it; and then let her
consider.

Song

Hark, hark, the lark at heaven's gate sings,
20   And Phoebus 'gins arise,
His steeds to water at those springs
     On chaliced flowers that lies;
And winking Mary-buds begin
     To ope their golden eyes;
With every thing that pretty is,
     My lady sweet, arise;
          Arise, arise!

Cloten. So, get you gone. If this penetrate, I will
consider your music the better; if it do not, it is a vice
30 in her ears, which horse-hairs and calf's-guts, nor the
voice of unpaved eunuch to boot, can never amend.

                                        [*musicians go*

Enter CYMBELINE *and Queen*

2 *Lord.* Here comes the king.

Cloten. I am glad I was up so late, for that's the
reason I was up so early. He cannot choose but take
this service I have done fatherly. Good morrow to
your majesty and to my gracious mother.

Cymbeline. Attend you here the door of our stern daughter? Will she not forth?

Cloten. I have assailed her with musics, but she vouchsafes no notice.   40

Cymbeline. The exile of her minion is too new;
She hath not yet forgot him. Some more time
Must wear the print of his remembrance out,
And then she's yours.

Queen.   You are most bound to th'king,
Who lets go by no vantages that may
Prefer you to his daughter. Frame yourself
To orderly solicits, and be friended
With aptness of the season; make denials
Increase your services; so seem as if
You were inspired to do those duties which   50
You tender to her; that you in all obey her,
Save when command to your dismission tends,
And therein you are senseless.

Cloten.   Senseless? not so.

Enter a Messenger

Messenger. So like you, sir, ambassadors from Rome;
The one is Caius Lucius.

Cymbeline.   A worthy fellow,
Albeit he comes on angry purpose now;
But that's no fault of his. We must receive him
According to the honour of his sender;
And towards himself, his goodness forespent on us,
We must extend our notice. Our dear son,   60
When you have given good morning to your mistress,
Attend the queen and us; we shall have need
T'employ you towards this Roman. Come, our queen.
                      [*all but Cloten go*

Cloten. If she be up, I'll speak with her; if not,

Let her lie still and dream. By your leave, ho! [*knocks*
I know her women are about her; what
If I do line one of their hands? 'Tis gold
Which buys admittance—oft it doth—yea, and makes
Diana's rangers false themselves, yield up
70 Their deer to th'stand o'th'stealer; and 'tis gold
Which makes the true man killed and saves the thief;
Nay, sometime hangs both thief and true man. What
Can it not do and undo? I will make
One of her women lawyer to me, for
I yet not understand the case myself.
By your leave.   [*knocks*

Enter a Lady

Lady. Who's there that knocks?
Cloten.   A gentleman.
Lady.   No more?
Cloten. Yes, and a gentlewoman's son.
Lady.   That's more
Than some whose tailors are as dear as yours
80 Can justly boast of. What's your lordship's pleasure?
Cloten. Your lady's person; is she ready?
Lady.   Ay,
To keep her chamber.
Cloten.   There is gold for you;
Sell me your good report.
Lady. How, my good name? or to report of you
What I shall think is good? The princess.   [*lady goes*

Enter IMOGEN

Cloten. Good morrow, fairest sister. Your sweet hand.
Imogen. Good morrow, sir. You lay out too much pains
For purchasing but trouble. The thanks I give
Is telling you that I am poor of thanks,
90 And scarce can spare them.

Cloten.　　　　　　　　　　Still I swear I love you.

Imogen. If you but said so, 'twere as deep with me.
If you swear still, your recompense is still
That I regard it not.

Cloten.　　　　　　　　This is no answer.

Imogen. But that you shall not say I yield being silent,
I would not speak. I pray you, spare me. Faith,
I shall unfold equal discourtesy
To your best kindness; one of your great knowing
Should learn, being taught, forbearance.

Cloten. To leave you in your madness, 'twere my sin.
I will not.　　　　　　　　　　　　　　　　100

Imogen. Fools are not mad folks.

Cloten.　　　　　　　　Do you call me fool?

Imogen. As I am mad, I do.
If you'll be patient, I'll no more be mad;
That cures us both. I am much sorry, sir,
You put me to forget a lady's manners
By being so verbal; and learn now for all
That I, which know my heart, do here pronounce
By th'very truth of it, I care not for you,
And am so near the lack of charity
To accuse myself I hate you; which I had rather　　110
You felt than make't my boast.

Cloten.　　　　　　　　You sin against
Obedience, which you owe your father. For
The contract you pretend with that base wretch,
One bred of alms and fostered with cold dishes,
With scraps o'th'court, it is no contract, none.
And though it be allowed in meaner parties—
Yet who than he more mean?—to knit their souls,
On whom there is no more dependency
But brats and beggary, in self-figured knot;
Yet you are curbed from that enlargement by　　120

The consequence o'th'crown, and must not foil
The precious note of it with a base slave,
A hilding for a livery, a squire's cloth,
A pantler—not so eminent.
   Imogen.   Profane fellow,
Wert thou the son of Jupiter, and no more.
But what thou art besides, thou wert too base
To be his groom; thou wert dignified enough,
Even to the point of envy, if 'twere made
Comparative for your virtues, to be styled
130 The under-hangman of his kingdom, and hated
For being preferred so well.
   Cloten.   The south fog rot him!
   Imogen. He never can meet more mischance than come
To be but named of thee. His meanest garment
That ever hath but clipped his body is dearer
In my respect than all the hairs above thee,
Were they all made such men. How now, Pisanio!

Enter PISANIO

   Cloten. 'His garment'! Now the devil—
   Imogen. To Dorothy my woman hie thee presently.
   Cloten. 'His garment'!
   Imogen.   I am sprited with a fool,
140 Frighted, and ang'red worse. Go bid my woman
Search for a jewel that too casually
Hath left mine arm. It was thy master's. 'Shrew me
If I would lose it for a revenue
Of any king's in Europe! I do think
I saw't this morning; confident I am
Last night 'twas on mine arm; I kissed it.
I hope it be not gone to tell my lord
That I kiss aught but he.
   Pisanio.   'Twill not be lost.

Imogen. I hope so; go and search.   [*Pisanio goes*
Cloten.   You have abused me.
'His meanest garment'!
Imogen.   Ay, I said so, sir.   150
If you will make't an action, call witness to't.
Cloten. I will inform your father.
Imogen.   Your mother too.
She's my good lady, and will conceive, I hope,
But the worst of me. So I leave you, sir,
To th'worst of discontent.   [*goes*
Cloten.   I'll be revenged.
'His meanest garment'! Well.   [*goes*

[2. 4.]   *Rome. Philario's house*

Enter POSTHUMUS *and* PHILARIO

Posthumus. Fear it not, sir; I would I were so sure
To win the king as I am bold her honour
Will remain hers.
Philario.   What means do you make to him?
Posthumus. Not any; but abide the change of time,
Quake in the present winter's state, and wish
That warmer days would come. In these fear'd hopes,
I barely gratify your love; they failing,
I must die much your debtor.
Philario. Your very goodness and your company
O'erpays all I can do. By this, your king   10
Hath heard of great Augustus. Caius Lucius
Will do's commission throughly. And I think
He'll grant the tribute, send th'arrearages,
Or look upon our Romans, whose remembrance
Is yet fresh in their grief.

Posthumus.   I do believe,
Statist though I am none, nor like to be,
That this will prove a war; and you shall hear
The legions now in Gallia sooner landed
In our not-fearing Britain than have tidings
20 Of any penny tribute paid. Our countrymen
Are men more ordered than when Julius Caesar
Smiled at their lack of skill, but found their courage
Worthy his frowning at. Their discipline,
Now mingled with their courage, will make known
To their approvers they are people such
That mend upon the world.

Enter JACHIMO

Philario.   See, Jachimo!
Posthumus. The swiftest harts have posted you
    by land,
And winds of all the corners kissed your sails,
To make your vessel nimble.
Philario.   Welcome, sir.
30 *Posthumus.* I hope the briefness of your answer made
The speediness of your return.
Jachimo.   Your lady
Is one the fairest that I have looked upon—
Posthumus. And therewithal the best, or let her beauty
Look through a casement to allure false hearts,
And be false with them.
Jachimo.   Here are letters for you.
Posthumus. Their tenour good, I trust.
Jachimo.   'Tis very like.
Philario. Was Caius Lucius in the Briton court
When you were there?
Jachimo.   He was expected then,
But not approached.

Posthumus.   All is well yet.
Sparkles this stone as it was wont, or is't not   40
Too dull for your good wearing?
     Jachimo.   If I have lost it,
I should have lost the worth of it in gold.
I'll make a journey twice as far t'enjoy
A second night of such sweet shortness which
Was mine in Britain; for the ring is won.
     Posthumus. The stone's too hard to come by.
     Jachimo.   Not a whit,
Your lady being so easy.
     Posthumus.   Make not, sir,
Your loss your sport. I hope you know that we
Must not continue friends.
     Jachimo.   Good sir, we must,
If you keep covenant. Had I not brought   50
The knowledge of your mistress home, I grant
We were to question farther; but I now
Profess myself the winner of her honour,
Together with your ring; and not the wronger
Of her or you, having proceeded but
By both your wills.
     Posthumus.   If you can make't apparent
That you have tasted her in bed, my hand
And ring is yours. If not, the foul opinion
You had of her pure honour gains or loses
Your sword or mine, or masterless leaves both   60
To who shall find them.
     Jachimo.   Sir, my circumstances,
Being so near the truth as I will make them,
Must first induce you to believe; whose strength
I will confirm with oath; which I doubt not
You'll give me leave to spare, when you shall find
You need it not.

Posthumus. Proceed.

Jachimo. First, her bedchamber—
Where I confess I slept not, but profess
Had that was well worth watching—it was hanged
With tapestry of silk and silver; the story
70 Proud Cleopatra when she met her Roman,
And Cydnus swelled above the banks, or for
The press of boats or pride; a piece of work
So bravely done, so rich, that it did strive
In workmanship and value; which I wondered
Could be so rarely and exactly wrought,
Since the true life was out on't.

Posthumus. This is true;
And this you might have heard of here, by me
Or by some other.

Jachimo. More particulars
Must justify my knowledge.

Posthumus. So they must,
80 Or do your honour injury.

Jachimo. The chimney
Is south the chamber, and the chimney-piece
Chaste Dian bathing. Never saw I figures
So likely to report themselves; the cutter
Was as another nature; dumb, outwent her,
Motion and breath left out.

Posthumus. This is a thing
Which you might from relation likewise reap,
Being, as it is, much spoke of.

Jachimo. The roof o'th'chamber
With golden cherubins is fretted; her andirons—
I had forgot them—were two winking Cupids
90 Of silver, each on one foot standing, nicely
Depending on their brands.

Posthumus. This is her honour!

Let it be granted you have seen all this—and praise
Be given to your remembrance—the description
Of what is in her chamber nothing saves
The wager you have laid.

 Jachimo.   Then, if you can
            [*showing the bracelet*
Be pale, I beg but leave to air this jewel. See!
And now 'tis up again; it must be married
To that your diamond; I'll keep them.

 Posthumus.   Jove!
Once more let me behold it. Is it that
Which I left with her?

 Jachimo. Sir, I thank her, that. 100
She stripped it from her arm; I see her yet;
Her pretty action did outsell her gift,
And yet enriched it too. She gave it me
And said she prized it once.

 Posthumus.   May be she plucked it off
To send it me.

 Jachimo. She writes so to you, doth she?
 Posthumus. O, no, no, no, 'tis true! Here, take
  this too;   [*gives the ring*
It is a basilisk unto mine eye,
Kills me to look on't. Let there be no honour
Where there is beauty; truth where semblance; love
Where there's another man. The vows of women 110
Of no more bondage be to where they are made
Than they are to their virtues, which is nothing.
O, above measure false!

 Philario.   Have patience, sir,
And take your ring again; 'tis not yet won.
It may be probable she lost it, or
Who knows if one her women, being corrupted,
Hath stol'n it from her?

Posthumus.   Very true;
And so I hope he came by't. Back my ring;
Render to me some corporal sign about her
120 More evident than this; for this was stol'n.
    Jachimo. By Jupiter, I had it from her arm.
    Posthumus. Hark you, he swears; by Jupiter
            he swears.
'Tis true, nay, keep the ring, 'tis true. I am sure
She would not lose it. Her attendants are
All sworn and honourable. They induced to steal it?
And by a stranger? No, he hath enjoyed her.
The cognizance of her incontinency
Is this. She hath bought the name of whore thus dearly.
There, take thy hire; and all the fiends of hell
130 Divide themselves between you!
    Philario.   Sir, be patient;
This is not strong enough to be believed
Of one persuaded well of.
    Posthumus.   Never talk on't;
She hath been colted by him.
    Jachimo.   If you seek
For further satisfying, under her breast—
Worthy the pressing—lies a mole, right proud
Of that most delicate lodging. By my life,
I kissed it, and it gave me present hunger
To feed again, though full. You do remember
This stain upon her?
    Posthumus.   Ay, and it doth confirm
140 Another stain, as big as hell can hold,
Were there no more but it.
    Jachimo.   Will you hear more?
    Posthumus. Spare your arithmetic; never count
            the turns.
Once, and a million!

Jachimo.   I'll be sworn.
Posthumus.   No swearing.
If you will swear you have not done't, you lie;
And I will kill thee if thou dost deny
Thou'st made me cuckold.
   Jachimo.   I'll deny nothing.
   Posthumus. O that I had her here to tear her
     limb-meal!
I will go there and do't i'th'court, before
Her father. I'll do something.   [*goes*
   Philario.   Quite besides
The government of patience! You have won.   150
Let's follow him and pervert the present wrath
He hath against himself.
   Jachimo.   With all my heart.   [*they go*

[2. 5.]   *Re-enter* POSTHUMUS

   Posthumus. Is there no way for men to be,
     but women
Must be half-workers? We are all bastards,
And that most venerable man which I
Did call my father was I know not where
When I was stamped. Some coiner with his tools
Made me a counterfeit; yet my mother seemed
The Dian of that time; so doth my wife
The nonpareil of this. O, vengeance, vengeance!
Me of my lawful pleasure she restrained,
And prayed me oft forbearance; did it with   10
A pudency so rosy, the sweet view on't
Might well have warmed old Saturn; that I thought her
As chaste as unsunned snow. O, all the devils!
This yellow Jachimo in an hour—was't not?—

Or less—at first? Perchance he spoke not, but
Like a full-acorned boar, a German one,
Cried 'O!' and mounted; found no opposition
But what he looked for should oppose and she
Should from encounter guard. Could I find out
20 The woman's part in me—for there's no motion
That tends to vice in man but I affirm
It is the woman's part; be it lying, note it,
The woman's; flattering, hers; deceiving, hers;
Lust and rank thoughts, hers, hers; revenges, hers;
Ambitions, covetings, change of prides, disdain,
Nice longing, slanders, mutability,
All faults that man may name, nay, that hell knows,
Why, hers, in part or all, but rather all;
For even to vice
30 They are not constant, but are changing still
One vice but of a minute old for one
Not half so old as that. I'll write against them,
Detest them, curse them; yet 'tis greater skill
In a true hate, to pray they have their will:
The very devils cannot plague them better.   [*goes*

[3. 1.]   *Britain. A hall in*
                          Cymbeline's palace

Enter in state, CYMBELINE, *Queen,* CLOTEN, *and Lords
at one door, and at another,* CAIUS LUCIUS *and attendants*

Cymbeline. Now say, what would Augustus Cæsar
      with us?
Lucius. When Julius Cæsar, whose remembrance yet
Lives in men's eyes, and will to ears and tongues
Be theme and hearing ever, was in this Britain,

And conquered it, Cassibelan, thine uncle,
Famous in Cæsar's praises no whit less
Than in his feats deserving it, for him
And his succession granted Rome a tribute,
Yearly three thousand pounds, which by thee lately
Is left untendered.
    Queen.   And, to kill the marvel,   10
Shall be so ever.
    Cloten.   There be many Cæsars
Ere such another Julius. Britain's a world
By itself, and we will nothing pay
For wearing our own noses.
    Queen.   That opportunity
Which then they had to take from's, to resume
We have again. Remember, sir, my liege,
The kings your ancestors, together with
The natural bravery of your isle, which stands
As Neptune's park, ribbed and paled in
With rocks unscalable and roaring waters,   20
With sands that will not bear your enemies' boats,
But suck them up to th'topmast. A kind of conquest
Cæsar made here, but made not here his brag
Of 'Came, and saw, and overcame'. With shame—
The first that ever touched him—he was carried
From off our coast, twice beaten; and his shipping,
Poor ignorant baubles, on our terrible seas,
Like egg-shells moved upon their surges, cracked
As easily 'gainst our rocks; for joy whereof
The famed Cassibelan, who was once at point—   30
O giglot fortune!—to master Cæsar's sword,
Made Lud's town with rejoicing fires bright,
And Britons strut with courage.
    Cloten. Come, there's no more tribute to be paid. Our
kingdom is stronger than it was at that time; and, as I

said, there is no moe such Cæsars. Other of them may
have crooked noses, but to owe such straight arms, none.

Cymbeline. Son, let your mother end.

Cloten. We have yet many among us can gripe as hard
40 as Cassibelan. I do not say I am one; but I have a hand.
Why tribute? why should we pay tribute? If Cæsar can
hide the sun from us with a blanket, or put the moon in
his pocket, we will pay him tribute for light; else, sir,
no more tribute, pray you now.

Cymbeline. You must know,
Till the injurious Romans did extort
This tribute from us, we were free. Cæsar's ambition,
Which swelled so much that it did almost stretch
The sides o'th'world, against all colour here
50 Did put the yoke upon's; which to shake off
Becomes a warlike people, whom we reckon
Ourselves to be. We do say then to Cæsar,
Our ancestor was that Mulmutius which
Ordained our laws, whose use the sword of Cæsar
Hath too much mangled; whose repair and franchise
Shall, by the power we hold, be our good deed,
Though Rome be therefore angry. Mulmutius made
      our laws,
Who was the first of Britain which did put
His brows within a golden crown, and called
60 Himself a king.

Lucius.   I am sorry, Cymbeline,
That I am to pronounce Augustus Cæsar—
Cæsar, that hath moe kings his servants than
Thyself domestic officers—thine enemy
Receive it from me, then: war and confusion
In Cæsar's name pronounce I 'gainst thee. Look
For fury not to be resisted. Thus defied,
I thank thee for myself.

Cymbeline.   Thou art welcome, Caius.
Thy Cæsar knighted me; my youth I spent
Much under him; of him I gathered honour;
Which he to seek of me again, perforce,   70
Behoves me keep at utterance. I am perfect
That the Pannonians and Dalmatians for
Their liberties are now in arms, a precedent
Which not to read would show the Britons cold;
So Cæsar shall not find them.
     Lucius.   Let proof speak.
     Cloten. His majesty bids you welcome. Make pastime
with us a day or two, or longer. If you seek us after-
wards in other terms, you shall find us in our salt-water
girdle. If you beat us out of it, it is yours, if you fall in
the adventure, our crows shall fare the better for you; 80
and there's an end.
     Lucius. So, sir.
     Cymbeline. I know your master's pleasure, and
       he mine.
All the remain is 'Welcome'.   [*they go*

[3. 2.]   *Enter* PISANIO, *reading of a letter*

     Pisanio. How? of adultery? Wherefore write you not
What monster's her accuser? Leonatus,
O master, what a strange infection
Is fall'n into thy ear! What false Italian,
As poisonous tongued as handed, hath prevailed
On thy too ready hearing? Disloyal? No.
She's punished for her truth, and undergoes,
More goddess-like than wife-like, such assaults
As would take in some virtue. O my master,
Thy mind to her is now as low as were   10

Thy fortunes. How? that I should murder her?
Upon the love and truth and vows which I
Have made to thy command? I, her? her blood?
If it be so to do good service, never
Let me be counted serviceable. How look I,
That I should seem to lack humanity
So much as this fact comes to? [*reading*] 'Do't.
    The letter
That I have sent her, by her own command
Shall give thee opportunity.' O damned paper,
20 Black as the ink that's on thee! Senseless bauble,
Art thou a fedary for this act, and look'st
So virgin-like without? Lo, here she comes.

Enter IMOGEN

I am ignorant in what I am commanded.
  Imogen. How now, Pisanio!
  Pisanio. Madam, here is a letter from my lord.
  Imogen. Who, thy lord? that is my lord Leonatus?
O, learned indeed were that astronomer
That knew the stars as I his characters;
He'ld lay the future open. You good gods,
30 Let what is here contained relish of love,
Of my lord's health, of his content—yet not
That we two are asunder; let that grieve him.
Some griefs are medicinable; that is one of them,
For it doth physic love—of his content
All but in that. Good wax, thy leave. Blest be
You bees that make these locks of counsel! Lovers
And men in dangerous bonds pray not alike;
Though forfeiters you cast in prison, yet
You clasp young Cupid's tables. Good news, gods!
40 [*reads*] 'Justice, and your father's wrath, should he
take me in his dominion, could not be so cruel to me,

as you, O the dearest of creatures, would even renew me
with your eyes. Take notice that I am in Cambria, at
Milford Haven. What your own love will out of this
advise you, follow. So he wishes you all happiness, that
remains loyal to his vow, and your increasing in love
                              LEONATUS POSTHUMUS.'
O, for a horse with wings! Hear'st thou, Pisanio?
He is at Milford Haven. Read, and tell me
How far 'tis thither. If one of mean affairs   50
May plod it in a week, why may not I
Glide thither in a day? Then, true Pisanio,
Who long'st like me to see thy lord, who long'st—
O let me bate—but not like me—yet long'st,
But in a fainter kind—O, not like me,
For mine's beyond beyond; say, and speak thick—
Love's counsellor should fill the bores of hearing,
To th'smothering of the sense—how far it is
To this same blessèd Milford. And by th'way
Tell me how Wales was made so happy as   60
T'inherit such a haven. But first of all,
How we may steal from hence; and for the gap
That we shall make in time from our hence-going
And our return, to excuse—but first, how get hence.
Why should excuse be born or ere begot?
We'll talk of that hereafter. Prithee speak,
How many score of miles may we well ride
'Twixt hour and hour?
  Pisanio.   One score 'twixt sun and sun,
Madam, 's enough for you, and too much too.
  Imogen. Why, one that rode to's execution, man,   70
Could never go so slow. I have heard of riding wagers
Where horses have been nimbler than the sands
That run i'th'clock's behalf. But this is fool'ry.
Go bid my woman feign a sickness, say

She'll home to her father; and provide me presently
A riding-suit, no costlier than would fit
A franklin's housewife.
    Pisanio.   Madam, you're best consider.
    Imogen. I see before me, man. Nor here, nor here,
Nor what ensues, but have a fog in them,
80 That I cannot look through. Away, I prithee;
Do as I bid thee. There's no more to say;
Accessible is none but Milford way.   *[they go*

[3. 3.]   *Wales: a mountainous country*
              with a cave

Enter BELARIUS, GUIDERIUS, and ARVIRAGUS

    Belarius. A goodly day not to keep house with such
Whose roof's as low as ours. Stoop, boys; this gate
Instructs you how t'adore the heavens, and bows you
To a morning's holy office. The gates of monarchs
Are arched so high that giants may jet through
And keep their impious turbans on, without
Good morrow to the sun. Hail, thou fair heaven!
We house i'th'rock, yet use thee not so hardly
As prouder livers do.
    Guiderius.   Hail, heaven!
    Arviragus.   Hail, heaven!
10   *Belarius.* Now for our mountain sport. Up to yond hill,
Your legs are young; I'll tread these flats. Consider,
When you above perceive me like a crow,
That it is place which lessens and sets off;
And you may then revolve what tales I have told you
Of courts, of princes, of the tricks in war;
This service is not service, so being done,

But being so allowed. To apprehend thus
Draws us a profit from all things we see;
And often to our comfort shall we find
The sharded beetle in a safer hold   20
Than is the full-winged eagle. O, this life
Is nobler than attending for a check,
Richer than doing nothing for a bauble,
Prouder than rustling in unpaid-for silk;
Such gain the cap of him that makes them fine,
Yet keeps his book uncrossed. No life to ours.
  Guiderius. Out of your proof you speak; we,
     poor unfledged,
Have never winged from view o'th'nest, nor know not
What air's from home. Haply this life is best,
If quiet life be best; sweeter to you   30
That have a sharper known; well corresponding
With your stiff age; but unto us it is
A cell of ignorance, travelling abed,
A prison, or a debtor that not dares
To stride a limit.
  Arviragus.   What should we speak of
When we are old as you? when we shall hear
The rain and wind beat dark December, how
In this our pinching cave shall we discourse
The freezing hours away? We have seen nothing;
We are beastly-subtle as the fox for prey,   40
Like warlike as the wolf for what we eat;
Our valour is to chase what flies; our cage
We make a choir, as doth the prisoned bird,
And sing our bondage freely.
  Belarius.   How you speak!
Did you but know the city's usuries,
And felt them knowingly; the art o'th'court,
As hard to leave as keep, whose top to climb

Is certain falling, or so slipp'ry that
The fear's as bad as falling; the toil o'th'war,
50 A pain that only seems to seek out danger
I'th'name of fame and honour, which dies i'th'search
And hath as oft a sland'rous epitaph
As record of fair act; nay, many times,
Doth ill deserve by doing well; what's worse,
Must curtsy at the censure. O, boys, this story
The world may read in me; my body's marked
With Roman swords, and my report was once
First with the best of note. Cymbeline loved me;
And when a soldier was the theme, my name
60 Was not far off. Then was I as a tree
Whose boughs did bend with fruit; but in one night
A storm, or robbery, call it what you will,
Shook down my mellow hangings, nay, my leaves,
And left me bare to weather.

    Guiderius.   Uncertain favour!

    Belarius. My fault being nothing, as I have told
       you oft,
But that two villains, whose false oaths prevailed
Before my perfect honour, swore to Cymbeline
I was confederate with the Romans. So
Followed my banishment, and this twenty years
70 This rock and these demesnes have been my world,
Where I have lived at honest freedom, paid
More pious debts to heaven than in all
The fore-end of my time. But up to th'mountains!
This is not hunters' language. He that strikes
The venison first shall be the lord o'th'feast;
To him the other two shall minister;
And we will fear no poison, which attends
In place of greater state. I'll meet you in the valleys.
                      [*Guiderius and Arviragus go*

How hard it is to hide the sparks of nature!
These boys know little they are sons to th'king,　　80
Nor Cymbeline dreams that they are alive.
They think they are mine; and though trained up
　　　thus meanly,
I'th'cave wherein they bow, their thoughts do hit
The roofs of palaces, and nature prompts them
In simple and low things to prince it much
Beyond the trick of others. This Polydore,
The heir of Cymbeline and Britain, who
The king his father called Guiderius—Jove!
When on my three-foot stool I sit and tell
The warlike feats I have done, his spirits fly out　　90
Into my story; say 'Thus mine enemy fell,
And thus I set my foot on's neck', even then
The princely blood flows in his cheek, he sweats,
Strains his young nerves, and puts himself in posture
That acts my words. The younger brother, Cadwal,
Once Arviragus, in as like a figure
Strikes life into my speech and shows much more
His own conceiving. Hark, the game is roused!
O Cymbeline, heaven and my conscience knows
Thou didst unjustly banish me; whereon,　　100
At three and two years old, I stole these babes,
Thinking to bar thee of succession as
Thou reft'st me of my lands. Euriphile,
Thou wast their nurse; they took thee for their mother,
And every day do honour to her grave.
Myself, Belarius, that am Morgan called,
They take for natural father. The game is up.　　[goes

[3. 4.]   *Country near Milford Haven*

Enter PISANIO *and* IMOGEN

Imogen. Thou told'st me, when we came from horse,
          the place
Was near at hand. Ne'er longed my mother so
To see me first as I have now. Pisanio, man,
Where is Posthumus? What is in thy mind,
That makes thee stare thus? Wherefore breaks
          that sigh
From th'inward of thee? One but painted thus
Would be interpreted a thing perplexed
Beyond self-explication. Put thyself
Into a haviour of less fear, ere wildness
10 Vanquish my staider senses. What's the matter?
Why tender'st thou that paper to me with
A look untender? If't be summer news,
Smile to't before; if winterly, thou need'st
But keep that countenance still. My husband's hand?
That drug-damned Italy hath out-craftied him,
And he's at some hard point. Speak, man; thy tongue
May take off some extremity, which to read
Would be even mortal to me.

Pisanio.   Please you read,
And you shall find me, wretched man, a thing
20 The most disdained of fortune.

Imogen. [*reads*] 'Thy mistress, Pisanio, hath played
the strumpet in my bed; the testimonies whereof lie
bleeding in me. I speak not out of weak surmises, but
from proof as strong as my grief and as certain as I
expect my revenge. That part thou, Pisanio, must act
for me, if thy faith be not tainted with the breach of hers.
Let thine own hands take away her life; I shall give thee

opportunity at Milford Haven. She hath my letter for
the purpose; where, if thou fear to strike, and to make
me certain it is done, thou art the pandar to her dis-　30
honour, and equally to me disloyal.'

 Pisanio. What shall I need to draw my sword?
  the paper
Hath cut her throat already. No, 'tis slander,
Whose edge is sharper than the sword, whose tongue
Outvenoms all the worms of Nile, whose breath
Rides on the posting winds and doth belie
All corners of the world. Kings, queens, and states,
Maids, matrons, nay, the secrets of the grave
This viperous slander enters. What cheer, madam?

 Imogen. False to his bed? What is it to be false?　40
To lie in watch there, and to think on him?
To weep 'twixt clock and clock? if sleep charge nature,
To break it with a fearful dream of him,
And cry myself awake? that's false to's bed, is it?

 Pisanio. Alas, good lady!

 Imogen. I false? Thy conscience witness. Jachimo,
Thou didst accuse him of incontinency;
Thou then look'dst like a villain; now, methinks,
Thy favour's good enough. Some jay of Italy,
Whose mother was her painting, hath betrayed him.　50
Poor I am stale, a garment out of fashion;
And, for I am richer than to hang by th'walls,
I must be ripped. To pieces with me! O,
Men's vows are women's traitors! All good seeming,
By thy revolt, O husband, shall be thought
Put on for villainy; not born where't grows,
But worn a bait for ladies.

 Pisanio.   Good madam, hear me.

 Imogen. True honest men being heard like false Æneas
Were in his time thought false; and Sinon's weeping

60 Did scandal many a holy tear, took pity
From most true wretchedness. So thou, Posthumus,
Wilt lay the leaven on all proper men;
Goodly and gallant shall be false and perjured
From thy great fail. Come, fellow, be thou honest;
Do thou thy master's bidding. When thou see'st him,
A little witness my obedience. Look,
I draw the sword myself; take it, and hit
The innocent mansion of my love, my heart.
Fear not; 'tis empty of all things but grief;
70 Thy master is not there, who was indeed
The riches of it. Do his bidding; strike.
Thou mayst be valiant in a better cause,
But now thou seem'st a coward.

Pisanio.   Hence, vile instrument!
Thou shalt not damn my hand.

Imogen.   Why, I must die;
And if I do not by thy hand, thou art
No servant of thy master's. Against self-slaughter
There is a prohibition so divine
That cravens my weak hand. Come, here's my heart:
Something's afore't. Soft, soft! we'll no defence;
80 Obedient as the scabbard. What is here?
The scriptures of the loyal Leonatus,
All turned to heresy? Away, away,
Corrupters of my faith! you shall no more
Be stomachers to my heart. Thus may poor fools
Believe false teachers; though those that are betrayed
Do feel the treason sharply, yet the traitor
Stands in worse case of woe. And thou, Posthumus,
That didst set up
My disobedience 'gainst the king my father,
90 And make me put into contempt the suits
Of princely fellows, shalt hereafter find

It is no act of common passage, but
A strain of rareness; and I grieve myself
To think, when thou shalt be disedged by her
That now thou tirest on, how thy memory
Will then be panged by me. Prithee, dispatch;
The lamb entreats the butcher. Where's thy knife?
Thou art too slow to do thy master's bidding
When I desire it too.

   Pisanio.   O gracious lady,
Since I received command to do this business   100
I have not slept one wink.

   Imogen.   Do't, and to bed then.

   Pisanio. I'll wake mine eye-balls out first.

   Imogen.   Wherefore then
Didst undertake it? Why hast thou abused
So many miles with a pretence? this place?
Mine action, and thine own? our horses' labour?
The time inviting thee? the perturbed court,
For my being absent? whereunto I never
Purpose return. Why hast thou gone so far,
To be unbent when thou hast ta'en thy stand,
Th'elected deer before thee?

   Pisanio.   But to win time   110
To lose so bad employment; in the which
I have considered of a course. Good lady,
Hear me with patience.

   Imogen.   Talk thy tongue weary; speak.
I have heard I am a strumpet, and mine ear,
Therein false struck, can take no greater wound,
Nor tent to bottom that.   But speak.

   Pisanio.   Then, madam,
I thought you would not back again.

   Imogen.   Most like,
Bringing me here to kill me.

Pisanio.   Not so, neither;
But if I were as wise as honest, then
120 My purpose would prove well. It cannot be
But that my master is abused. Some villain,
Ay, and singular in his art, hath done you both
This curséd injury.
    Imogen. Some Roman courtezan.
    Pisanio.   No, on my life.
I'll give but notice you are dead, and send him
Some bloody sign of it; for 'tis commanded
I should do so. You shall be missed at court,
And that will well confirm it.
    Imogen.   Why, good fellow,
What shall I do the while? where bide? how live?
130 Or in my life what comfort, when I am
Dead to my husband?
    Pisanio.   If you'll back to th'court—
    Imogen. No court, no father, nor no more ado
With that harsh, feeble, noble, simple nothing,
That Cloten, whose love-suit hath been to me
As fearful as a siege.
    Pisanio.   If not at court,
Then not in Britain must you bide.
    Imogen.   Where then?
Hath Britain all the sun that shines? Day, night,
Are they not but in Britain? I'th'world's volume
Our Britain seems as of it, but not in't;
140 In a great pool a swan's nest. Prithee think
There's livers out of Britain.
    Pisanio.   I am most glad
You think of other place. Th'ambassador,
Lucius the Roman, comes to Milford Haven
To-morrow. Now if you could wear a mind
Dark as your fortune is, and but disguise

That which t'appear itself must not yet be
But by self-danger, you should tread a course
Pretty and full of view; yea, haply, near
The residence of Posthumus; so nigh, at least,
That though his actions were not visible, yet 150
Report should render him hourly to your ear
As truly as he moves.

Imogen.　　　　　　O, for such means,
Though peril to my modesty, not death on't,
I would adventure.

Pisanio.　　　　　Well then, here's the point:
You must forget to be a woman; change
Command into obedience; fear and niceness—
The handmaids of all women, or, more truly,
Woman it pretty self—into a waggish courage,
Ready in gibes, quick-answered, saucy and
As quarrelous as the weasel. Nay, you must 160
Forget that rarest treasure of your cheek,
Exposing it—but, O, the harder heart!
Alack, no remedy!—to the greedy touch
Of common-kissing Titan, and forget
Your laboursome and dainty trims, wherein
You made great Juno angry.

Imogen.　　　　　　　　Nay, be brief.
I see into thy end, and am almost
A man already.

Pisanio.　　　　First, make yourself but like one.
Forethinking this, I have already fit—
'Tis in my cloak-bag—doublet, hat, hose, all 170
That answer to them. Would you, in their serving,
And with what imitation you can borrow
From youth of such a season, 'fore noble Lucius
Present yourself, desire his service, tell him
Wherein you're happy—which will make him know

If that his head have ear in music—, doubtless
With joy he will embrace you; for he's honourable,
And, doubling that, most holy. Your means abroad—
You have me, rich; and I will never fail
180 Beginning nor supplyment.

    Imogen.   Thou art all the comfort
The gods will diet me with. Prithee away;
There's more to be considered; but we'll even
All that good time will give us. This attempt
I am soldier to, and will abide it with
A prince's courage. Away, I prithee.

    Pisanio. Well, madam, we must take a short farewell,
Lest, being missed, I be suspected of
Your carriage from the court. My noble mistress,
Here is a box—I had it from the queen—
190 What's in't is precious; if you are sick at sea,
Or stomach-qualmed at land, a dram of this
Will drive away distemper. To some shade,
And fit you to your manhood; may the gods
Direct you to the best!

    Imogen.   Amen. I thank thee.

                [*they go in opposite directions*

   [3. 5.]   *A room in Cymbeline's palace*

     Enter CYMBELINE, *Queen,* CLOTEN,
        LUCIUS, *and Lords*

    Cymbeline. Thus far, and so farewell.

    Lucius.   Thanks, royal sir.
My emperor hath wrote I must from hence;
And am right sorry that I must report ye
My master's enemy.

    Cymbeline.   Our subjects, sir,

Will not endure his yoke; and for ourself
To show less sovereignty than they, must needs
Appear unkinglike.

  Lucius.   So, sir. I desire of you
A conduct over land to Milford Haven.
Madam, all joy befall your grace, and you.

  Cymbeline. My lords, you are appointed for that office; 10
The due of honour in no point omit.
So farewell, noble Lucius.

  Lucius.   Your hand, my lord.

  Cloten. Receive it friendly; but from this time forth
I wear it as your enemy.

  Lucius.   Sir, the event
Is yet to name the winner. Fare you well.

  Cymbeline. Leave not the worthy Lucius, good
    my lords,
Till he hath crossed the Severn. Happiness!

                     [*Lucius and lords go*

  Queen. He goes hence frowning; but it honours us
That we have given him cause.

  Cloten.   'Tis all the better;
Your valiant Britons have their wishes in it.   20

  Cymbeline. Lucius hath wrote already to the emperor
How it goes here. It fits us therefore ripely
Our chariots and our horsemen be in readiness.
The powers that he already hath in Gallia
Will soon be drawn to head, from whence he moves
His war for Britain.

  Queen.   'Tis not sleepy business,
But must be looked to speedily and strongly.

  Cymbeline. Our expectation that it would be thus
Hath made us forward. But, my gentle queen,
Where is our daughter? She hath not appeared   30
Before the Roman, nor to us hath tendered

The duty of the day. She looks us like
A thing more made of malice than of duty;
We have noted it. Call her before us, for
We have been too slight in sufferance.

[*an attendant goes*

Queen.   Royal sir,
Since the exile of Posthumus, most retired
Hath her life been; the cure whereof, my lord,
'Tis time must do. Beseech your majesty,
Forbear sharp speeches to her. She's a lady
40 So tender of rebukes that words are strokes,
And strokes death to her.

Re-enter Attendant

Cymbeline.   Where is she, sir? How
Can her contempt be answered?
Attendant.   Please you, sir,
Her chambers are all locked, and there's no answer
That will be given to th'loud'st of noise we make.
Queen. My lord, when last I went to visit her,
She prayed me to excuse her keeping close;
Whereto constrained by her infirmity
She should that duty leave unpaid to you,
Which daily she was bound to proffer. This
50 She wished me to make known; but our great court
Made me to blame in memory.
Cymbeline.   Her doors locked?
Not seen of late? Grant, heavens, that which I fear
Prove false!   [*goes*
Queen. Son, I say, follow the king.
Cloten. That man of hers, Pisanio, her old servant,
I have not seen these two days.
Queen.   Go, look after.

[*Cloten goes*

Pisanio, thou that stand'st so for Posthumus!
He hath a drug of mine. I pray his absence
Proceed by swallowing that; for he believes
It is a thing most precious. But for her,   60
Where is she gone? Haply despair hath seized her;
Or, winged with fervour of her love, she's flown
To her desired Posthumus. Gone she is
To death or to dishonour, and my end
Can make good use of either. She being down,
I have the placing of the British crown.

Re-enter CLOTEN

How now, my son?
  Cloten.   'Tis certain she is fled.
Go in and cheer the king; he rages, none
Dare come about him.
  (*Queen.*   All the better. May
This night forestall him of the coming day!   [*goes* 70
  Cloten. I love and hate her. For she's fair and royal,
And that she hath all courtly parts more exquisite
Than lady, ladies, woman—from every one
The best she hath, and she, of all compounded,
Outsells them all—I love her therefore; but
Disdaining me and throwing favours on
The low Posthumus slanders so her judgement
That what's else rare is choked; and in that point
I will conclude to hate her, nay, indeed,
To be revenged upon her. For when fools   80
Shall—
              Enter PISANIO

          Who is here? What, are you packing, sirrah?
Come hither. Ah, you precious pandar! Villain,
Where is thy lady? In a word, or else
Thou art straightway with the fiends.

Pisanio.   O, good my lord!
Cloten.   Where is thy lady? or, by Jupiter,
I will not ask again. Close villain,
I'll have this secret from thy heart, or rip
Thy heart to find it. Is she with Posthumus?
From whose so many weights of baseness cannot
90 A dram of worth be drawn.
   Pisanio.   Alas, my lord,
How can she be with him? When was she missed?
He is in Rome.
   Cloten.   Where is she, sir? Come nearer.
No farther halting; satisfy me home
What is become of her.
   Pisanio. O, my all-worthy lord!
   Cloten.   All-worthy villain,
Discover where thy mistress is at once,
At the next word; no more of 'worthy lord'!
Speak, or thy silence on the instant is
Thy condemnation and thy death.
   Pisanio.   Then, sir,
100 This paper is the history of my knowledge
Touching her flight.   [*presenting a letter*
   Cloten.   Let's see't. I will pursue her
Even to Augustus' throne.
   (*Pisanio.*   Or this or perish.
She's far enough, and what he learns by this
May prove his travel, not her danger.
   Cloten.   Hum!
   (*Pisanio.* I'll write to my lord she's dead. O Imogen,
Safe mayst thou wander, safe return again!
   Cloten. Sirrah, is this letter true?
   Pisanio. Sir, as I think.
   Cloten. It is Posthumus' hand; I know't. Sirrah, if
110 thou wouldst not be a villain, but do me true service,

undergo those employments wherein I should have cause
to use thee with a serious industry—that is, what villainy
soe'er I bid thee do, to perform it directly and truly—
I would think thee an honest man; thou shouldst neither
want my means for thy relief, nor my voice for thy
preferment.

Pisanio. Well, my good lord.

Cloten. Wilt thou serve me? for since patiently and
constantly thou hast stuck to the bare fortune of that
beggar Posthumus, thou canst not in the course of 120
gratitude but be a diligent follower of mine. Wilt thou
serve me?

Pisanio. Sir, I will.

Cloten. Give me thy hand; here's my purse. Hast
any of thy late master's garments in thy possession?

Pisanio. I have, my lord, at my lodging the same suit
he wore when he took leave of my lady and mistress.

Cloten. The first service thou dost me, fetch that suit
hither. Let it be thy first service; go.

Pisanio. I shall, my lord.   [*goes* 130

Cloten. Meet thee at Milford Haven! I forgot to ask
him one thing; I'll remember't anon. Even there, thou
villain Posthumus, will I kill thee. I would these garments were come. She said upon a time—the bitterness
of it I now belch from my heart—that she held the very
garment of Posthumus in more respect than my noble
and natural person, together with the adornment of my
qualities. With that suit upon my back will I ravish her;
first kill him, and in her eyes; there shall she see my
valour, which will then be a torment to her contempt. 140
He on the ground, my speech of insultment ended on
his dead body, and when my lust hath dined—which,
as I say, to vex her I will execute in the clothes that she
so praised—to the court I'll knock her back, foot her

home again. She hath despised me rejoicingly, and I'll
be merry in my revenge.

        Re-enter PISANIO, *with the clothes*

Be those the garments?
   Pisanio. Ay, my noble lord.
   Cloten. How long is't since she went to Milford
150 Haven?
   Pisanio. She can scarce be there yet.
   Cloten. Bring this apparel to my chamber; that is the
second thing that I have commanded thee. The third is
that thou wilt be a voluntary mute to my design. Be but
duteous and true, preferment shall tender itself to thee.
My revenge is now at Milford; would I had wings to
follow it! Come, and be true.   *[goes*
   Pisanio. Thou bid'st me to my loss; for, true to thee
Were to prove false, which I will never be
160 To him that is most true. To Milford go,
And find not her whom thou pursuest. Flow, flow,
You heavenly blessings, on her. This fool's speed
Be crossed with slowness; labour be his meed.   *[goes*

[3.6.]   *Wales: before the cave of* BELARIUS

        Enter IMOGEN *alone, in boy's clothes*

   Imogen. I see a man's life is a tedious one.
I have tired myself, and for two nights together
Have made the ground my bed. I should be sick,
But that my resolution helps me. Milford,
When from the mountain-top Pisanio showed thee,
Thou wast within a ken. O Jove, I think
Foundations fly the wretched: such, I mean,

Where they should be relieved. Two beggars
   told me
I could not miss my way. Will poor folks lie,
That have afflictions on them, knowing 'tis 10
A punishment or trial? Yes; no wonder,
When rich ones scarce tell true. To lapse in fulness
Is sorer than to lie for need; and falsehood
Is worse in kings than beggars. My dear lord,
Thou art one o'th'false ones. Now I think on thee
My hunger's gone; but even before, I was
At point to sink for food. But what is this?
Here is a path to't; 'tis some savage hold.
I were best not call; I dare not call; yet famine,
Ere clean it o'erthrow nature, makes it valiant. 20
Plenty and peace breeds cowards; hardness ever
Of hardiness is mother. Ho! who's here?
If any thing that's civil, speak; if savage,
Take or lend. Ho! no answer? then I'll enter.
Best draw my sword; and if mine enemy
But fear the sword like me, he'll scarcely look on't.
Such a foe, good heavens!   [goes into the cave

Enter BELARIUS, GUIDERIUS, *and* ARVIRAGUS

Belarius. You, Polydore, have proved best
   woodman and
Are master of the feast. Cadwal and I
Will play the cook and servant; 'tis our match. 30
The sweat of industry would dry and die
But for the end it works to. Come, our stomachs
Will make what's homely savoury; weariness
Can snore upon the flint, when resty sloth
Finds the down pillow hard. Now peace be here,
Poor house, that keep'st thyself.
  Guiderius.   I am throughly weary.

Arviragus. I am weak with toil, yet strong in appetite.

Guiderius. There is cold meat i'th'cave; we'll browse
    on that
Whilst what we have killed be cooked.

Belarius. [*looking into the cave*]   Stay, come not in.
40 But that it eats our victuals, I should think
Here were a fairy.

Guiderius.   What's the matter, sir?

Belarius. By Jupiter, an angel; or, if not,
An earthly paragon. Behold divineness
No elder than a boy.

IMOGEN *comes from the cave*

Imogen. Good masters, harm me not.
Before I entered here I called, and thought
To have begged or bought what I have took.
    Good troth,
I have stol'n nought; nor would not though I
    had found
Gold strewed i'th'floor. Here's money for my meat.
50 I would have left it on the board so soon
As I had made my meal, and parted
With prayers for the provider.

Guiderius.   Money, youth?

Arviragus. All gold and silver rather turn to dirt,
As 'tis no better reckoned but of those
Who worship dirty gods.

Imogen.   I see you're angry.
Know, if you kill me for my fault, I should
Have died had I not made it.

Belarius.   Whither bound?

Imogen. To Milford Haven.

Belarius. What's your name?

60 *Imogen.* Fidele, sir. I have a kinsman who

Is bound for Italy; he embarked at Milford;
To whom being going, almost spent with hunger,
I am fall'n in this offence.
 Belarius.   Prithee, fair youth,
Think us no churls, nor measure our good minds
By this rude place we live in. Well encountered.
'Tis almost night; you shall have better cheer
Ere you depart, and thanks to stay and eat it.
Boys, bid him welcome.
 Guiderius.   Were you a woman, youth,
I should woo hard but be your groom in honesty;
I bid for you as I'ld buy.
 Arviragus.   I'll make't my comfort 70
He is a man, I'll love him as my brother:
And such a welcome as I'ld give to him
After long absence, such is yours. Most welcome.
Be sprightly, for you fall 'mongst friends.
 Imogen.   'Mongst friends?
—If brothers. [*aside*] Would it had been so that they
Had been my father's sons! then had my prize
Been less, and so more equal ballasting
To thee, Posthumus.
 Belarius.   He wrings at some distress.
 Guiderius. Would I could free't!
 Arviragus.   Or I; whate'er it be,
What pain it cost, what danger! Gods!
 Belarius.   Hark, boys. 80
           [*whispering*

 Imogen. Great men
That had a court no bigger than this cave,
That did attend themselves, and had the virtue
Which their own conscience sealed them, laying by
That nothing-gift of differing multitudes,
Could not outpeer these twain. Pardon me, gods,

I'ld change my sex to be companion with them,
Since Leonatus' false.

 Belarius.   It shall be so.

Boys, we'll go dress our hunt. Fair youth, come in;
90 Discourse is heavy, fasting; when we have supped,
We'll mannerly demand thee of thy story,
So far as thou wilt speak it.

 Guiderius.   Pray draw near.

 Arviragus. The night to th'owl and morn to th'lark
  less welcome.

 Imogen. Thanks, sir.

 Arviragus. I pray draw near.   *[they go*

[3. 7.]   *Rome. A public place*

Enter two Roman Senators and Tribunes

 1 *Senator.* This is the tenour of the emperor's writ:
That since the common men are now in action
'Gainst the Pannonians and Dalmatians,
And that the legions now in Gallia are
Full weak to undertake our wars against
The fall'n-off Britons, that we do incite
The gentry to this business. He creates
Lucius proconsul; and to you the tribunes,
For this immediate levy, he commends
10 His absolute commission. Long live Cæsar!

 1 *Tribune.* Is Lucius general of the forces?

 2 *Senator.*   Ay.

 1 *Tribune.* Remaining now in Gallia?

 1 *Senator.*   With those legions
Which I have spoke of, whereunto your levy
Must be supplyant. The words of your commission

Will tie you to the numbers and the time
Of their dispatch.

1 *Tribune.*   We will discharge our duty. [*they go*

[4. 1.]   *Wales: near the cave of Belarius*

Enter CLOTEN alone

Cloten. I am near to th'place where they should meet,
if Pisanio have mapped it truly. How fit his garments
serve me! Why should his mistress, who was made by
him that made the tailor, not be fit too? the rather—
saving reverence of the word—for 'tis said a woman's
fitness comes by fits. Therein I must play the workman.
I dare speak it to myself, for it is not vain-glory for a man
and his glass to confer in his own chamber; I mean, the
lines of my body are as well drawn as his; no less young,
more strong, not beneath him in fortunes, beyond him 10
in the advantage of the time, above him in birth, alike
conversant in general services, and more remarkable in
single oppositions; yet this imperceiverant thing loves
him in my despite. What mortality is! Posthumus, thy
head, which now is growing upon thy shoulders, shall
within this hour be off; thy mistress enforced; thy garments cut to pieces before her face; and all this done,
spurn her home to her father, who may haply be a little
angry for my so rough usage; but my mother, having
power of his testiness, shall turn all into my commenda- 20
tions. My horse is tied up safe; out, sword, and to a
sore purpose! Fortune put them into my hand. This is
the very description of their meeting-place; and the
fellow dares not deceive me.   [*goes*

[4. 2.]   *Before the cave of Belarius*

Enter BELARIUS, GUIDERIUS, ARVIRAGUS,
and IMOGEN *from the cave*

Belarius. [*to Imogen*] You are not well. Remain
     here in the cave;
We'll come to you after hunting.
     Arviragus. [*to Imogen*]   Brother, stay here.
Are we not brothers?
     Imogen.   So man and man should be;
But clay and clay differs in dignity,
Whose dust is both alike. I am very sick.
     Guiderius. Go you to hunting; I'll abide with him.
     Imogen. So sick I am not, yet I am not well;
But not so citizen a wanton as
To seem to die ere sick. So please you, leave me;
10 Stick to your journal course: the breach of custom
Is breach of all. I am ill, but your being by me
Cannot amend me. Society is no comfort
To one not sociable. I am not very sick,
Since I can reason of it. Pray you trust me here:
I'll rob none but myself; and let me die,
Stealing so poorly.
     Guiderius.   I love thee, I have spoke it,
How much the quantity, the weight as much,
As I do love my father.
     Belarius.   What? how, how?
     Arviragus. If it be sin to say so, sir, I yoke me
20 In my good brother's fault. I know not why
I love this youth, and I have heard you say,
Love's reason's without reason. The bier at door,
And a demand who is't shall die, I'ld say
'My father, not this youth'.

(*Belarius*.   O noble strain!
O worthiness of nature, breed of greatness!
"Cowards father cowards and base things sire base;
"Nature hath meal and bran, contempt and grace.
I'm not their father; yet who this should be
Doth miracle itself, loved before me.
[*to Guiderius and Arviragus*] 'Tis the ninth hour
        o'th'morn.
    Arviragus.   Brother, farewell.   30
    Imogen. I wish ye sport.
    Arviragus.   You health. [*to Belarius*] So
        please you, sir.
(*Imogen*. These are kind creatures. Gods, what lies
        I have heard!
Our courtiers say all's savage but at court.
Experience, O, thou disprovest report!
Th'imperious seas breeds monsters; for the dish
Poor tributary rivers as sweet fish.
I am sick still, heart-sick. Pisanio,
I'll now taste of thy drug.   [*swallows some*
    Guiderius.   I could not stir him.
He said he was gentle, but unfortunate;
Dishonestly afflicted, but yet honest.   40
    Arviragus. Thus did he answer me; yet said hereafter
I might know more.
    Belarius.   To th'field, to th'field.
We'll leave you for this time; go in and rest.
    Arviragus. We'll not be long away.
    Belarius.   Pray be not sick,
For you must be our housewife.
    Imogen.   Well or ill,
I am bound to you.
    Belarius.   And shalt be ever.
                                    [*Imogen goes into the cave*

This youth, howe'er distress'd, appears he hath had
Good ancestors.

Arviragus. How angel-like he sings!

Guiderius. But his neat cookery! he cut our roots
in characters;

50 And sauced our broths, as Juno had been sick,
And he her dieter.

Arviragus. Nobly he yokes
A smiling with a sigh, as if the sigh
Was that it was for not being such a smile;
The smile mocking the sigh that it would fly
From so divine a temple to commix
With winds that sailors rail at.

Guiderius. I do note
That grief and patience, rooted in him both,
Mingle their spurs together.

Arviragus. Grow patience,
And let the stinking elder, grief, untwine
60 His perishing root with the increasing vine.

Belarius. It is great morning. Come away.
Who's there?

Enter CLOTEN

Cloten. I cannot find those runagates; that villain
Hath mocked me. I am faint.

Belarius. 'Those runagates'?
Means he not us? I partly know him; 'tis
Cloten, the son o'th'queen. I fear some ambush.
I saw him not these many years, and yet
I know 'tis he. We are held as outlaws. Hence!

Guiderius. He is but one; you and my brother search
What companies are near; pray you, away;
70 Let me alone with him. [*Belarius and Arviragus go*

Cloten. Soft, what are you

That fly me thus? some villain mountaineers?
I have heard of such. What slave art thou?
Guiderius.　　　　　　　　　　A thing
More slavish did I ne'er than answering
A slave without a knock.
Cloten.　　　　　　　Thou art a robber,
A law-breaker, a villain. Yield thee, thief.
Guiderius. To who? to thee? What art thou?
　　　Have not I
An arm as big as thine, a heart as big?
Thy words, I grant, are bigger; for I wear not
My dagger in my mouth. Say what thou art,
Why I should yield to thee.
Cloten.　　　　　　Thou villain base,　　80
Know'st me not by my clothes?
Guiderius.　　　　　No, nor thy tailor, rascal,
Who is thy grandfather. He made those clothes,
Which, as it seems, make thee.
Cloten.　　　　　　　Thou precious varlet,
My tailor made them not.
Guiderius.　　　　　Hence then, and thank
The man that gave them thee. Thou art some fool;
I am loath to beat thee.
Cloten.　　　　　Thou injurious thief,
Hear but my name, and tremble.
Guiderius.　　　　　　What's thy name?
Cloten. Cloten, thou villain.
Guiderius. Cloten, thou double villain, be
　　　thy name,
I cannot tremble at it: were it Toad, or Adder, Spider, 90
'Twould move me sooner.
Cloten.　　　　　To thy further fear,
Nay, to thy mere confusion, thou shalt know
I am son to th'queen.

Guiderius.   I am sorry for't; not seeming
So worthy as thy birth.
Cloten.   Art not afeard?
Guiderius. Those that I reverence, those I fear,
     the wise.
At fools I laugh, not fear them.
Cloten.   Die the death.
When I have slain thee with my proper hand,
I'll follow those that even now fled hence,
And on the gates of Lud's town set your heads.
100 Yield, rustic mountaineer.   [*they go out fighting*

Re-enter BELARIUS and ARVIRAGUS

Belarius. No company's abroad?
Arviragus. None in the world; you did mistake
     him, sure.
Belarius. I cannot tell; long is it since I saw him,
But time hath nothing blurred those lines of favour
Which then he wore; the snatches in his voice,
And burst of speaking, were as his; I am absolute
'Twas very Cloten.
Arviragus.   In this place we left them;
I wish my brother make good time with him,
You say he is so fell.
Belarius.   Being scarce made up,
110 I mean to man, he had not apprehension
Of roaring terrors: for defect of judgement
Is oft the cease of fear.

Re-enter GUIDERIUS with Cloten's head

                         But see, thy brother.
Guiderius. This Cloten was a fool, an
     empty purse;
There was no money in't. Not Hercules

Could have knocked out his brains, for he had none.
Yet I not doing this, the fool had borne
My head as I do his.

 Belarius.   What hast thou done?

 Guiderius. I am perfect what: cut off one
   Cloten's head,
Son to the queen, after his own report,
Who called me traitor, mountaineer, and swore   120
With his own single hand he'ld take us in,
Displace our heads where—thank the gods—they grow,
And set them on Lud's town.

 Belarius.   We are all undone.

 Guiderius. Why, worthy father, what have we
   to lose
But that he swore to take, our lives? The law
Protects not us; then why should we be tender
To let an arrogant piece of flesh threat us,
Play judge and executioner all himself,
For we do fear the law? What company
Discover you abroad?

 Belarius.   No single soul   130
Can we set eye on; but in all safe reason
He must have some attendants. Though his humour
Was nothing but mutation, ay, and that
From one bad thing to worse, not frenzy, not
Absolute madness could so far have raved,
To bring him here alone. Although perhaps
It may be heard at court that such as we
Cave here, hunt here, are outlaws, and in time
May make some stronger head, the which
   he hearing—
As it is like him—might break out, and swear   140
He'ld fetch us in; yet is't not probable
To come alone, either he so undertaking,

Or they so suffering. Then on good ground
    we fear,
If we do fear this body hath a tail
More perilous than the head.

   Arviragus.   Let ordinance
Come as the gods foresay it; howsoe'er,
My brother hath done well.

   Belarius.   I had no mind
To hunt this day. The boy Fidele's sickness
Did make my way long forth.

   Guiderius.   With his own sword,
150 Which he did wave against my throat, I have ta'en
His head from him. I'll throw't into the creek
Behind our rock, and let it to the sea,
And tell the fishes he's the queen's son, Cloten.
That's all I reck.   *[goes*

   Belarius.   I fear 'twill be revenged.
Would, Polydore, thou hadst not done't,
    though valour
Becomes thee well enough.

   Arviragus.   Would I had done't,
So the revenge alone pursued me. Polydore,
I love thee brotherly, but envy much
Thou hast robbed me of this deed. I would revenges
160 That possible strength might meet would seek
    us through
And put us to our answer.

   Belarius.   Well, 'tis done.
We'll hunt no more to-day, nor seek for danger
Where there's no profit. I prithee to our rock;
You and Fidele play the cooks; I'll stay
Till hasty Polydore return, and bring him
To dinner presently.

   Arviragus.   Poor sick Fidele,

I'll willingly to him. To gain his colour
I'ld let a parish of such Clotens blood,
And praise myself for charity.   [*goes*

  Belarius.   O thou goddess,
Thou divine Nature, how thyself thou blazon'st   170
In these two princely boys! They are as gentle
As zephyrs blowing below the violet,
Not wagging his sweet head; and yet as rough,
Their royal blood enchafed, as the rud'st wind
That by the top doth take the mountain pine
And make him stoop to th'vale. 'Tis wonder
That an invisible instinct should frame them
To royalty unlearned, honour untaught,
Civility not seen from other, valour
That wildly grows in them, but yields a crop   180
As if it had been sowed. Yet still it's strange
What Cloten's being here to us portends,
Or what his death will bring us.

Re-enter GUIDERIUS

  Guiderius.   Where's my brother?
I have sent Cloten's clotpoll down the stream,
In embassy to his mother; his body's hostage
For his return.   [*solemn music*

  Belarius.   My ingenious instrument!
Hark, Polydore, it sounds. But what occasion
Hath Cadwal now to give it motion? Hark!

  Guiderius. Is he at home?

  Belarius.   He went hence even now.

  Guiderius. What does he mean? Since death of my
      dear'st mother   190
It did not speak before. All solemn things
Should answer solemn accidents. The matter?
Triumphs for nothing and lamenting toys

Is jollity for apes and grief for boys.
Is Cadwal mad?

Re-enter ARVIRAGUS *with* IMOGEN, *dead,*
bearing her in his arms

Belarius.   Look, here he comes,
And brings the dire occasion in his arms
Of what we blame him for.
        Arviragus.   The bird is dead
That we have made so much on. I had rather
Have skipped from sixteen years of age to sixty,
200 To have turned my leaping time into a crutch,
Than have seen this.
        Guiderius.   O sweetest, fairest lily!
My brother wears thee not the one half so well
As when thou grew'st thyself.
        Belarius.   O melancholy!
Who ever yet could sound thy bottom? find
The ooze, to show what coast thy sluggish crare
Might easiliest harbour in? Thou blessed thing,
Jove knows what man thou mightst have made; but I,
Thou diedst, a most rare boy, of melancholy.
How found you him?
        Arviragus.   Stark, as you see;
210 Thus smiling, as some fly had tickled slumber,
Not as death's dart being laughed at; his right cheek
Reposing on a cushion.
        Guiderius.   Where?
        Arviragus.   O'th'floor,
His arms thus leagued; I thought he slept, and put
My clouted brogues from off my feet, whose rudeness
Answered my steps too loud.
        Guiderius.   Why, he but sleeps.
If he be gone, he'll make his grave a bed;

With female fairies will his tomb be haunted,
And worms will not come to thee.

　Arviragus.　　　　　　　　With fairest flowers,
Whilst summer lasts, and I live here, Fidele,
I'll sweeten thy sad grave. Thou shalt not lack　　　220
The flower that's like thy face, pale primrose, nor
The azured harebell, like thy veins; no, nor
The leaf of eglantine, whom not to slander,
Out-sweet'ned not thy breath. The ruddock would
With charitable bill—O bill sore shaming
Those rich-left heirs that let their fathers lie
Without a monument!—bring thee all this;
Yea, and furred moss besides, when flowers are none,
To winter-ground thy corse.

　Guiderius.　　　　　　　Prithee have done,
And do not play in wench-like words with that　　　230
Which is so serious. Let us bury him,
And not protract with admiration what
Is now due debt. To th'grave.

　Arviragus.　　　　　　Say, where shall's lay him?
　Guiderius. By good Euriphile, our mother.

　Arviragus.　　　　　　　　　　Be't so;
And let us, Polydore, though now our voices
Have got the mannish crack, sing him to th'ground,
As once our mother; use like note and words,
Save that 'Euriphile' must be 'Fidele'.

　Guiderius. Cadwal,
I cannot sing. I'll weep, and word it with thee;　　　240
For notes of sorrow out of tune are worse
Than priests and fanes that lie.

　Arviragus.　　　　　　We'll speak it then.
　Belarius. Great griefs, I see, medicine the less;
　　　for Cloten
Is quite forgot. He was a queen's son, boys;

And though he came our enemy, remember
He was paid for that; though mean and mighty rotting
Together have one dust, yet reverence,
That angel of the world, doth make distinction
Of place 'tween high and low. Our foe was princely,
250 And though you took his life as being our foe,
Yet bury him as a prince.
    Guiderius.   Pray you fetch him hither.
Thersites' body is as good as Ajax'
When neither are alive.
    Arviragus.   If you'll go fetch him,
We'll say our song the whilst. Brother, begin.
                           [*Belarius goes*
    Guiderius. Nay, Cadwal, we must lay his head
        to th'east;
My father hath a reason for it.
    Arviragus.   'Tis true.
    Guiderius. Come on then and remove him.
    Arviragus.   So. Begin.

SONG

    Guiderius. Fear no more the heat o'th'sun,
           Nor the furious winter's rages;
260   Thou thy worldly task hast done,
           Home art gone and ta'en thy wages.
      Golden lads and girls all must,
      As chimney-sweepers, come to dust.

    Arviragus. Fear no more the frown o'th'great;
           Thou art past the tyrant's stroke;
      Care no more to clothe and eat;
           To thee the reed is as the oak.
      The sceptre, learning, physic, must
      All follow this and come to dust.

Guiderius.	Fear no more the lightning flash,	270
Arviragus.	Nor th'all-dreaded thunder-stone;	
Guiderius.	Fear not slander, censure rash;	
Arviragus.	Thou hast finished joy and moan.	
Both.	All lovers young, all lovers must	
	Consign to thee and come to dust.	

Guiderius.	No exorciser harm thee!	
Arviragus.	Nor no witchcraft charm thee!	
Guiderius.	Ghost unlaid forbear thee!	
Arviragus.	Nothing ill come near thee!	
Both.	Quiet consummation have;	280
	And renownéd be thy grave!	

Re-enter BELARIUS *with the body of Cloten*

Guiderius. We have done our obsequies. Come,
    lay him down.
Belarius. Here's a few flowers, but 'bout
    midnight more:
The herbs that have on them cold dew o'th'night
Are strewings fitt'st for graves. Upon their faces.
You were as flowers, now wither'd; even so
These herblets shall, which we upon you strew.
Come on, away; apart upon our knees.
The ground that gave them first has them again.
Their pleasures here are past, so is their pain.   290
       [*Belarius, Guiderius and Arviragus go*
  Imogen. [*awaking*] Yes, sir, to Milford Haven;
    which is the way?—
I thank you. By yond bush? Pray, how far thither?
'Ods pittikins, can it be six mile yet?
I have gone all night. Faith, I'll lie down and sleep.
But, soft, no bedfellow! O gods and goddesses!
           [*seeing the body of Cloten*

These flowers are like the pleasures of the world;
This bloody man, the care on't. I hope I dream;
For so I thought I was a cave-keeper,
And cook to honest creatures. But 'tis not so;
300 'Twas but a bolt of nothing, shot at nothing,
Which the brain makes of fumes. Our very eyes
Are sometimes like our judgements, blind.
     Good faith,
I tremble still with fear; but if there be
Yet left in heaven as small a drop of pity
As a wren's eye, feared gods, a part of it!
The dream's here still; even when I wake, it is
Without me, as within me; not imagined, felt.
A headless man? The garments of Posthumus?
I know the shape of's leg; this is his hand;
310 His foot Mercurial; his Martial thigh;
The brawns of Hercules; but his Jovial face—
Murder in heaven? How? 'Tis gone. Pisanio,
All curses madded Hecuba gave the Greeks,
And mine to boot, be darted on thee! Thou,
Conspired with that irregulous devil, Cloten,
Hath here cut off my lord. To write and read
Be henceforth treacherous! Damned Pisanio
Hath with his forgéd letters—damned Pisanio—
From this most bravest vessel of the world
320 Struck the main-top. O Posthumus, alas,
Where is thy head? where's that? Ay me! where's that?
Pisanio might have killed thee at the heart,
And left this head on. How should this be? Pisanio?
'Tis he and Cloten; malice and lucre in them
Have laid this woe here. O, 'tis pregnant, pregnant!
The drug he gave me, which he said was precious
And cordial to me, have I not found it
Murd'rous to th'senses? That confirms it home.

This is Pisanio's deed, and Cloten's. O!
Give colour to my pale cheek with thy blood,   330
That we the horrider may seem to those
Which chance to find us. O, my lord, my lord!

                         [falls on the body

      Enter LUCIUS, a Captain and other Officers,
                and a Soothsayer

  Captain. To them the legions garrisoned in Gallia
After your will have crossed the sea, attending
You here at Milford Haven with your ships.
They are here in readiness.
  Lucius.   But what from Rome?
  Captain. The senate hath stirred up the confiners
And gentlemen of Italy, most willing spirits
That promise noble service; and they come
Under the conduct of bold Jachimo,   340
Siena's brother.
    Lucius.   When expect you them?
  Captain. With the next benefit o'th'wind.
  Lucius.   This forwardness
Makes our hopes fair. Command our present numbers
Be mustered; bid the captains look to't. Now, sir,
What have you dreamed of late of this war's purpose?
  Soothsayer. Last night the very gods showed me
      a vision—
I fast and prayed for their intelligence—thus:
I saw Jove's bird, the Roman eagle, winged
From the spongy south to this part of the west,
There vanished in the sunbeams; which portends,   350
Unless my sins abuse my divination,
Success to th'Roman host.
  Lucius.   Dream often so,
And never false. Soft, ho, what trunk is here

Without his top? The ruin speaks that sometime
It was a worthy building. How? a page?
Or dead or sleeping on him? But dead rather;
For nature doth abhor to make his bed
With the defunct, or sleep upon the dead.
Let's see the boy's face.

 Captain.   He's alive, my lord.

360 *Lucius.* He'll then instruct us of this body.
    Young one,
Inform us of thy fortunes, for it seems
They crave to be demanded. Who is this
Thou makest thy bloody pillow? Or who was he
That, otherwise than noble nature did,
Hath altered that good picture? What's thy interest
In this sad wreck? How came't? Who is't?
What art thou?

 Imogen.   I am nothing; or if not,
Nothing to be were better. This was my master,
A very valiant Briton and a good,

370 That here by mountaineers lies slain. Alas,
There is no more such masters. I may wander
From east to occident; cry out for service;
Try many, all good; serve truly; never
Find such another master.

 Lucius.   'Lack, good youth,
Thou mov'st no less with thy complaining than
Thy master in bleeding. Say his name, good friend.

 Imogen. Richard du Champ. [*aside*] If I do lie, and do
No harm by it, though the gods hear, I hope
They'll pardon it. [*to Lucius*] Say you, sir?

380 *Lucius.* Thy name?

 Imogen. Fidele, sir.

 Lucius. Thou dost approve thyself the very same:
Thy name fits well thy faith, thy faith thy name.

Wilt take thy chance with me? I will not say
Thou shalt be so well mastered, but be sure,
No less beloved. The Roman emperor's letters
Sent by a consul to me should not sooner
Than thine own worth prefer thee. Go with me.

  Imogen. I'll follow, sir. But first, an't please the gods,
I'll hide my master from the flies, as deep   390
As these poor pickaxes can dig; and when
With wild wood-leaves and weeds I ha' strewed
      his grave
And on it said a century of prayers,
Such as I can, twice o'er, I'll weep and sigh,
And leaving so his service, follow you,
So please you entertain me.

  Lucius.   Ay, good youth,
And rather father thee than master thee.
My friends,
The boy hath taught us manly duties; let us
Find out the prettiest daisied plot we can,   400
And make him with our pikes and partisans
A grave. Come, arm him. Boy, he is preferred
By thee to us, and he shall be interred
As soldiers can. Be cheerful; wipe thine eyes.
Some falls are means the happier to arise.   [*they go*

[4. 3.]   *A room in Cymbeline's palace*

  Enter CYMBELINE, *Lords*, PISANIO, *and attendants*

  Cymbeline. Again; and bring me word how 'tis
      with her.   [*an attendant goes*
A fever with the absence of her son;
A madness, of which her life's in danger. Heavens,

How deeply you at once do touch me! Imogen,
The great part of my comfort, gone; my queen
Upon a desperate bed, and in a time
When fearful wars point at me; her son gone,
So needful for this present. It strikes me past
The hope of comfort. But for thee, fellow,

10 Who needs must know of her departure and
Dost seem so ignorant, we'll enforce it from thee
By a sharp torture.
    Pisanio.   Sir, my life is yours;
I humbly set it at your will; but for my mistress,
I know nothing where she remains, why gone,
Nor when she purposes return. Beseech your highness,
Hold me your loyal servant.
    1 Lord.   Good my liege,
The day that she was missing he was here;
I dare be bound he's true and shall perform
All parts of his subjection loyally. For Cloten,

20 There wants no diligence in seeking him,
And will no doubt be found.
    Cymbeline.   The time is troublesome.
[*to Pisanio*] We'll slip you for a season, but our jealousy
Does yet depend.
    1 Lord.   So please your majesty,
The Roman legions, all from Gallia drawn,
Are landed on your coast, with a supply
Of Roman gentlemen by the senate sent.
    Cymbeline. Now for the counsel of my son
         and queen!
I am amazed with matter.
    1 Lord.   Good my liege,
Your preparation can affront no less

30 Than what you hear of. Come more, for more
         you're ready.

The want is but to put those powers in motion
That long to move.

Cymbeline.　　　　I thank you. Let's withdraw,
And meet the time as it seeks us. We fear not
What can from Italy annoy us, but
We grieve at chances here. Away!

　　　　　　　　　　　　　　　[all but Pisanio go

　Pisanio. I heard no letter from my master since
I wrote him Imogen was slain. 'Tis strange.
Nor hear I from my mistress, who did promise
To yield me often tidings. Neither know I
What is betid to Cloten, but remain　　　　　　40
Perplexed in all. The heavens still must work.
Wherein I am false I am honest; not true, to be true.
These present wars shall find I love my country,
Even to the note o'th'king, or I'll fall in them.
All other doubts, by time let them be cleared:
Fortune brings in some boats that are not steered.

　　　　　　　　　　　　　　　　　　　　[goes

[4. 4.]　　*Wales: Before the cave of Belarius*

Enter BELARIUS, GUIDERIUS, *and* ARVIRAGUS

Guiderius. The noise is round about us.
Belarius.　　　　　　　　　Let us from it.
Arviragus. What pleasure, sir, find we in life, to
　lock it
From action and adventure?
Guiderius.　　　　　　　　Nay, what hope
Have we in hiding us? This way the Romans
Must or for Britons slay us or receive us
For barbarous and unnatural revolts
During their use, and slay us after.

Belarius. Sons,
We'll higher to the mountains; there secure us.
To the king's party there's no going. Newness
10 Of Cloten's death—we being not known, not mustered
Among the bands—may drive us to a render
Where we have lived, and so extort from's that
Which we have done, whose answer would be death
Drawn on with torture.

Guiderius. This is, sir, a doubt
In such a time nothing becoming you,
Nor satisfying us.

Arviragus. It is not likely
That when they hear the Roman horses neigh,
Behold their quartered fires, have both their eyes
And ears so cloyed importantly as now,
20 That they will waste their time upon our note,
To know from whence we are.

Belarius. O, I am known
Of many in the army. Many years,
Though Cloten then but young, you see, not wore him
From my remembrance. And besides, the king
Hath not deserved my service nor your loves,
Who find in my exile the want of breeding,
The certainty of this hard life; aye hopeless
To have the courtesy your cradle promised,
But to be still hot summer's tanlings and
30 The shrinking slaves of winter.

Guiderius. Than be so
Better to cease to be. Pray, sir, to th'army.
I and my brother are not known; yourself
So out of thought, and thereto so o'ergrown,
Cannot be questioned.

Arviragus. By this sun that shines
I'll thither. What thing is't that I never

Did see man die, scarce ever looked on blood,
But that of coward hares, hot goats, and venison,
Never bestrid a horse, save one that had
A rider like myself, who ne'er wore rowel
Nor iron on his heel! I am ashamed   40
To look upon the holy sun, to have
The benefit of his blest beams, remaining
So long a poor unknown.
    Guiderius.   By heavens, I'll go;
If you will bless me sir, and give me leave,
I'll take the better care; but if you will not,
The hazard therefore due fall on me by
The hands of Romans!
    Arviragus.   So say I; amen.
    Belarius. No reason I, since of your lives you set
So slight a valuation, should reserve
My cracked one to more care. Have with you, boys! 50
If in your country wars you chance to die,
That is my bed too, lads, and there I'll lie.
Lead, lead. [*aside*] The time seems long; their
        blood thinks scorn
Till it fly out and show them princes born.   [*they go*

[5. 1.]   *Britain. The Roman camp*

    Enter POSTHUMUS alone, with a bloody handkerchief

    Posthumus. Yea, bloody cloth, I'll keep thee; for
        I wished
Thou shouldst be coloured thus. You married ones,
If each of you should take this course, how many
Must murder wives much better than themselves
For wrying but a little! O Pisanio,

Every good servant does not all commands;
No bond but to do just ones. Gods, if you
Should have ta'en vengeance on my faults, I never
Had lived to put on this; so had you saved
10 The noble Imogen to repent, and struck
Me, wretch, more worth your vengeance. But alack,
You snatch some hence for little faults; that's love,
To have them fall no more; you some permit
To second ills with ills, each elder worse,
And make them dread it, to the doers' thrift.
But Imogen is your own; do your best wills,
And make me blest to obey. I am brought hither
Among th'Italian gentry, and to fight
Against my lady's kingdom. 'Tis enough
20 That, Britain, I have killed thy mistress; peace,
I'll give no wound to thee. Therefore, good heavens,
Hear patiently my purpose. I'll disrobe me
Of these Italian weeds, and suit myself
As does a Briton peasant. So I'll fight
Against the part I come with; so I'll die
For thee, O Imogen, even for whom my life
Is every breath a death; and thus, unknown,
Pitied nor hated, to the face of peril
Myself I'll dedicate. Let me make men know
30 More valour in me than my habits show.
Gods, put the strength o'th'Leonati in me.
To shame the guise o'th'world, I will begin
The fashion—less without and more within. [goes

[5. 2.]   *Field of battle between the British*
and Roman camps

Enter from one side, LUCIUS, JACHIMO, *and the*
Roman Army; from the other side, the British Army;
LEONATUS POSTHUMUS *following, like a poor soldier.*
They march over and go out. Then enter again, in skirmish,
JACHIMO *and* POSTHUMUS: *he vanquisheth and dis-*
armeth JACHIMO, *and then leaves him*

Jachimo. The heaviness and guilt within my bosom
Takes off my manhood. I have belied a lady,
The princess of this country, and the air on't
Revengingly enfeebles me; or could this carl,
A very drudge of nature's, have subdued me
In my profession? Knighthoods and honours borne
As I wear mine are titles but of scorn.
If that thy gentry, Britain, go before
This lout as he exceeds our lords, the odds
Is that we scarce are men and you are gods.   [*goes* 10

The battle continues; the Britons fly; CYMBELINE *is*
taken: then enter, to his rescue, BELARIUS, GUIDERIUS
and ARVIRAGUS

Belarius. Stand, stand, we have the advantage of
        the ground;
The lane is guarded; nothing routs us but
The villainy of our fears.
  Guiderius }
  and Arviragus.}   Stand, stand, and fight.

Re-enter POSTHUMUS, *and seconds the Britons: they*
rescue CYMBELINE *and go out. Then re-enter* LUCIUS,
JACHIMO, *with* IMOGEN

Lucius. Away, boy, from the troops, and save thyself;
For friends kill friends, and the disorder's such
As war were hoodwinked.
    Jachimo.   'Tis their fresh supplies.
    Lucius. It is a day turned strangely; or betimes
Let's reinforce, or fly.   [*they go*

[5.3.]   *Another part of the field*

Enter POSTHUMUS *and a British Lord*

    Lord. Cam'st thou from where they made the stand?
    Posthumus.   I did;
Though you, it seems, come from the fliers?
    Lord.   I did.
    Posthumus. No blame be to you, sir; for all was lost,
But that the heavens fought. The king himself
Of his wings destitute, the army broken,
And but the backs of Britons seen, all flying
Through a strait lane; the enemy full-hearted,
Lolling the tongue with slaught'ring, having work
More plentiful than tools to do't, struck down
10 Some mortally, some slightly touched, some falling
Merely through fear, that the strait pass was dammed
With dead men hurt behind, and cowards living
To die with length'ned shame.
    Lord.   Where was this lane?
    Posthumus. Close by the battle, ditched, and walled
            with turf;
Which gave advantage to an ancient soldier,
An honest one, I warrant, who deserved
So long a breeding as his white beard came to,
In doing this for's country. Athwart the lane

He, with two striplings—lads more like to run
The country base than to commit such slaughter;   20
With faces fit for masks, or rather fairer
Than those for preservation cased, or shame—
Made good the passage; cried to those that fled,
'Our Britain's harts die flying, not our men:
To darkness fleet souls that fly backwards. Stand,
Or we are Romans, and will give you that
Like beasts which you shun beastly, and may save
But to look back in frown. Stand, stand'. These three,
Three thousand confident, in act as many—
For three performers are the file when all   30
The rest do nothing—with this word 'Stand, stand',
Accommodated by the place, more charming
With their own nobleness, which could have turned
A distaff to a lance, gilded pale looks;
Part shame, part spirit renewed, that some,
        turned coward
But by example—O, a sin in war,
Damned in the first beginners!—'gan to look
The way that they did and to grin like lions
Upon the pikes o'th'hunters. Then began
A stop i'th'chaser, a retire; anon   40
A rout, confusion thick; forthwith they fly
Chickens, the way which they stooped eagles; slaves,
The strides they victors made; and now our cowards,
Like fragments in hard voyages, became
The life o'th'need. Having found the back-door open
Of the unguarded hearts, heavens, how they wound!
Some slain before, some dying, some their friends
O'er-borne i'th'former wave, ten chased by one,
Are now each one the slaughterman of twenty.
Those that would die or ere resist are grown   50
The mortal bugs o'th'field.

Lord.   This was strange chance:
A narrow lane, an old man, and two boys.

Posthumus. Nay, do not wonder at it; you are made
Rather to wonder at the things you hear
Than to work any. Will you rhyme upon't,
And vent it for a mock'ry? Here is one:
'Two boys, an old man—twice a boy—a lane,
Preserved the Britons, was the Romans' bane.'

Lord. Nay, be not angry, sir.

Posthumus.   'Lack, to what end?
60 Who dares not stand his foe, I'll be his friend;
For if he'll do as he is made to do,
I know he'll quickly fly my friendship too.
You have put me into rhyme.

Lord.   Farewell; you're angry.
                          [*goes*

Posthumus. Still going? This is a lord! O noble misery,
To be i'th'field, and ask 'what news?' of me!
To-day how many would have given their honours
To have saved their carcasses! took heel to do't,
And yet died too! I, in mine own woe charmed,
Could not find death where I did hear him groan,
70 Nor feel him where he struck. Being an ugly monster,
'Tis strange he hides him in fresh cups, soft beds,
Sweet words; or hath moe ministers than we
That draw his knives i'th'war. Well, I will find him;
For being now a favourer to the Briton,
No more a Briton, I have resumed again
The part I came in. Fight I will no more,
But yield me to the veriest hind that shall
Once touch my shoulder. Great the slaughter is
Here made by th'Roman; great the answer be
80 Britons must take. For me, my ransom's death;
On either side I come to spend my breath,

Which neither here I'll keep nor bear again,
But end it by some means for Imogen.

Enter two British Captains and Soldiers

1 *Captain.* Great Jupiter be praised, Lucius
        is taken.
'Tis thought the old man and his sons were angels.
  2 *Captain.* There was a fourth man, in a silly habit,
That gave th'affront with them.
  1 *Captain.*   So 'tis reported;
But none of 'em can be found. Stand, who's there?
  Posthumus. A Roman,
Who had not now been drooping here if seconds   90
Had answered him.
  2 *Captain.*   Lay hands on him; a dog!
A leg of Rome shall not return to tell
What crows have pecked them here. He brags
        his service
As if he were of note: bring him to th'king.

Enter CYMBELINE, BELARIUS, GUIDERIUS, ARVIRAGUS,
PISANIO, *and Roman Captives. The Captains present*
POSTHUMUS *to* CYMBELINE, *who delivers him over to a
Gaoler: then all go*

[5.4.]   *A British prison*

Enter POSTHUMUS *and two Gaolers*

1 *Gaoler.* You shall not now be stol'n, you have
        locks upon you;
So graze as you find pasture.
  2 *Gaoler.*   Ay, or a stomach.
                              [*the gaolers go*

Posthumus. Most welcome, bondage, for thou art
  a way,
I think, to liberty. Yet am I better
Than one that's sick o'th'gout, since he had rather
Groan so in perpetuity than be cured
By th'sure physician, death, who is the key
T'unbar these locks. My conscience, thou art fettered
More than my shanks and wrists. You good gods, give me
10 The penitent instrument to pick that bolt,
Then, free for ever. Is't enough I am sorry?
So children temporal fathers do appease;
Gods are more full of mercy. Must I repent,
I cannot do it better than in gyves,
Desired more than constrained. To satisfy,
If of my freedom 'tis the main part, take
No stricter render of me than my all.
I know you are more clement than vile men,
Who of their broken debtors take a third,
20 A sixth, a tenth, letting them thrive again
On their abatement; that's not my desire.
For Imogen's dear life take mine; and though
'Tis not so dear, yet 'tis a life; you coined it.
'Tween man and man they weigh not every stamp;
Though light, take pieces for the figure's sake;
You rather mine, being yours. And so, great powers,
If you will take this audit, take this life,
And cancel these cold bonds. O Imogen,
I'll speak to thee in silence.   [*sleeps*

Solemn music. Enter, as in an apparition, SICILIUS
LEONATUS, *father to Posthumus, an old man, attired like
a warrior; leading in his hand an ancient matron, his
wife and mother to Posthumus, with music before them.
Then, after other music, follow the two young* LEONATI,

brothers to Posthumus, with wounds as they died in the
wars. They circle Posthumus round as he lies sleeping

Sicilius.　　No more, thou thunder-master, show　　　30
　　　　　　　Thy spite on mortal flies.
　　　　　With Mars fall out, with Juno chide,
　　　　　　　That thy adulteries
　　　　　　　　Rates and revenges.
　　　　　Hath my poor boy done aught but well,
　　　　　　　Whose face I never saw?
　　　　　I died whilst in the womb he stayed
　　　　　　　Attending nature's law;
　　　　　Whose father then—as men report
　　　　　　　Thou orphans' father art—　　　　40
　　　　　Thou shouldst have been, and shielded him
　　　　　　　From this earth-vexing smart.

Mother.　　Lucina lent not me her aid,
　　　　　　　But took me in my throes,
　　　　　That from me was Posthumus ripped,
　　　　　　　Came crying 'mongst his foes,
　　　　　　　　A thing of pity.

Sicilius.　　Great nature like his ancestry
　　　　　　　Moulded the stuff so fair
　　　　　That he deserved the praise o'th'world,　　50
　　　　　　　As great Sicilius' heir.

1 Brother.　When once he was mature for man,
　　　　　　　In Britain where was he
　　　　　That could stand up his parallel,
　　　　　　　Or fruitful object be
　　　　　In eye of Imogen, that best
　　　　　　　Could deem his dignity?

Mother.　　With marriage wherefore was he mocked,
　　　　　　　To be exiled, and thrown

60   From Leonati seat, and cast
              From her his dearest one,
              Sweet Imogen?

Sicilius. Why did you suffer Jachimo,
              Slight thing of Italy,
          To taint his nobler heart and brain
              With needless jealousy,
          And to become the geck and scorn
              O'th'other's villainy?

2 *Brother.* For this from stiller seats we came,
70   Our parents and us twain,
          That striking in our country's cause
              Fell bravely and were slain,
          Our fealty and Tenantius' right
              With honour to maintain.

1 *Brother.* Like hardiment Posthumus hath
              To Cymbeline performed.
          Then, Jupiter, thou king of gods,
              Why hast thou thus adjourned
          The graces for his merits due,
80   Being all to dolours turned?

Sicilius. Thy crystal window ope; look out;
              No longer exercise
          Upon a valiant race thy harsh
              And potent injuries.

Mother. Since, Jupiter, our son is good,
              Take off his miseries.

Sicilius. Peep through thy marble mansion; help;
              Or we poor ghosts will cry
          To th'shining synod of the rest
90   Against thy deity.

Both Brothers. Help, Jupiter, or we appeal,
    And from thy justice fly.

JUPITER descends in thunder and lightning, sitting upon an eagle; he throws a thunderbolt. The ghosts fall on their knees

Jupiter. No more, you petty spirits of region low,
    Offend our hearing; hush! How dare you
      ghosts
Accuse the thunderer, whose bolt, you know,
    Sky-planted, batters all rebelling coasts?
Poor shadows of Elysium, hence, and rest
    Upon your never-withering banks
      of flowers.
Be not with mortal accidents oppressed;
    No care of yours it is; you know 'tis ours.   100
Whom best I love I cross; to make my gift,
    The more delayed, delighted. Be content;
Your low-laid son our godhead will uplift;
    His comforts thrive, his trials well are spent.
Our Jovial star reigned at his birth, and in
    Our temple was he married. Rise,
      and fade.
He shall be lord of lady Imogen,
    And happier much by his affliction made.
This tablet lay upon his breast, wherein
    Our pleasure his full fortune doth confine;   110
And so away; no farther with your din
    Express impatience, lest you stir up mine.
    Mount, eagle, to my palace crystalline.
                    [ascends

Sicilius. He came in thunder; his celestial breath
Was sulphurous to smell; the holy eagle

Stooped, as to foot us. His ascension is
More sweet than our blest fields. His royal bird
Prunes the immortal wing and cloys his beak,
As when his god is pleased.

All.   Thanks, Jupiter.

120 *Sicilius.* The marble pavement closes, he is entered
His radiant roof. Away, and, to be blest,
Let us with care perform his great behest.

> [*the ghosts vanish*

Posthumus. [*waking*] Sleep, thou hast been a grand-
        sire, and begot
A father to me; and thou hast created
A mother and two brothers. But, O scorn,
Gone! they went hence so soon as they were born;
And so I am awake. Poor wretches that depend
On greatness' favour dream as I have done;
Wake, and find nothing. But, alas, I swerve;
130 Many dream not to find, neither deserve,
And yet are steeped in favours; so am I,
That have this golden chance, and know not why.
What fairies haunt this ground? A book? O rare one,
Be not, as is our fangled world, a garment
Nobler than that it covers. Let thy effects
So follow to be most unlike our courtiers,
As good as promise.   [*reads*

   'When as a lion's whelp shall, to himself unknown,
without seeking find, and be embraced by a piece of
140 tender air, and when from a stately cedar shall be
lopped branches which, being dead many years, shall
after revive, be jointed to the old stock, and freshly
grow; then shall Posthumus end his miseries, Britain
be fortunate and flourish in peace and plenty.'
'Tis still a dream; or else such stuff as madmen
Tongue, and brain not; either both, or nothing,

Or senseless speaking, or a speaking such
As sense cannot untie. Be what it is,
The action of my life is like it, which
I'll keep, if but for sympathy.　　　　　　　　　　150

Re-enter Gaolers

1 *Gaoler.* Come, sir, are you ready for death?

Posthumus. Over-roasted rather; ready long ago.

1 *Gaoler.* Hanging is the word, sir; if you be ready
for that you are well cooked.

Posthumus. So, if I prove a good repast to the specta-
tors, the dish pays the shot.

1 *Gaoler.* A heavy reckoning for you, sir. But the
comfort is, you shall be called to no more payments,
fear no more tavern bills, which are as often the sadness
of parting, as the procuring of mirth. You come in faint 160
for want of meat, depart reeling with too much drink;
sorry that you have paid too much, and sorry that you
are paid too much; purse and brain both empty: the
brain the heavier for being too light, the purse too light,
being drawn of heaviness. Of this contradiction you
shall now be quit. O, the charity of a penny cord! it
sums up thousands in a trice; you have no true debitor-
and-creditor but it; of what's past, is, and to come, the
discharge; your neck, sir, is pen, book, and counters; so
the acquittance follows.　　　　　　　　　　　　170

Posthumus. I am merrier to die than thou art to live.

1 *Gaoler.* Indeed, sir, he that sleeps feels not the
toothache; but a man that were to sleep your sleep, and
a hangman to help him to bed, I think he would change
places with his officer; for look you, sir, you know not
which way you shall go.

Posthumus. Yes indeed do I, fellow.

1 *Gaoler.* Your death has eyes in's head then; I have

not seen him so pictured. You must either be directed
180 by some that take upon them to know, or take upon
yourself that which I am sure you do not know, or
jump the after-inquiry on your own peril; and how you
shall speed in your journey's end, I think you'll never
return to tell on.

Posthumus. I tell thee, fellow, there are none want eyes
to direct them the way I am going, but such as wink
and will not use them.

1 *Gaoler.* What an infinite mock is this, that a man
should have the best use of eyes to see the way of blind-
190 ness! I am sure hanging's the way of winking.

Enter a Messenger

Messenger. Knock off his manacles; bring your
prisoner to the king.

Posthumus. Thou bringest good news, I am called to
be made free.

1 *Gaoler.* I'll be hanged then.

Posthumus. Thou shalt be then freer than a gaoler;
no bolts for the dead.   [*all but* 1 *Gaoler go*

1 *Gaoler.* Unless a man would marry a gallows and
beget young gibbets, I never saw one so prone. Yet, on
200 my conscience there are verier knaves desire to live, for
all he be a Roman; and there be some of them too that
die against their wills; so should I, if I were one. I
would we were all of one mind, and one mind good. O,
there were desolation of gaolers and gallowses! I speak
against my present profit, but my wish hath a preferment in't.   [*goes*

[5. 5.]   *Cymbeline's tent*

Enter CYMBELINE, BELARIUS, GUIDERIUS, ARVIRAGUS,
    PISANIO, *Lords, Officers, and Attendants*

  Cymbeline. Stand by my side, you whom the gods
        have made
Preservers of my throne. Woe is my heart
That the poor soldier that so richly fought,
Whose rags shamed gilded arms, whose
        naked breast
Stepped before targes of proof, cannot be found.
He shall be happy that can find him, if
Our grace can make him so.
  Belarius.   I never saw
Such noble fury in so poor a thing;
Such precious deeds in one that promised nought
But beggary and poor looks.
  Cymbeline.   No tidings of him?   10
  Pisanio. He hath been searched among the dead
        and living,
But no trace of him.
  Cymbeline.   To my grief, I am
The heir of his reward; [*to Belarius, Guiderius, and
        Arviragus*] which I will add
To you, the liver, heart, and brain of Britain,
By whom I grant she lives. 'Tis now the time
To ask of whence you are. Report it.
  Belarius.   Sir,
In Cambria are we born, and gentlemen;
Further to boast were neither true nor modest,
Unless I add, we are honest.
  Cymbeline.   Bow your knees.
Arise my knights o'th'battle; I create you   20

Companions to our person, and will fit you
With dignities becoming your estates.

Enter CORNELIUS *and Ladies*

There's business in these faces. Why so sadly
Greet you our victory? you look like Romans,
And not o'th'court of Britain.
    Cornelius.   Hail, great king!
To sour your happiness, I must report
The queen is dead.
    Cymbeline.   Who worse than a physician
Would this report become? But I consider,
By medicine life may be prolonged, yet death
30 Will seize the doctor too. How ended she?
    Cornelius. With horror, madly dying, like
        her life,
Which, being cruel to the world, concluded
Most cruel to herself. What she confessed
I will report, so please you; these her women
Can trip me if I err, who with wet cheeks
Were present when she finished.
    Cymbeline.   Prithee say.
    Cornelius. First, she confessed she never loved
        you; only
Affected greatness got by you, not you;
Married your royalty, was wife to your place;
40 Abhorred your person.
    Cymbeline.   She alone knew this;
And but she spoke it dying, I would not
Believe her lips in opening it. Proceed.
    Cornelius. Your daughter whom she bore in hand
        to love
With such integrity, she did confess
Was as a scorpion to her sight; whose life,

But that her flight prevented it, she had
Ta'en off by poison.

   Cymbeline.   O most delicate fiend!
Who is't can read a woman? Is there more?

   Cornelius. More, sir, and worse. She did confess
         she had
For you a mortal mineral, which, being took,   50
Should by the minute feed on life, and, ling'ring,
By inches waste you. In which time she purposed,
By watching, weeping, tendance, kissing, to
O'ercome you with her show; and in time,
When she had fitted you with her craft, to work
Her son into th'adoption of the crown;
But failing of her end by his strange absence,
Grew shameless-desperate; opened, in despite
Of heaven and men, her purposes; repented
The evils she hatched were not effected; so   60
Despairing died.

   Cymbeline.   Heard you all this, her women?
   Ladies. We did, so please your highness.

   Cymbeline.   Mine eyes
Were not in fault, for she was beautiful;
Mine ears that heard her flattery, nor my heart
That thought her like her seeming. It had
         been vicious
To have mistrusted her; yet, O my daughter,
That it was folly in me thou mayst say,
And prove it in thy feeling. Heaven mend all!

*Enter LUCIUS, JACHIMO, the Soothsayer, and other
Roman Prisoners, guarded; POSTHUMUS behind, and
IMOGEN*

Thou com'st not, Caius, now for tribute; that
The Britons have razed out, though with the loss   70

Of many a bold one; whose kinsmen have made suit
That their good souls may be appeased with slaughter
Of you their captives, which ourself have granted;
So think of your estate.
   Lucius. Consider, sir, the chance of war; the day
Was yours by accident; had it gone with us,
We should not, when the blood was cool, have threatened
Our prisoners with the sword. But since the gods
Will have it thus, that nothing but our lives
80 May be called ransom, let it come. Sufficeth
A Roman with a Roman's heart can suffer.
Augustus lives to think on't; and so much
For my peculiar care. This one thing only
I will entreat: my boy, a Briton born,
Let him be ransomed. Never master had
A page so kind, so duteous, diligent,
So tender over his occasions, true,
So feat, so nurse-like; let his virtue join
With my request, which I'll make bold your highness
90 Cannot deny; he hath done no Briton harm
Though he have served a Roman. Save him, sir,
And spare no blood beside.
   Cymbeline.   I have surely seen him.
His favour is familiar to me. Boy,
Thou hast looked thyself into my grace,
And art mine own. I know not why, wherefore,
To say, 'Live, boy'. Ne'er thank thy master; live;
And ask of Cymbeline what boon thou wilt,
Fitting my bounty and thy state, I'll give it;
Yea, though thou do demand a prisoner,
100 The noblest ta'en.
   Imogen.   I humbly thank your highness.

Lucius. I do not bid thee beg my life, good lad,
And yet I know thou wilt.

Imogen.   No, no; alack,
There's other work in hand. I see a thing
Bitter to me as death; your life, good master,
Must shuffle for itself.

Lucius.   The boy disdains me,
He leaves me, scorns me. Briefly die their joys
That place them on the truth of girls and boys.
Why stands he so perplexed?

Cymbeline.   What wouldst thou, boy?
I love thee more and more; think more and more
What's best to ask. Know'st him thou look'st
    on? speak,   110
Wilt have him live? Is he thy kin? thy friend?

Imogen. He is a Roman, no more kin to me
Than I to your highness; who, being born your vassal,
Am something nearer.

Cymbeline.   Wherefore ey'st him so?

Imogen. I'll tell you, sir, in private, if you please
To give me hearing.

Cymbeline.   Ay, with all my heart,
And lend my best attention. What's thy name?

Imogen. Fidele, sir.

Cymbeline.   Thou'rt my good youth, my page;
I'll be thy master. Walk with me; speak freely.

               [*Cymbeline and Imogen walk aside*

Belarius. Is not this boy revived from death?

Arviragus.   One sand another 120
Not more resembles—that sweet rosy lad
Who died, and was Fidele. What think you?

Guiderius. The same dead thing alive.

Belarius. Peace, peace, see further; he eyes us
    not; forbear;

Creatures may be alike; were't he, I am sure
He would have spoke to us.

Guiderius.   But we saw him dead.

Belarius. Be silent; let's see further.

(*Pisanio.*   It is my mistress.
Since she is living, let the time run on
To good or bad. [*Cymbeline and Imogen come forward*

Cymbeline.   Come, stand thou by our side;
130 Make thy demand aloud. [*to Jachimo*] Sir, step
          you forth;
Give answer to this boy, and do it freely,
Or, by our greatness and the grace of it,
Which is our honour, bitter torture shall
Winnow the truth from falsehood. On, speak to him.

Imogen. My boon is that this gentleman may render
Of whom he had this ring.

(*Posthumus.*   What's that to him?

Cymbeline. That diamond upon your finger, say
How came it yours?

Jachimo. Thou'lt torture me to leave unspoken that
140 Which, to be spoke, would torture thee.

Cymbeline.   How? me?

Jachimo. I am glad to be constrained to utter that
Torments me to conceal. By villainy
I got this ring; 'twas Leonatus' jewel,
Whom thou didst banish; and—which more may
          grieve thee,
As it doth me—a nobler sir ne'er lived
'Twixt sky and ground. Wilt thou hear more,
          my lord?

Cymbeline. All that belongs to this.

Jachimo.   That paragon, thy daughter,
For whom my heart drops blood, and my false spirits
Quail to remember—Give me leave; I faint.

Cymbeline. My daughter? what of her? Renew
　　thy strength;　　　　　　　　　　　　　　150
I had rather thou shouldst live while nature will
Than die ere I hear more. Strive, man, and speak.
　Jachimo. Upon a time—unhappy was the clock
That struck the hour!—it was in Rome—accursed
The mansion where!—'twas at a feast—O, would
Our viands had been poisoned, or at least
Those which I heaved to head!—the good Posthumus—
What should I say? he was too good to be
Where ill men were, and was the best of all
Amongst the rar'st of good ones—sitting sadly,　　160
Hearing us praise our loves of Italy
For beauty that made barren the swelled boast
Of him that best could speak; for feature, laming
The shrine of Venus or straight-pight Minerva,
Postures beyond brief Nature; for condition,
A shop of all the qualities that man
Loves woman for; besides that hook of wiving,
Fairness which strikes the eye—
　Cymbeline.　　　　　　　　I stand on fire.
Come to the matter.
　Jachimo.　　　　　　　All too soon I shall,
Unless thou wouldst grieve quickly. This Posthumus,　170
Most like a noble lord in love and one
That had a royal lover, took his hint,
And not dispraising whom we praised—therein
He was as calm as virtue—he began
His mistress' picture; which by his tongue
　　being made,
And then a mind put in't, either our brags
Were cracked of kitchen-trulls, or his description
Proved us unspeaking sots.
　Cymbeline.　　　　　　　Nay, nay, to th'purpose.

N.S.C. – 10

Jachimo. Your daughter's chastity—there it begins.
180 He spake of her as Dian had hot dreams
And she alone were cold; whereat I, wretch,
Made scruple of his praise, and wagered with him
Pieces of gold 'gainst this which then he wore
Upon his honoured finger, to attain
In suit the place of's bed and win this ring
By hers and mine adultery. He, true knight,
No lesser of her honour confident
Than I did truly find her, stakes this ring;
And would so, had it been a carbuncle
190 Of Phœbus' wheel; and might so safely, had it
Been all the worth of's car. Away to Britain
Post I in this design. Well may you, sir,
Remember me at court; where I was taught
Of your chaste daughter the wide difference
'Twixt amorous and villainous. Being thus quenched
Of hope, not longing, mine Italian brain
'Gan in your duller Britain operate
Most vilely; for my vantage, excellent.
And, to be brief, my practice so prevailed,
200 That I returned with simular proof enough
To make the noble Leonatus mad,
By wounding his belief in her renown
With tokens thus and thus; averring notes
Of chamber-hanging, pictures, this her bracelet—
☉ cunning, how I got it!—nay, some marks
Of secret on her person, that he could not
But think her bond of chastity quite cracked,
I having ta'en the forfeit. Whereupon—
Methinks I see him now—
    Posthumus. [*advancing*] Ay, so thou dost,
210 Italian fiend! Ay me, most credulous fool,
Egregious murderer, thief, any thing

That's due to all the villains past, in being,
To come! O, give me cord, or knife, or poison,
Some upright justicer! Thou, king, send out
For torturers ingenious: it is I
That all th'abhorréd things o'th'earth amend
By being worse than they. I am Posthumus,
That killed thy daughter; villain-like, I lie;
That caused a lesser villain than myself,
A sacrilegious thief, to do't. The temple   220
Of virtue was she; yea, and she herself.
Spit, and throw stones, cast mire upon me, set
The dogs o'th'street to bay me. Every villain
Be called Posthumus Leonatus, and
Be 'villain' less than 'twas! O Imogen!
My queen, my life, my wife! O Imogen,
Imogen, Imogen!

    Imogen.   Peace, my lord; hear, hear.

    Posthumus. Shall's have a play of this? Thou
        scornful page,

There lie thy part.   [*strikes her: she falls*

    Pisanio.   O gentlemen, help!

Mine and your mistress! O my lord Posthumus,   230
You ne'er killed Imogen till now. Help, help!
Mine honoured lady!

    Cymbeline.   Does the world go round?

    Posthumus. How comes these staggers on me?

    Pisanio.   Wake, my mistress!

    Cymbeline. If this be so, the gods do mean to strike me
To death with mortal joy.

    Pisanio.   How fares my mistress?

    Imogen. O, get thee from my sight;
Thou gavest me poison. Dangerous fellow, hence!
Breathe not where princes are.

    Cymbeline.   The tune of Imogen.

Pisanio. Lady,

240 The gods throw stones of sulphur on me, if
That box I gave you was not thought by me
A precious thing; I had it from the queen.
    Cymbeline. New matter still.
    Imogen.   It poisoned me.
    Cornelius.   O gods!
I left out one thing which the queen confessed,
Which must approve thee honest: 'If Pisanio
Have' said she 'given his mistress that confection
Which I gave him for a cordial, she is served
As I would serve a rat.'
    Cymbeline.   What's this, Cornelius?
    Cornelius. The queen, sir, very oft importuned me

250 To temper poisons for her, still pretending
The satisfaction of her knowledge only
In killing creatures vile, as cats and dogs,
Of no esteem. I, dreading that her purpose
Was of more danger, did compound for her
A certain stuff which being ta'en would cease
The present power of life, but in short time
All offices of nature should again
Do their due functions. Have you ta'en of it?
    Imogen. Most like I did, for I was dead.
    Belarius.   My boys,

260 There was our error.
    Guiderius.   This is, sure, Fidele.
    Imogen. Why did you throw your wedded lady
        from you?
Think that you are upon a lock, and now
Throw me again.   *[embracing him*
    Posthumus.   Hang there like fruit, my soul,
Till the tree die!
    Cymbeline.   How now, my flesh? my child?

What, mak'st thou me a dullard in this act?
Wilt thou not speak to me?

  Imogen.   [*kneeling*] Your blessing, sir.

  Belarius. [*to Guiderius and Arviragus*] Though you
     did love this youth, I blame ye not;
You had a motive for't.

  Cymbeline.   My tears that fall
Prove holy water on thee! Imogen,
Thy mother's dead.

  Imogen.   I am sorry for't, my lord.   270

  Cymbeline. O, she was naught; and long of her it was
That we meet here so strangely; but her son
Is gone, we know not how or where.

  Pisanio.   My lord,
Now fear is from me, I'll speak troth. Lord Cloten,
Upon my lady's missing, came to me
With his sword drawn, foamed at the mouth,
     and swore,
If I discovered not which way she was gone,
It was my instant death. By accident,
I had a feignéd letter of my master's
Then in my pocket, which directed him   280
To seek her on the mountains near to Milford;
Where, in a frenzy, in my master's garments,
Which he enforced from me, away he posts
With unchaste purpose, and with oath to violate
My lady's honour. What became of him
I further know not.

  Guiderius.   Let me end the story:
I slew him there.

  Cymbeline.   Marry, the gods forfend!
I would not thy good deeds should from my lips
Pluck a hard sentence. Prithee, valiant youth,
Deny't again.

290 *Guiderius*.   I have spoke it, and I did it.
    Cymbeline. He was a prince.
    Guiderius. A most incivil one. The wrongs he
       did me
Were nothing prince-like; for he did provoke me
With language that would make me spurn the sea,
If it could so roar to me. I cut off's head,
And am right glad he is not standing here
To tell this tale of mine.
    Cymbeline.   I am sorrow for thee.
By thine own tongue thou art condemned, and must
Endure our law. Thou'rt dead.
    Imogen.   That headless man
300 I thought had been my lord.
    Cymbeline.   Bind the offender,
And take him from our presence.
    Belarius.   Stay, sir king.
This man is better than the man he slew,
As well descended as thyself, and hath
More of thee merited than a band of Clotens
Had ever scar for. [*to the guard*] Let his arms alone;
They were not born for bondage.
    Cymbeline.   Why, old soldier:
Wilt thou undo the worth thou art unpaid for,
By tasting of our wrath? How of descent
As good as we?
    Arviragus.   In that he spake too far.
310 *Cymbeline*. And thou shalt die for't.
    Belarius.   We will die all three
But I will prove that two on's are as good
As I have given out him. My sons, I must
For mine own part unfold a dangerous speech,
Though haply well for you.
    Arviragus.   Your danger's ours.

Guiderius.　And our good his.

Belarius.　　　　　　　Have at it then; by leave,
Thou hadst, great king, a subject who
Was called Belarius.

Cymbeline.　　　　What of him? he is
A banished traitor.

Belarius.　　　　　He it is that hath
Assumed this age; indeed a banished man,
I know not how a traitor.

Cymbeline.　　　　　　Take him hence;　　　320
The whole world shall not save him.

Belarius.　　　　　　　　Not too hot;
First pay me for the nursing of thy sons,
And let it be confiscate all, so soon
As I have received it.

Cymbeline.　　　　Nursing of my sons?

Belarius.　I am too blunt and saucy: here's my knee.
Ere I arise I will prefer my sons,
Then spare not the old father. Mighty sir,
These two young gentlemen that call me father,
And think they are my sons, are none of mine;
They are the issue of your loins, my liege,　　　330
And blood of your begetting.

Cymbeline.　　　　　　How? my issue?

Belarius.　So sure as you your father's. I, old Morgan,
Am that Belarius whom you sometime banished.
Your pleasure was my mere offence, my punishment
Itself, and all my treason; that I suffered
Was all the harm I did. These gentle princes—
For such and so they are—these twenty years
Have I trained up; those arts they have as I
Could put into them. My breeding was, sir, as
Your highness knows. Their nurse, Euriphile,　　　340
Whom for the theft I wedded, stole these children

Upon my banishment; I moved her to't,
Having received the punishment before
For that which I did then. Beaten for loyalty
Excited me to treason. Their dear loss,
The more of you 'twas felt, the more it shaped
Unto my end of stealing them. But gracious sir,
Here are your sons again, and I must lose
Two of the sweet'st companions in the world.
350 The benediction of these covering heavens
Fall on their heads like dew! for they are worthy
To inlay heaven with stars.

    Cymbeline.   Thou weep'st, and speak'st.
The service that you three have done is more
Unlike than this thou tell'st. I lost my children;
If these be they, I know not how to wish
A pair of worthier sons.

    Belarius.   Be pleased awhile.
This gentleman, whom I call Polydore,
Most worthy prince, as yours, is true Guiderius;
This gentleman, my Cadwal, Arviragus,
360 Your younger princely son; he, sir, was lapped
In a most curious mantle, wrought by th'hand
Of his queen mother, which for more probation
I can with ease produce.

    Cymbeline.   Guiderius had
Upon his neck a mole, a sanguine star;
It was a mark of wonder.

    Belarius.   This is he,
Who hath upon him still that natural stamp.
It was wise nature's end in the donation,
To be his evidence now.

    Cymbeline.   O, what am I?
A mother to the birth of three? Ne'er mother
370 Rejoiced deliverance more. Blest pray you be,

That, after this strange starting from your orbs,
You may reign in them now! O Imogen,
Thou hast lost by this a kingdom.

   Imogen.   No, my lord;
I have got two worlds by't. O my gentle brothers,
Have we thus met? O, never say hereafter
But I am truest speaker: you called me brother,
When I was but your sister; I you brothers,
When ye were so indeed.

   Cymbeline.   Did you e'er meet?

   Arviragus. Ay, my good lord.

   Guiderius.   And at first meeting loved,
Continued so until we thought he died.   380

   Cornelius. By the queen's dram she swallowed.

   Cymbeline.   O rare instinct!
When shall I hear all through? This fierce abridgement
Hath to it circumstantial branches which
Distinction should be rich in. Where? how lived you?
And when came you to serve our Roman captive?
How parted with your brothers? how first met them?
Why fled you from the court? and whither? These,
And your three motives to the battle, with
I know not how much more, should be demanded,
And all the other by-dependences,   390
From chance to chance; but nor the time nor place
Will serve our long inter'gatories. See
Posthumus anchors upon Imogen;
And she, like harmless lightning, throws her eye
On him, her brothers, me, her master, hitting
Each object with a joy; the counterchange
Is severally in all. Let's quit this ground,
And smoke the temple with our sacrifices.
[*to Belarius*] Thou art my brother; so we'll hold
      thee ever.

400 *Imogen.* You are my father too, and did relieve me
To see this gracious season.

Cymbeline.   All o'erjoyed,
Save these in bonds; let them be joyful too,
For they shall taste our comfort.

Imogen.   My good master,
I will yet do you service.

Lucius.   Happy be you!

Cymbeline. The forlorn soldier that so
      nobly fought,
He would have well becomed this place and graced
The thankings of a king.

Posthumus.   I am, sir,
The soldier that did company these three
In poor beseeming; 'twas a fitment for
410 The purpose I then followed. That I was he,
Speak, Jachimo. I had you down, and might
Have made you finish.

Jachimo.   [*kneeling*] I am down again;
But now my heavy conscience sinks my knee,
As then your force did. Take that life, beseech you,
Which I so often owe; but your ring first,
And here the bracelet of the truest princess
That ever swore her faith.

Posthumus.   Kneel not to me.
The power that I have on you is to spare you;
The malice towards you to forgive you. Live,
420 And deal with others better.

Cymbeline.   Nobly doomed!
We'll learn our freeness of a son-in-law;
Pardon's the word to all.

Arviragus.   You holp us, sir,
As you did mean indeed to be our brother;
Joyed are we that you are.

Posthumus. Your servant, princes. Good my lord
    of Rome,
Call forth your soothsayer. As I slept, methought
Great Jupiter, upon his eagle backed,
Appeared to me, with other spritely shows
Of mine own kindred. When I waked, I found
This label on my bosom; whose containing   430
Is so from sense in hardness that I can
Make no collection of it. Let him show
His skill in the construction.

Lucius.   Philarmonus!
Soothsayer. Here, my good lord.
Lucius.   Read, and declare the meaning.
Soothsayer. [*reads*] 'When as a lion's whelp shall, to
himself unknown, without seeking find, and be em-
braced by a piece of tender air; and when from a stately
cedar shall be lopped branches which, being dead many
years, shall after revive, be jointed to the old stock, and
freshly grow; then shall Posthumus end his miseries, 440
Britain be fortunate and flourish in peace and plenty.'
Thou, Leonatus, art the lion's whelp;
The fit and apt construction of thy name,
Being Leo-natus, doth import so much.
[*to Cymbeline*] The piece of tender air, thy
    virtuous daughter,
Which we call 'mollis aer'; and 'mollis aer'
We term it 'mulier'; [*to Posthumus*] which 'mulier'
    I divine
Is this most constant wife; who even now,
Answering the letter of the oracle,
Unknown to you, unsought, were clipped about   450
With this most tender air.

Cymbeline.   This hath some seeming.
Soothsayer. The lofty cedar, royal Cymbeline,

Personates thee; and thy lopped branches point
Thy two sons forth, who, by Belarius stol'n,
For many years thought dead, are now revived,
To the majestic cedar joined, whose issue
Promises Britain peace and plenty.

 Cymbeline.   Well;
My peace we will begin. And, Caius Lucius,
Although the victor, we submit to Cæsar

460 And to the Roman empire, promising
To pay our wonted tribute, from the which
We were dissuaded by our wicked queen,
Whom heavens in justice both on her and hers
Have laid most heavy hand.

 Soothsayer. The fingers of the powers above do tune
The harmony of this peace. The vision,
Which I made known to Lucius ere the stroke
Of this yet scarce-cold battle, at this instant
Is full accomplished; for the Roman eagle,

470 From south to west on wing soaring aloft,
Lessened herself, and in the beams o'th'sun
So vanished; which foreshowed our princely eagle,
Th'imperial Cæsar, should again unite
His favour with the radiant Cymbeline,
Which shines here in the west.

 Cymbeline.   Laud we the gods,
And let our crookéd smokes climb to their nostrils
From our blest altars. Publish we this peace
To all our subjects. Set we forward; let
A Roman and a British ensign wave

480 Friendly together; so through Lud's town march,
And in the temple of great Jupiter
Our peace we'll ratify; seal it with feasts.
Set on there. Never was a war did cease,
Ere bloody hands were washed, with such a peace.

            [they go

THE COPY FOR
CYMBELINE, 1623

'The Tragedie of Cymbeline' is the last play in the First Folio. It is certainly not what we should call a tragedy, and it has been suggested that its appearance in this class may have been 'the result of late receipt of the "copy" in the printing-house'.[1] Greg, indeed, thinks that it may have been 'through a misunderstanding that Jaggard placed it at the end of the volume instead of the section [containing the comedies]'[2] to which *The Winter's Tale* was added at a late stage. This is possible, but it cannot be regarded as certain. Heminge and Condell had denied themselves the convenient category of 'tragi-comedy', and, though *Cymbeline* seems to us to fall naturally into the same class as *The Tempest* and *The Winter's Tale*, it contains weightier public and historical matter, so that it is not inconceivable that the placing of it among the tragedies was the deliberate choice of what seemed the lesser evil.

The Folio text is free from any marked idiosyncrasies. In 1942, it suggested to Greg 'a prompt-book that has taken over progressively more of the author's original directions for production'.[3] In 1955, while still seeing 'behind F the company's prompt-book as it stood in the early twenties', he thought that 'the actual copy may, of course, have been an *ad hoc* transcript'.[4] Further reasons for believing in a transcript, and for doubting if what it transcribed was actually a prompt-

[1] J. M. Nosworthy, Arden edition (1955), p. xiii.
[2] *The Shakespeare First Folio* (1955), p. 80, n. 8.
[3] *The Editorial Problem in Shakespeare*, p. 150.
[4] *The Shakespeare First Folio*, p. 414.

book, are given by Nosworthy in his Arden edition of
1955, citing the unpublished views of Dr Alice Walker.
She notes certain anomalies that one would not expect
to survive in a prompt-book, such as the superfluous
Dutchman and Spaniard of 1. 4, and—perhaps less
significant—the absence of flourishes, alarums, etc.
Her conclusion is 'that the actual copy was a scribe's
transcript of difficult foul papers which had preceded
the prompt-book' (p. xii). I find nothing to invalidate
this view, and some further evidence to support it.
There is such a minor, and easily corrigible, anomaly as
the speech-prefix '2. Gao.' at 5. 4. 2, following an
entry for a single 'Gaoler' and an opening speech pre-
fixed simply 'Gao.'. The elaborate and sometimes melo-
dramatic punctuation, particularly lavish with question-
marks, though it has its parallels elsewhere in F, and
though the nature of the play helps to explain it, has
a literary rather than a theatrical flavour. The text does
not, on the other hand, have all the peculiarities that
have caused the copy for the first four comedies, and
for *The Winter's Tale*, to be attributed to Ralph
Crane.[1] There is, for instance, a strong taste for hyphens,
including epithet plus substantive (2. 4. 19, 'not-
fearing-Britaine', 4. 2. 226, 'rich-left-heyres', 5. 5.
468, 'ſcarſe-cold-Battaile'), but no examples of the
hyphenated verb plus pronominal object, as in *Tp.* 1. 2.
295, 'peg-thee', 343, 'ſty-me', or verb plus preposition
(or adverb) as in *Gent.* 2. 5. 6, 'Come-on', 5. 4. 114,
'falls-off'.[2]

There are a number of places where the corruptions
seem to reflect not just the carelessness for which
Compositor B is notorious, but a certain perverse in-

[1] See *The Winter's Tale* in this edition, pp. 111–19;
Greg, *The Shakespeare First Folio*, Index, s.v. 'Crane'.

[2] See W. W. Greg, *The Library*, 4th ser. XXII (1941–2),
215–16.

genuity. I think that 2. 4. 76 is an example of this,
though it must be admitted that editors generally retain
the Folio text. Similarly the punctuation at 4. 2. 228–9
looks like a deliberate attempt to solve a textual problem
—here again, there are those who would accept it.

Apart from such passages, F seems to offer a fairly
normal text, as far as the kind and frequency of its
errors is concerned. There are, according to the present
text, omissions at 1. 4. 45, 72; 1. 5. 28; 2. 1. 31; 2. 5.
27; 3. 4. 102, 133; 5. 4. 159; 5. 5. 205; additions,
some caught from the context, at 2. 4. 32; 4. 2. 237;
5. 1. 1; 5. 4. 81, 165, 180; 5. 5. 142 (and perhaps also
3. 5. 105); substitutions, by anticipation or repetition of
a word or part thereof, at 1. 1. 15; 2. 1. 24; 2. 3. 47;
2. 4. 135; 3. 3. 25; 4. 1. 17; 4. 2. 170, 206; 4. 4. 17;
5. 5. 126; other substitutions of similar or related words,
sometimes aided by the context, and sometimes substituting a commoner word for a rare one, at 1. 3. 9; 1.
6. 108; 2. 1. 13; 2. 3. 29, 154; 2. 4. 47; 3. 2. 2, 78; 3.
5. 44; 4. 2. 57, 205, 290; 5. 3. 43; 5. 5. 378, 405. The
addition or omission of final *s* is particularly common:
1. 1. 3; 1. 4. 126; 1. 6. 7, 27, 167; 2. 3. 137; 2. 4. 24,
60; 3. 3. 28; 3. 4. 22, 90; 3. 5. 32; 4. 2. 122, 329;
5. 5. 386. There are almost certain transpositions at
4. 4. 2; 5. 5. 468.

By contrast with these errors, all of which can be
abundantly paralleled in other plays set by Compositor
B,[1] clear errors of which the most plausible explanation
is misreading of handwriting (in the strict sense of mis-

---

[1] See, for example, Alice Walker's analysis of *Henry V* in
Studies in Bibliography, VIII (1956), especially p. 98. Unlike
Dr Walker, I am not here dealing with literals, or with
other errors that do not produce words at all. On the other
hand, I am including places where the fact of error, and the
correction, are uncertain. But the general pattern of causes
of error is similar.

taking one letter or group of letters for another) are relatively few. There are probable minim errors at 1. 4. 70; 2. 3. 43; 2. 4. 24; 4. 2. 132; 5. 5. 225, 334; an 'ſ:f' error at 1. 6. 168; an 'e:d' error at 5. 5. 64; and misreading may also be responsible, though it is not always clear how, for errors at 1. 6. 103; 3. 1. 20; 3. 3. 2, 23; 3. 4. 79; 3. 6. 70; 4. 2. 58; 5. 5. 262.

On proof-correction, all that can be done pending the publication of Dr Hinman's findings is to record the variants noted by the Cambridge editors and by W. J. Craig in his *New Shakspere Society* edition (1883): 1. 6. 79, 'Tallents|Talents'; 1. 6. 103, 'dampn'd|damn'd'; 2. 1. 57, 'expuſion|expulſion'; 2. 2. 2, 'houe|houre'; 2. 2. 23, 'deſigne?|deſigne.'; 2. 2. 26, 'adronement|adornement'; 2. 2. 43, 'riuete| riueted'. The first two are on one page, and the other five on another. Comparison with the other variants on the same page shows—what might not have been quite certain otherwise—that the corrected state at 2. 2. 23 is 'deſigne.'.

NOTES

All significant departures from F are recorded, the source of the accepted reading being indicated in brackets. Square brackets about an author's name mean that he is responsible for the substance of the note that precedes; round brackets a verbatim quotation from him. Line-numeration for references to plays not yet issued in this edition is that found in Bartlett's *Concordance* (1894) and the *Globe Shakespeare*.

F stands for First Folio (1623); F2, F3, F4 for Second, Third and Fourth Folios (1632, 1663, 1685); G. for Glossary; O.E.D. for the *Oxford English Dictionary*; S.D. for stage-direction; Sh. for Shakespeare or Shakespearian; sp.-pref. for speech-prefix. Common words are also usually abbreviated: e.g. sp. = spelling or spelt, prob. = probable or probably, om. = omitted, etc.

The following is a list of other works cited in abridged form:

Abbott = *A Shakespearian Grammar*, by E. A. Abbott (3rd ed. 1870).

Al. = ed. of Sh. by Peter Alexander, 1951.

Anders = *Shakespeare's Books*, by H. R. D. Anders, 1900.

Baldwin = *William Shakspere's Small Latine and Lesse Greeke*, 1944.

B.C.P. = Book of Common Prayer.

Beaumont and Fletcher = *Works of Francis Beaumont and John Fletcher*, Variorum ed., 1904–12 [incomplete]; for other plays, *Works*, ed. A. Glover and A. R. Waller, 1905–12.

Boswell-Stone = *Sh.'s Holinshed*, by W. G. Boswell-Stone, 1896.

Camb. = *The Cambridge Sh.* (2nd ed. 1892).

Cap. = ed. of Sh. by Edward Capell, 1768.

Chambers, *Wm. Sh.* = *William Sh.*, by E. K. Chambers, 1930.

Clarke = ed. of Sh. by Charles and Mary Cowden Clarke [1864–8].

Collier = ed. of Sh. by J. P. Collier, 1842–4, 1858.

Deighton = ed. by K. Deighton, 1889.

Dekker = *Dramatic Works of Thomas Dekker*, ed. by F. Bowers, 1953– (in progress).

Delius = ed. of Sh. by N. Delius (3rd ed. 1872).

Douce = *Illustrations of Sh.*, by F. Douce, 1807.

Dowd. = ed. by E. Dowden (*Arden Sh.*), 1903.

D'Urfey = *The Injured Princess, or the Fatal Wager*, by Thomas D'Urfey, 1682.

Dyce = ed. of Sh. by A. Dyce, 1857, 1864–6.

Dyce, *Remarks* = *Remarks on Collier's and Knight's Editions of Sh.*, by A. Dyce, 1844.

Eccles = ed. by A. Eccles, 1794.

E.E.T.S. = Early English Text Society.

Evans = ed. by H. A. Evans (*Henry Irving Sh.*), 1890.

Franz = *Die Sprache Shakespeares*, by W. Franz (4th ed. of *Shakespeare-Grammatik*), 1939.

Furn. = ed. by H. H. Furness, 1913.

Globe = ed. by W. G. Clark and W. A. Wright (*Globe Sh.*), 1864.

Grant White = ed. of Sh. by R. Grant White, 1865.

Han. = ed. of Sh. by Sir Thomas Hanmer, 1743–4.

Heath = *Revisal of Sh.'s Text*, by B. Heath, 1765.

Her. = ed. by C. H. Herford (*Eversley Sh.*), 1899.

Hol. = R. Holinshed, *Chronicles of England* (1587).

Ingleby = ed. by C. M. Ingleby, 1886.

J. = ed. of Sh. by Samuel Johnson, 1765.

Jonson = *Works of Ben Jonson*, ed. by C. H. Herford and Percy and Evelyn Simpson, 1925–52.

K. = ed. of Sh. by G. L. Kittredge, 1936.

Kökeritz = *Sh.'s Pronunciation*, by H. Kökeritz, 1953.

Lyly = *Works of John Lyly*, ed. by R. W. Bond, 1902.

Mal. = ed. of Sh. by E. Malone, 1790 (notes incorporated in final form in 1821 Variorum, ed. J. Boswell).

Mason = *Comments on the Several Editions of Sh.'s Plays*, by J. M. Mason, 1807 (expanded from edd. 1785, 1798).

Middleton = *Works of Thomas Middleton*, ed. by A. H. Bullen, 1885–6.

MSH. = *The Manuscript of Sh.'s 'Hamlet'*, by J. D. Wilson, 1934.

M.S.R. = Malone Society Reprint.

Nashe = *Works of Thomas Nashe*, ed. by R. B. McKerrow, 1904–10.

Neilson and Hill = ed. of Sh. by W. A. Neilson and C. J. Hill, 1942.

N. & Q. = *Notes and Queries*.

Nos. = ed. by J. M. Nosworthy (*Arden Sh.*), 1955.

On. = *A Sh. Glossary*, by C. T. Onions, 1911 (last corrected impression, 1946).

Pope = ed. of Sh. by Alexander Pope, 1723–5.

R.E.S. = *Review of English Studies*.

Rowe = ed. of Sh. by N. Rowe, 1709–10 (2 edd.), 1714.

Schmidt = *Sh.-Lexikon*, by A. Schmidt (3rd ed. 1902).

Sh. Eng. = *Shakespeare's England*, 1916.

Simpson = *Sh.'s Punctuation*, by P. Simpson, 1911.

Sisson = ed. of Sh. by C. J. Sisson [1954].

Sisson, *Readings* = *New Readings in Sh.*, by C. J. Sisson, 1956.

Steev. = ed. of Sh. by G. Steevens, 1773 (supplemented in later edd. up to 1803).

Theob. = ed. of Sh. by L. Theobald, 1733.

Thiselton = *Textual Notes on 'Cymbeline'*, by A. E. Thiselton, 1902.

Tilley = *A Dictionary of the Proverbs in England in the Sixteenth and Seventeenth Centuries*, by M. P. Tilley, 1950.

T.L.S. = *Times Literary Supplement*.

Var. = Variorum ed. of Sh., ed. by J. Boswell, 1821.

Vaughan = *New Readings and New Renderings of Sh.'s Tragedies*, by H. H. Vaughan, vol. iii, 1886.

Verity = ed. by A. W. Verity, 1923.

S. Walker = *A Critical Examination of the Text of Sh.*, by W. S. Walker, 1860.

Warb. = ed. of Sh. by W. Warburton, 1747.

Webster = *Works of John Webster*, ed. by F. L. Lucas, 1927.

Wyatt = ed. by A. J. Wyatt (*Warwick Sh.*) [1897].

Yale = ed. by S. B. Hemingway (*Yale Sh.*), 1924.

The above list does not include a number of names occasionally cited from the Cambridge Shakespeare critical apparatus, or from the notes in Furness's edition.

Names of the Characters. First given, imperfectly, by Rowe. The only characters who correspond closely to Hol. both in name and function are Cymbeline (Kymbeline or Cimbeline in Hol.; the historical Cuno-bellinus), and his two sons. But a number of the other names could have come from Hol. (Boswell-Stone, pp. 17–18), and the following probably did: Cadwal (Cadwallo, King of Britain from 635 A.D.), Cloten (Cloton or Clotenus, King of Cornwall and father of Mulmucius; cf. 3. 1. 53), and Morgan (cf. 3. 3. 106 n.). Less certain is Posthumus, but Sh. is likely to have looked at the account in Hol. ii, i of Posthumus the son of Aeneas and Lavinia. Leonatus, as Mal. noted, is the name of the good son of the Paphlagonian king in Sidney's *Arcadia*: the prototype of Edgar in *King Lear*.

Common names such as Cornelius and Helen occur in Hol. but may have come from anywhere. F. G. Stokes, *Dictionary of the Characters and Proper Names in the Works of Sh.* (1924), cites two medical bearers of the name Cornelius. Each of the elements of the name Caius [the customary mis-spelling of Gaius] Lucius could be found in Hol., and each is common; the combination of two praenomina is un-Latin. Polydore may derive from Polydore Vergil, frequently cited as an authority by Hol. Dowd., p. xxi, notes that a Polydorus occurs in Young's translation of Montemayor's *Diana* (1598). Jachimo is the Italian 'Giacomo'. F's initial 'I' is ambiguous. F4, the first edition to differentiate initial 'J' from 'I', has 'Jachimo' (and 'Jago' in *Othello*), and so does D'Urfey in *The Injured Princess* (see Stage-history, p. xliv). Rowe introduced the now traditional spelling 'Iachimo', while perversely retaining 'Jago', which, unlike 'Jachimo', is not in accordance with the metre. For Belarius, cf. Bellario in *Philaster* and Bellaria in Greene's *Pandosto*, the prototype of Hermione in *Wint.* (Chambers, *Wm. Sh.* 1, 485); also Bellario in *M.V.* [J.D.W.]. The name 'Imogen' is found only here. The wife of Brute in Hol. is 'Innogen', which is also the name of the (mute) wife of Leonato in the initial S.D. of *Ado*, 1.1. This coincidence of two pairs of names in Sh.'s two slander-plays is suggestive (cf. F. D. Hoeniger, *Sh. Quarterly*, VIII (1957), 132–3). Forman's report also has 'Innogen' (see Stage-history, p. xliii). Though it is not exactly paralleled by invented significant names like Marina, Perdita and Miranda, 'Innogen' might also be appropriate as carrying a suggestion of 'innocence', as H. H. Furness long ago remarked; her assumed name 'Fidele' is, of course, overtly significant. It is probable that F is wrong, but it would scarcely be tolerable to dislodge the familiar form for anything less than a certainty.

correctly understood, and emended (see next note), by
Tyrwhitt. Cf. *Ant.* 1. 5. 55–6 [Mal.].

2–3. *courtiers...king* (Tyrwhitt) F 'Courtiers:
...Kings'. All accept the change of punctuation, but
some recent edd. have reverted to 'king's'. The confusion may be Sh.'s but more prob. the compositor's,
perh. from the endings of the preceding lines in F
[Verity].

9. *outward* Dowd. glosses 'insincere' and compares
Cor. 1. 6. 77. But the word may be more neutrally
used, with the sense '*merely* outward' emerging only by
contrast with the following clause.

15. *of* (Staunton conj.) F 'at', prob. caught from
the end of the line; Sh. never elsewhere has 'glad at'.

22. *compare* see G.

24. *speak him far* go far in what you say of him.
Cf. Fletcher, *Wild Goose Chase*, 1. 1. (IV, 317), 'To
speak him farther is beyond my Charter' [Dowd.]; and,
in a similar context, *H. VIII*, 1. 1. 38, 'you go far'.

25. *extend...himself* 'my praise, however extensive, is within his merit' (J.).

29. *Sicilius* The name of a much earlier King of
Britain, from 430 B.C., in Hol.

29–30. *did...Cassibelan* 'brought his renowned
soldiership to the service of C.' (Her.).

31. *Tenantius* Also called Theomantius (Boswell-
Stone, p. 7 and n. 1).

33. *sur-addition* Cf. 'addition' in *Cor.* 1. 9. 66
[Verity].

37. *fond of issue* doting on his children. Collier read
'of's' for 'of', but the F text presents his state as
typical of old age.

42. *of his bedchamber* i.e. a chamberlain; cf. *Mac.* 1.
7. 75–6 [Delius]; *Per.* 1. 1. 152.

43. *Puts to* see G., and cf. the bawdy pun in
L.L.L. 4. 2. 83 [Dowd.]. *time* see G.

46. *And* Cap., perh. rightly, transferred this to the end of l. 45. *harvest* i.e. ripe (in learning); so (of bounty) *Ant.* 5. 2. 87, 'an autumn 'twas' [Ingleby].

49. *glass...them* O.E.D. gives the conjectural gloss 'constrained to propriety' for 'feated'. The meaning seems to be 'a glass that reflected them as feat—i.e. elegant—', with the implication that they then proceeded to emulate what they saw.

50–2. *To...him* 'The construction with "to", caught from the preceding sentence, is broken' (Dowd.). So already Cap., who put a dash after 'banished'.

51. *her own price* i.e. the price—imprisonment and her father's displeasure—that she has had to pay for him; cf. *M.V.* 3. 2. 314, 'Since you are dear bought, I will love you dear'. This is more satisfactory than 'her own worth', which could not in the same way prove her esteem for him.

52. *him; ...virtue* (F; Nos., following Thiselton, who first explained it) Pope, most edd., 'him...virtue.'. But 'his virtue' is parallel in construction to 'her price', and the whole passage 'and...is' (ll. 52–4) is a typically 'licentious' piece of late-Sh. syntax, with 'what...is' an afterthought expanding 'his virtue'.

60–1. *guess...went* The exact relation of 'in knowledge' to the rest of the phrase is not clear. Perh. 'guess enabling anyone to know' [Ingleby, substantially].

63. *conveyed* see G.

65. *That* Perh. rel. pron. [Deighton, citing Abbott, §279]. But the conj. after 'so', with ellipse of subj., is also idiomatic; cf. 3. 4. 77–8; *Ado*, 4. 1. 152–3, 'Who loved her so, that, speaking of her foulness, | Washed it with tears'; *Hyckescorner* (ed. Manly), 962–3.

68. *forbear* see G.

69. After this line, F has 'Scena Secunda', presum-

ably because there is an empty stage. But there is no break, and it is reasonable with modern edd. (except Nos.) to continue the scene. S.D. F 'Exeunt' *Entry* (F, after 'Scena Secunda').

71. *slander* see G.

72. *Evil-eyed* 'Evil', as usu. in Sh., is monosyllabic.

74. *lock...restraint.* Some edd. take 'restraint' concretely = 'prison', but more prob. the phrase combines concrete and abstract, and virtually = 'lock up and confine you'.

78. *leaned unto* see G.

79. *inform* see G. The usual gloss 'instruct' is less apt. As often (cf. Abbott, §394) a second 'with' at the end of the clause is omitted.

83. S.D. F 'Exit'. *O* Here in Cap.; at beginning of l. 84 in F.

87. *duty* As Delius saw, this must be her duty to her husband, which would be violated by a divorce imposed by the king, especially if followed by a command to marry again. Interpretations which treat it as her duty to her father make nonsense of the very point Imogen insists on: the contrast between fearing her father and fearing the consequences of his rage.

97. *Rome* Keightley 'Rome's', but the omission of the vb. is natural in hasty speech.

Philario's (Rowe). F '*Filorio's*'.

101. S.D. (Pope) F 'Enter Queene'.

103. S.D. (Rowe).

104–5. *I...friends* whenever I do him wrong, he pays for the injuries I do him (as if they were benefits) in order to be friends with me again.

106. S.D. (Rowe).

113. *But* only; slightly heightening the force of the imper. (cf. *Oth.* 3. 3. 434; 4. 1. 75, 87) rather than closely with 'till', as Wyatt thinks.

116. *cere* (Steev.) F 'ſeare'. See G.; there may be

play on the sealing of a document with wax. O.E.D.
accepts Steev.'s interpretation; On., less plausibly,
equates with 'sear' = 'cause to wither'.

117. S.D. (Rowe).

117–18. *thou...it* Nicholson (*ap.* Furn.) well ex-
plains the change of person (for which Mal. cites 3. 3.
104–5): at 'Remain thou here', Post. 'kisses it, and
then while continuing his words, he naturally looks
towards Imogen'.

123. S.D. (Rowe).

124. *see* see G. S.D. (F).

125. *avoid* (F, Nos.) Most edd. since Rowe
(though Dowd. noted that F 'may be right') take it
absolutely, and insert a comma or exclamation-mark,
unnecessarily.

126. *fraught* Subjunctive.

130. S.D. F 'Exit'.

133. *A year's age* F 'A yeares age'. Many have
been dissatisfied with the obvious meaning, and have
emended or offered forced interpretations. The least
violent solution, accepted by Al., is 'A years' age',
which Schmidt glosses 'an age advanced in years', and
Thiselton 'an age of years'. But, as Cap. notes, Cym. is
an old man to whom a year is a long time, and he may
be grimly understating.

135. *a touch more rare* 'the "sweet pain" of parting
with Posthumus' (Wyatt).

137. *that...grace* The exclusion of grace by
despair is a Christian (not, as some have thought, a
purely Calvinist) doctrine.

139. *might not* was able not to. Takes up, and
plays on, Cym.'s 'mightst'.

141–2. *Thou...baseness* Divided by Rowe; after
'my' in F.

142–3. *No...it* Divided by Rowe; one line in F.

143. *vile* F 'vilde', as often.

146–7. *overbuys...pays* almost all of what he pays for me (himself and his sufferings) is in excess of my value.

150. *neighbour shepherd's* Hyphenated in F. S.D. (Cap.) F 'Enter Queene'. Dyce transferred to the end of the line, to show that 'Thou foolish thing' is not addressed to the queen.

151. S.D. (Theob.).

156–7. *languish...day* Cf. *Oth.* 5.2.158–9, 'may his pernicious soul | Rot half a grain a day!' [Steev.].

156. *languish* see G. Sometimes trans., as Dowd. notes, but here most naturally taken as 'languish at the rate of'.

158. S.D. (i) after Dyce; F 'Exit'. (ii) (F), unnecessarily transferred by Dyce to the end of the line. *Fie...way* Flung after the departing Cym., but designed to delude Im. into a belief in her friendship.

165. *takes his part* behaves as might be expected of him. This interpretation, given by Nos. as preferable to 'sides with my father', is supported by Greene, *Pandosto*, ed. P. G. Thomas, p. 23, 'it was her part to deny such a monstrous crime'. *part* (F) J., most edd., 'part.', with 'To...exile' an independent exclamation. But F, with 'To draw'='in drawing', is preferable [Thiselton].

167. *in Afric* The notion of conflict in a desert place, with no one to part the combatants, occurs also in *R. II*, 4. 1. 74; *Mac.* 3. 4. 104 [Clarke]; cf. *R. II*, 1. 1. 65 n.

168. *needle* Monosyllabic; cf. *M.N.D.* 3. 2. 204 n.

177. *About...me* Arranged by Rowe; divided after 'hence' in F. Cap., followed by most later edd., made 'Pray...hence' a single line, and then had to emend 'Pray' in this line to 'I pray' to regularize a line ending at 'least'. H. F. Brooks, *ap.* Nos. (who also follows Rowe in preference to Cap.), suggests that

'pray' (opening a line in F) may have been caught from 'Pray' in l. 176, replacing 'an irrecoverable disyllable'. (The obvious candidate would be 'Beseech'.) The lines would then end as in Cap.

179. S.D. F 'Exeunt'.

I. 2

S.D. *Loc.* (Camb.) *Entry* (F). CLOTEN F 'Clotten'; so up to 4. 1.: thereafter 'Cloten'. The pronunciation is evidently 'ŏ': cf. 4. 2. 184, 'Cloten's clotpoll'.

3–4. *Where...vent* If he does not cease reeking, 'he must take air in to supply what he loses, and the outer air is less wholesome than that of his own sweet body' (Dowd.).

5–6. *If...him* Prose in Cap.; two lines, divided after 'it', in F.

7. S.D. (Theob.); so at ll. 11, 14. Asides of this kind are 'specially beloved by the companions of a *miles gloriosus*' (W. Creizenach, *Eng. Drama in the Age of Sh.* (1916), p. 275).

8. *passable* 'penetrable, without rupture, as a fluid' (Ingleby, citing *Tp.* 3. 3. 62–4), perh. with a quibble on the sense 'tolerably good'. So 'throughfare' in l. 9 carries the implication of unimpeded passage.

11–12. *o'th' backside the town* in the back streets, so as to avoid creditors.

18. S.D. (Pope); so at ll. 21, 25, 30, 34.

19. *As...oceans* 'that is, none at all' (Deighton).

21–2. *measured...ground M.N.D.* 3. 2. 429 is the earliest O.E.D. quotation for 'measure (out) one's length'.

25–6. *election...damned* A mild theological pun; cf. 1. 1. 137 n.

28. *go not together* 'are not on a par' (Clarke). Cf. Tilley, B 164, 'Beauty and folly are often matched

together'. *sign* see G. There may, as Steev. thought, be
a more specific reference to an inn-sign, but if so, the
contrast is scarcely with 'a motto, or some attempt at a
witticism, underneath it', but simply with what is in-
side the building: cf. 1. 6. 15–17 [Mal.].

29–30. *reflection...reflection* The meaning the first
time is simply 'shining', but the Second Lord plays on
it in a more specific sense: 'lest she should be injured by
the beams of her wit being thrown back from the
surface of folly' (Deighton).

30–1. *She...her* Prose in Rowe; two lines, divided
after 'reflection', in F.

36. *You'll...us* Perh. addressed to the Second Lord
(whom he has ignored up to now), in which case 'First
Lord intervenes with his assurance of attendance;
Cloten still presses for the company of Second Lord,
who then submits with a reluctant "Well, my lord"'
(Dowd.). Or else he addresses both, and when only
one replies he urges the other to join them.

39. S.D. F 'Exeunt'.

1. 3

S.D. *Loc.* (Mal.) *Entry* (F).

4. *offered mercy* Either pardon to a criminal
[Heath, Steev., citing *All's*, 5. 3. 58], or the mercy of
heaven [Warb.].

9. *this* (Warb. *ap.* Theob.) F 'his'. *ear* This has
caused difficulty, as 'Pis. describes no address made to
the ear' (J.), but the notion of straining both senses at
once is natural. I find Warb.'s correction satisfactory,
but J.D.W. believes Sh. wrote 'mark (Han.) me with
his eye, or mine (Deighton) Distinguish'. Earlier,
Han. had read 'I' for 'ear'.

14–21. *Thou...air* Recalls *Lr.* 4. 6. 13–20
[Steev.].

17–18. Divided by Pope; after 'eye-strings' in F.

17. *broke...them* So Nashe, 'I haue crackt mine eye-strings with excessiue staring and stedfast heauen-gazing' (II, 56, ll. 36–7); 'my eyes haue broken their strings with staring' (II, 324, ll. 24–5) [Thiselton].

19. *Of space* caused by (increasing) space [Heath; J.].

32–3. *T'encounter...him* The meeting of their prayers in heaven will be a sort of meeting of themselves.

35. *charming* see G.; the earliest O.E.D. quotation for the weakened mod. sense is 1663.

37. S.D. (F).

39. *bid* Past tense.

40. S.D. F 'Exeunt'.

1.4

S.D. *Loc.* (Camb.) *Entry* (F). The initial of F's 'Iachimo' is evidently a consonant, as Douce (II, 98) noted; cf. Names of the Characters, p. 133. The name is Ital. 'Giacomo', and wherever the metre is unambiguous, three, not four, syllables are called for. The Dutchman and the Spaniard show Sh.'s use of *Frederick of Jennen*, which has two foreign and two Italian merchants, whereas all are Italian in Boccaccio; cf. Introd., p. xviii. For Sh.'s habit of occasionally jotting down characters not subsequently used in dialogue, see Chambers, *Wm. Sh.* I, 203, 231.

9. *makes* see G.

12. *behold the sun* The traditional prerogative of the eagle [Ingleby, noting that Post. is an eagle at I. I. 139]. Deighton cites *L.L.L.* 4. 3. 222, and Dowd. *3 H. VI*, 2. 1. 91–2, paraphrasing, 'we had many eagles as true of breed as he'.

15–16. *words...matter* 'makes the description of him very distant from the truth' (J.).

18–19. *those . . . under her colours* 'her partisans'
(Clarke). Dowd. notes the continuation of the military
imagery in 'fortify' and 'battery'. *are* By 'confusion
of proximity' (Abbott, §412), or with 'banishment and
approbation' as implied subject. *are to* 'are of a nature
to' (Dowd.); a usage not recognized in O.E.D., but cf.
Jonson, *Volpone*, 2. 4. 30–1, 'Is not the colour o' my
beard, and eye-browes, | To make me knowne?'; 'he
was naturally to follow such counsel as was given him',
'he was naturally to be much in his presence' (World's
Classics *Selections from Clarendon*, pp. 71, 92); Donne,
Paradoxes and Problems, Prob. IX (Nonesuch ed.,
p. 351), 'her *prostitute disciples*, who so often . . . are to
take *new names*'; Kyd, *S.T.* 2. 1. 13 [1966].

22. *without less* A frequent confusion; cf. *Wint.* 3.
2. 55–7 [Mal.], *Cor.* 1. 4. 14.

23. *how creeps acquaintance?* 'How have you stolen
into acquaintance? "Creeps" hints at the stealthy
process implied in the unexpected result' (Her.). The
phrase remains odd, and I suspect a glance at the prov.,
Tilley, K 49, 'Kindness (Love, Kind) will creep where
it cannot go', or at least at the 'creep | go' antithesis; cf.
Gent. 4. 2. 19–20.

25. *S.D.* (F). Postponed to l. 28, after 'quality', by
Dyce, but he can quite well make his first appearance as
Phil. calls attention to him; cf. *Ham.* 2. 2. 168.

26. *Briton* F 'Britaine'; see 1. 6. 60 n.

27. *knowing* 'experience in society; cf. 2. 3. 96
[=97]' (Wyatt). Virtually, *savoir faire*.

33. *Orleans* F 'Orleance'; cf. *1 H. VI*, 1. 1. 59–
61 n.

35. *which . . . still* for which I shall always remain
in debt though I go on repaying them for ever; a
favourite notion: cf. *Son.* 30. 12, 'Which I new pay as
if not paid before'.

38. *put together* sc., in combat.

42–4. *rather...experiences* rather avoided acquiescing in what I was told than ⟨allowed myself to⟩ be guided by others' experience. Most edd. agree substantially on the sense, but fail to point out that a verb of opposite meaning to 'shun' has to be understood in the second half. See G. 'go even'.

44–5. *offend not* (Rowe; so, already, D'Urfey) F 'offend', which not even Sh.'s capacity for getting confused about negatives can make tolerable.

53. *without contradiction* without any objection being raised; cf. *R. II*, 3. 3. 124.

55–6. *country mistresses* Hyphenated in F. *mistresses;* (Theob., with colon) F 'Miſtreſſes.'.

58. *constant, qualified* Hyphenated by Cap. (Errata), unnecessarily; see G. 'qualified'.

66–7. *though...friend* One of the main cruces of the play. The implication of 'though' is that such praise is more surprising from an 'adorer' than from a 'friend', which is at first sight odd. Perh. the simplest explanation is that an 'adorer' might be expected to regard her as too exalted to have her name bandied about, whereas a 'friend' (=lover) would naturally fly to the defence of his loved one's reputation; similarly Thiselton, 'though, as a goddess, she does not need my defence'. I think Steev. was wrong in seeing an adorer's praises as 'the result of reason, not of amorous dotage'. J.D.W. prefers the emendation 'professed' (Ingleby, Vaughan, who, however, interpreted it as an unfulfilled condition)—when he was in France, he was her worshipper in the 'courtly' sense, *not yet* her accepted lover. For other interpretations see Furn., also Wyatt, and J. Derocquigny, *Revue Anglo-Américaine*, II (1924–5), 430–2. The notion mentioned by Furn. that 'though'='because' is groundless.

70. *Britain* (J.) F 'Britanie', which many edd. retain, with sp. 'Britany'. But as the form occurs no-

where else in Sh., it is better to assume a minim error.
Britain. (Pope, with colon) ...*others I* (Pope;
Rowe 'others, I') F 'Britanie;...others. I'.

72. *not but* (Mal.) F 'not'.

79. *mistress* F 'Miſtirs'.

82. *or if* either if. Rowe unnecessarily (so, already,
D'Urfey) deleted 'or'. *purchase* (Rowe; D'Urfey) F
'purchaſes'.

84. *only...of the gods* of the gods alone.

88. *neighbouring ponds* Cf. the 'peculiar river' of
Meas. 1. 2. 88 [Nos.], and *Wint.* 1. 2. 195, 'his pond
fished by his next neighbour' [J.D.W.].

89. *your* Theob. 'of your', but the looser syntax is
natural.

90. *casual* see G.   94. *convince* see G.

95. *frail.* (Pope) F 'fraile,'.

101. *at first* right from the beginning; cf. Abbott,
§90.

103. *get ground* 'get an advantage' (Deighton);
cf. 2 *H. IV*, 2. 3. 53. The sexual application of phrases
of combat is continued in 'go back'.

104. *admittance* Dowd. rightly retains F's comma
after this: 'to friend' goes only with 'opportunity'.

111. *herein too* F 'heerein to'. If the text is sound,
'and...too' prob.='and moreover'; but Grant
White's 'herein-to' is attractive, though the compound
is unrecorded. At 1. 6. 166 'into'='unto'. The anon.
conj. (*ap.* Camb.) 'hereunto' would give a more usual
form. Vaughan's 'herein, so' is also possible.

113. *abused* see G.

114. *sustain* Subjunctive; cf. Abbott, §368. *you're*
F 'y'are', as frequently.

116. *that* (F 2) F 'rhat'.

123. *spoke—* (J.C.M.) F 'ſpoke,', which I take
as a sign that Post. interrupts; cf. Simpson, p. 32; *K.J.*
3. 1. 201.

125. *whom* Cf. Franz, §324, Abbott, §410.

126. *thousand* (F 3) F 'thouſands'.

130. *reserved* see G.

133. *You are a friend* you know her intimately—
a sneer calculated to draw Post. on, by imputing his
refusal to lack of confidence. Theob.'s 'afraid' for 'a
friend' is less forceful, though it gains some support
from ll. 135–6.

134. *lady's* (J.C.M.) F 'Ladies' Edd. 'ladies'',
but the sing. is normal in such expressions; cf. *L.L.L.* 3.
1. 134, *Wint.* 2. 1. 138.

135. *preserve* (F 2) F 'preſeure'.

135–6. *some religion...fear* A cynical jest on
Psalm iii. 10, 'the fear of the Lord is the beginning of
wisdom' [Dowd.].

137. *custom...tongue* Cf. *Cor.* 3. 2. 55–6, 'roted
in | Your tongue'.

140. *undergo* see G.

147–152. *If...yours* Jach. twice describes the
conditions under which Post. will win, in order to lead
him on. Arbitrary emendations have been proposed so
that both outcomes may be stated, but 'one condition
of a wager implies the other' (J.).

157. *voyage* Cf. *Wiv.* 2. 1. 164 [Dyce]. *directly*
see G.

167. S.D. (after Theob.) Implied in Phil.'s closing
words.

170. S.D. F 'Exeunt'.

1. 5

S.D. *Loc.* (Camb.) *Entry* (F).

1. One line in Rowe; divided after 'ground' in F.
Whiles...ground Recommended as the best time by
Arderne, *Treatises of Fistula in Ano* (E.E.T.S. (1910),
p. 92) [Furn.].

3. S.D.   F 'Exit Ladies'.

5. S.D. (Mal.).

17. *did*   Cf. 2. 1. 40, Abbott, §370.

18. *conclusions*   see G.

22. *them*   In sense, the 'conclusions' of l. 18, though there need not be a specific reference back to the word.

26. S.D. (F).

27. S.D. (Rowe).

28. *factor for* (S. Walker) F 'for'. Cf. l. 76; an easy haplographic error. Besides regularizing the metre, 'factor' gives a noun for 'enemy' to answer.

31–2. S.D.s (Rowe).

33. S.D. (Cap.).

43–4. *truer...false*   A favourite Sh. notion; cf. *L.L.L.* 4. 3. 359–61; *K.J.* 3. 1. 263–87.

45. S.D.   F 'Exit'.

46. One line in Rowe: divided after 'thou' in F.

53. *at last gasp*   O.E.D. has no other exx. without either 'the' or a possessive.

54. *being*   see G.

56–7. *decay...work*   Perh. 'waste the work of a day, so far as he is concerned' (Deighton). But 'work' is obscure; J.D.W. conj. 'worth'.

58. *leans*   'inclines towards its fall' (J.).

60. S.D. (Camb.).

68. *what...on*   'with what a fair prospect of mending your fortunes you now change your present service' (Steev. after Heath). J.D.W. thinks Daniel's 'hangest' for 'changest' is supported by 'depender' in l. 58; 'chance' then = 'uncertain fortune'.

69. *still;* (Rowe) F 'ſtill,'.

73. *desert*   see G.

75. S.D.   Placed here by Cap.; F 'Exit Piſa.' after l. 74.

80. *liegers...sweet*   see G.

82. S.D. (Camb. after Cap.) F 'Enter Piſanio, and Ladies'.

85. *words* Dowd. conj. the addition of 'Pisanio', which could have dropped out before the following sp.-prefix. S.D. F 'Exit Qu. and Ladies'.

87. S.D. F 'Exit'.

I. 6

S.D. *Loc.* (Camb.) *Entry* (F).

4. *repeated* see G.

7. *the...glorious* 'the ungratified want and longing of a person in a most exalted position. The abstract for the concrete' (Vaughan). A characteristic Sh. usage. The usual interpretation, 'the desire for what is glorious', fails to give the contrast with the lowly status of her brothers that is needed. *desire* (F 2) F 'deſires'. *Blest* (Pope) F 'Bleſſed'.

9. *seasons* 'bestows an additional relish on' (Steev.). S.D. (F).

11. *Comes* who comes. *madam?* (Rowe) F 'Madam:'.

13. S.D. (Cap. after J.).

15. S.D. (Pope).

19. *me audacity* (F) Theob. 'me, audacity,', but a third pers. imper. is required, as in l. 18.

22. Sp.-pref. and S.D. F 'Imogen reads', centred.

22–4. *He...LEONATUS* Edd. have speculated, with little profit, on which parts of the letter she reads out. Prob. a fragment from the middle, plus the signature, though no one in the theatre would raise the question.

23. *Reflect* see G.

24. *your trust* 'the charge entrusted to you as my wife and representative' (Dowd.). But Han's 'truest' (with 'Leonatus') has many adherents.

27. *takes* (Pope) F 'take', which Vaughan retains
as parallel to 'read' in l. 25, with 'But...rest'
parenthetic.

32–3. *crop...land* Either 'what sea and land
produce' or 'the rich harvest which the eye gathers in,
consisting of sea and land' (Vaughan).

34. *twinned* see G.

35. *numbered* 'abounding in numbers of stones'
(Mal., after J.). Theob.'s 'unnumbered' (which
J.D.W. accepts) has some support in *Lr.* 4. 6. 21. See
Furn. (on l. 44 in his ed.) for the anon. (?Lettsom)
interpretation 'on which the pebbles can be numbered'.
F. D. Hoeniger, *Sh. Quart.* VIII (1957), 131, prints a
jotting of Dowd., referring to 'Th'unnumbered *Beach*'
in a poem of *c.* 1621.

36. *spectacles* (F 3) F 'Spectales'; see G; cf.
2 H. VI, G., 'spectacles'. *precious* Cf. *Lr.* 1. 1. 76,
'the most precious square of sense'.

39. *chatter this way* chatter in the direction of the
one, to show approval.

41. *case of favour* 'question of relative beauty'
(Her.); or perh. 'question which to prefer'. For the
whole phrase, cf. *Ham.* 3. 4. 76, 'in such a difference'.

44. *vomit emptiness* 'feel the convulsions of eructa-
tion without plenitude' (J., 1773 edn).

47–8. *tub...running* Prob. (cf. *Tim.* 4. 3. 245 n.)
with a reference to the leaky tub the Danaïdes were
condemned to keep filling in Hades; a symbol of
appetite since Plato, *Gorgias*, 493 B (not specifically
referring to the Danaïdes); see the edition by W. H.
Thompson, who quotes the present passage; cf. T.
Cooper, *Thesaurus*, s.v. 'Belides', 'whereof ariseth this
proverbe, *Danaidum dolium*, spoken of an unsatiable
man, whose greedie desire is neuer satisfied'.

50–1. *Thanks...sir* Divided by Camb., one line in
F.

51. S.D. (Rowe).

52. *Desire...abode* i.e. tell him to stay.

53. *strange and peevish* 'a foreigner, and easily fretted' (J.).

54. S.D. F 'Exit'.

60. *Briton* F 'Britaine'; so throughout for both sb. and adj., cf. 1. 4. 26 n. A case can be made out for retaining 'Britain' as an adj.—cf. Hol. cited in 2. 4. 20–6 n., *M.N.D.* 1. 1. 173, 'the Carthage queen', *Cor.* 1. 8. 8, 'your Corioli walls', 3. 3. 104, 'our Rome gates' [Deighton on 2. 4. 37, citing Abbott, §22]; but the sb., as in 1. 4. 26, must be modernized, and uniformity is desirable.

62. *Not knowing why* Like Antonio in *M.V.* 1. 1. 1; see New Arden (1955) note.

65. *furnaces* Cf. *A.Y.L.* 2. 7. 148, 'sighing like furnace' [Mal.].

66. *thick* see G.

71. *will's* Rowe 'will his', but 'hours' can be disyllabic [Nos.]. *languish* (J.) F 'languiſh:'. *for* Placed here by Steev.; at beginning of l. 72 in F.

72. *Assurèd* see G.

76. *to* F 'too', as often; cf. *Err.* 4. 1. 47 n.; Abbott, §73.

78–9. *In...talents* What it has given to him in his own person is much; what it has given indirectly in giving you to him, is inestimable [Hudson]. Some editors misinterpret as concerned with Post.'s behaviour, not his endowments. *his,* (Cap.) F 'his'.

96. *timely knowing* when one knows in time. The impressionistic syntax has worried some.

98. *What...stop* what you both urge to utterance and hold in.

103. *Fixing* (F2) F 'Fiering', defended by some edd., e.g. Dowd., 'from her alone does the passion of

my eye catch fire'. For me, 'Takes...motion' irresistibly points to 'fixing' as the climax. Cf. *Oth.* 2. 1.
15, 'th'ever-fixéd [Q: euer fired] pole'.

104. *Slaver* F catchword 'Slauer' F text 'Slauuer'.
common...stairs As Steev. notes, a variant on 'common as the highway'; cf. Tilley, H 457, and *2 H. IV*,
2. 2. 166–7 n.

106–7. *as | With labour* 'as much as if they had
been (literally) hardened by honest labour' (Ingleby).

107. *by-peeping* Hyphenated by Knight. See G. This
is prob. right. Delius, on the analogy of *1 H. IV*, 3. 3.
74, 'by-drinkings', glossed 'peeping at intervals'; and
it is conceivable that F as it stands is right, with a
rather stronger anacoluthon after 'tallow'.

108. *illustrous* (Collier) F 'illuſtrious'. The
meaning must be 'without lustre', and it is improbable
that Sh. would have used such a common word as
'illustrious' in a sense opposite to the usual one, and
very natural that the coinage 'illustrous' should be
corrupted. The correction is sometimes credited to
Tieck, who quotes the word so in his note, but this
must be a misprint as he translates 'glorreich', taking it
that 'illustrious' is used ironically.

111. *revolt* see G., and *L.L.L.* 5. 2. 74.

112. *himself.* (Pope; Rowe with semi-colon). F
'himſelfe,'.

112–13. *Not...pronounce* it is not from any
inclination that I pronounce. Furn. may be right in
seeing the bolder assertion, 'what pronounces it is not
I but your graces', though he is certainly wrong in
suggesting that Jach. admits that he is inclined.

119–20. *empery | Would...double* empire which
would double the power of the greatest of kings. Rowe
and many edd. read 'empery,', making 'lady' the
subject of 'would'. But then 'to be partnered' follows
awkwardly. The only difficulty about the F punctuation

is that the tribute to Cym.'s 'empery' is hyperbolical, and a digression from the praise of Im. herself.

122. *ventures* Prob. 'things risked in the way of trade' (Dowd., citing *M.V.* 1. 1. 42), rather than 'traders' (Cap.).

124. *boiled stuff* see G.

129. *As* Introducing a parenthesis; cf. *Per.* 4. 2. 14 n.

134. *purse*— (Nos.) F 'purſe:' Pope 'purse?'. But it is more effective to take 'Should...purse' as a conditional clause, with anacoluthon.

146. *Solicits* Cf. Franz, §152; the awkward sequence *tst* encourages the use of this form here.

150. *A...mart* that a saucy stranger should mart; cf. Abbott, §354.

150–1. *saucy...stew* For the associative link by which 'the word "stew" revived cooking imagery', cf. E. A. Armstrong, *Sh.'s Imagination* (1946), p. 99 [Nos.].

164. *one* above all others. The emphatic force of this 'one' with a superlative is noted by Abbott, §18, but ignored by O.E.D., 'one', 2 b. Cf. E. J. Dobson, *R.E.S.* n.s. vi (1955), 201.

165. *truest mannered* 'most honestly disposed' (On.).

166. *societies* social gatherings. *into* unto; but perh. there is a suggestion of attracting them 'into his magic circle' (Clarke).

167. *men's* (F 2) F 'men'.

168. *descended* (F 2) F 'defended'; cf. *Tim.* 5. 4. 55 [Mal.].

170. *seeming* Poss. as a pple, but more natural as a verbal noun, parallel to 'honour' [Eccles].

175. *Which* The antecedent is surely, as Nos. says, 'sir', not 'judgement'. Jach.'s cue is to overpraise Post., and it would strike a false note to refer to Im.'s *knowledge* of her own infallibility.

176–7. *fan*...*chaffless* A favourite image with Sh.;
cf. *Ham.* 5. 2. 193; *Troil.* 1. 3. 27–30 (with note,
citing Luke, xxii. 31; similarly Matthew, iii. 12), 3. 2.
166; *2 H. IV*, 4. 1. 194–6 (with R. Noble, *Sh.'s
Biblical Knowledge* (1935), p. 179) [J.D.W.].

178. One line in Rowe; divided after 'sir' in F.

181–2. *concerns*   (F4; so, already, D'Urfey)
...*lord;* (Rowe) F 'concernes: ...Lord,'. Nos., after
H. Ingleby and Furn., defends F, with 'it concerns' =
'it is of importance'. But it is nonsense to say that it is
of moment *because* it is of importance. Dyce may be
right in retaining only a comma after 'lord', and
interpreting 'Are' as 'who are'.

185. *The*...*wing* 'the choicest spirit of our fellow-
ship' (Wyatt); cf. O.E.D. 'wing', 4. Tilley, F156,
cites as prov., but with no earlier instance.

190. *curious* see G.

192–5. *Willingly*...*bedchamber* For a similar
speech in *Frederick of Jennen* see Nos.

201. *on promise* because I had promised Posthumus.

209. S.D. F 'Exeunt'.

2. 1

S.D. *Loc.* (Camb.) *Entry* (Rowe) F 'Enter
Clotten, and the two Lords'.

2. *jack*...*upcast*, (F) The uncertain meaning of
'upcast' makes it difficult to decide on the punctuation.
O.E.D. cites this passage, Drayton, *Pierce Gaveston*
(1619), cvii [l. 640], and a 19th c. source for the sense
'chance or accident'. But the earlier [1594?] version
of Drayton's line, 'Now at the up-cast of mine over-
throw' (l. 1551), suggests rather a metaph. phrase for
the crucial stage of a process. If it is technical for the
final shot at bowls, the punct. of Mason and many edd.,
'jack, ...upcast', seems preferable. J.D.W., accepting

O.E.D.'s gloss, thinks that Clot. is, with characteristic absurdity, admitting it was a fluke but grumbling at having been dislodged. F could also be right if 'upcast' corresponds to 'upshoot' in archery, 'the best shot, up to any point in the contest' (*Sh. Eng.* II, 383, citing *L.L.L.* 4. 1. 135, on which see Arden (1951) note): Clot. would then have been hit away when he 'lay', as bowlers say. But 'kissed the jack' already expresses that.

8. S.D. (Theob.); so ll. 12, 33.

8–9. *If...out* Han. read 'like his', and even edd. who retain the F text interpret, 'would have run out, so thin and watery are Clot.'s brains' (Dowd.). But the Second Lord may still be harping on Clot.'s cowardice as in 1. 2, and ll. 15 and 26–7, 'commit offence', suggest an unsavoury quibble in 'run out'.

11. *curtail* F 'curtall', conveying the pronunciation; cf. *R. III*, 1. 1. 18.

12. *crop the ears*. A ludicrous parallel to the literal meaning of 'curtail', by which the speaker shows his contempt for Cloten's metaphor.

13. *give* (F 2) F 'gaue', retained by Boswell (Var.), B. Nicholson *ap.* Camb., and some recent edd. (Neilson and Hill, Nos., Sisson), who treat the blow on the head as the 'satisfaction'. But the next clause strongly suggests that Clot. is affronted by the very notion of giving satisfaction.

14–15. *rank...smelt* Cf. *A.Y.L.* 1. 2. 100–1 [Steev.].

15. S.D. (Pope).

21. S.D. (Rowe).

21–2. *crow cock* (J.C.M.) F 'crow Cock,' Theob., edd., 'crow, cock,'; but the vocative rings false; 'crow cock' is not recorded, but sounds a natural expression for 'crow like a cock'. Perh. Sh. is playing on the phrase, recorded only in Scots, 'cry cock' = confess defeat (W. A. Craigie, *Dictionary of the Older Scottish*

Tongue, 'cok', n², O.E.D. 'cock', sb. 7); the form 'cry creak' is not uncommon, and is sometimes used of cocks, as in *Euphues* (Lyly, 1, 247), 'though he be a Cocke of the game, yet *Euphues* is content to bee crauen and crye creeke'. *capon...comb on*. A complicated insult, involving play on 'capon' = castrated cock, 'coxcomb' = fool's cap, and prob. (Cap.) on 'capon' read as 'cap on'.

23. *Sayest thou?* What do you say? So *Ham*. 4. 5. 28, and frequently.

24. *your* (F 3) F 'you', from l. 25.

27. *offence* see G.

31. *to-night* (F 2) F 'night'.

40. *went* Cf. 1. 5. 17 n.

42. *You...derogate* with the implication, 'you are as low as you can be already'.

44. S.D. (Pope). *a fool granted* 'admitted on all hands to be a fool' (Deighton). But there is prob. also an implication, following the semi-technical 'derogate', that the title of fool has been formally bestowed on him [J.D.W.]. *issues* 'deed[s] (in relation to the doer)' (O.E.D. 8 b, citing also *J.C.* 3. 1. 295); cf. M. M. Mahood, *Sh.'s Wordplay* (1957), p. 150.

48. S.D. (after Cap.) F 'Exit'.

49. *devil* As often, monosyllabic.

50–1. *ass...bears* W. Whiter, *Specimen of a Commentary on Sh.* (1794), pp. 117–20, notes the collocation of these words also in *Ham*. 5. 2. 43, 46, *Cor*. 2. 1. 64–5, as examples of association arising from the notion of the ass as a beast of burden.

51. *Bears all down* carries all before her. That 'all' = 'everything' rather than 'everyone' is confirmed by *2 H. IV*, 1. 1. 11, 'bears down all before him' and *Sir Thomas More*, Addition D, l. 40, 'bear down all things', cited in note there.

52. *for his heart* see G. 'heart'.

58–60. *husband, than* (F 3, sp. 'then') ...*divorce he'ld make*. (Theob.) ...*honour,* (Rowe, with semicolon) F 'Husband. Then...diuorce, heel'd make... Honour.'. One error evidently led to another in F.

62. S.D. F 'Exeunt'.

2. 2

S.D. *Loc.* (Camb.) *Entry* (Camb.) F 'Enter Imogen, in her Bed, and a Lady'. A 'discovery' on the inner stage.

1. *woman* (F 3) F 'woman:'.

2. *hour* Disyllabic; so 'hours' in l. 3.

7. S.D. (after Rowe).

10. S.D. F; 'comes' added by Collier.

12. *Our* 'The speaker is an Italian' (J.).

16. *whiter than the sheets* Cf. *Ven.* 398, 'Teaching the sheets a whiter hue than white' [Dowd.].

18. *do't* kiss each other; cf. *Ven.* 505, 'Long may they kiss each other' [Ingleby].

20. *lids* (Camb.; Rowe with comma) F 'lids.'.

22. *windows* see G. *azure-laced* (B. Nicholson *ap.* Camb.; so already interpreted by Staunton, without hyphen) F 'Azure lac'd' Cap. (J. with exclamation-mark) 'azure, lac'd', which most edd. accept; but to call the eyelids 'white and azure' and then add that they are 'laced with blue' is awkward, and the compound that F prob. intends is typical of Sh. P. B. Stroup, *English Studies*, XVII (1935), 144–5, noted the echo in Keats, *Eve of St. Agnes*, XXX, 1, 'azure-lidded'.

23–4. *design—...chamber.* (K.) F 'deſigne. [Cap.'s copy, 'deſigne?']...Chamber,'. Some less appropriately weaken to a comma (Collier) or delete (Steev., 1773) the punct. after 'design'.

27. *contents...story* Prob. 'what the story represented in the arras is'; but Nos. notes that 'story' could

mean 'room' (or 'set of rooms'), and J.D.W. thinks that 'contents' fits this interpretation better, citing 'Her chambers' (3. 5. 43).

31. *sleep...death* Cf. Tilley, S 527, 'Sleep is the image of death'.

33. S.D. (Rowe).

34. *slippery* see G. For the antithesis, cf. Donne, *A Litanie*, 31, 'Most slipperinesse, yet most entanglings hath'.

38. *mole* A link with Boccaccio; cf. Introd., p. xix.

45. *tale of Tereus* In Ovid, *Met.* vi; cf. *Tit.* 4. 1. 42–9.

48. *dragons* Cf. Marlowe, *Hero and Leander*, 1, 108 [Anders], *M.N.D.* 3. 2. 379 [Steev.], *2 H. VI*, 4. 1. 3–7 n.

49. *bare* (Theob. conj.) F 'beare'. Dowd. gives references for the raven as a bird that wakes early.

50. S.D. (F).

51. S.D. (Camb.) F 'Exit'.

2. 3

S.D. *Loc.* (Camb.) *Entry* (F).

2. *ace* see G.

7. sp.-pref. (F 4); om. F.

12. *o'* F 'a', as often. *penetrate* see G.; 'fingering' carries on the quibble. S.D. (F).

14. *so* see G.; for this usage, following an 'if'-clause, cf. *Gent.* 2. 1. 125, *Wiv.* 3. 4. 64.

16. *good-conceited* Hyphenated by Cap.

19–27. *Hark...arise* For an early 17th c. setting, see Nos., Appendix C.

19. *at heaven's gate* Cf. *Son.* 29. 12 [Steev.].

23–6. *And...arise* Arranged by Pope; two lines in F, defended by R. Noble, *Sh.'s Use of Song* (1923), p. 137.

23. *winking* see G.

25. *is* Han.'s 'bin', to regularize the rhyme-scheme, has perh. been unduly decried: Al. accepts it; 'is' may be the transcriber's grammatical 'correction'. (Han. himself corrected 'every thing' to 'all the things'.)

29. *consider* see G. *vice* (Rowe) F 'voyce'; 'vice' and 'voice' provide a homophonic pun, cf. Kökeritz, p. 151, *M.V.* 3. 2. 81 n.

30. *horse-hairs and calf's-guts* bow-strings and fiddle-strings. *calf's-guts* F 'calues-guts' Edd. 'calves'-guts', but the sing. gives the normal usage (cf. 1. 4. 134 n.), and F's sp. is ambiguous. Cf. *K.J.* 3. 1. 129 (F 'Calues skin'); but in *Ham.* 5. 1. 112, the following 'Calues' may point to 'calves'-skins' as the equivalent of Q 2's 'Calues-skinnes' (F 'Calue-skinnes').

31. *eunuch* R. Noble, *Sh.'s Use of Song* (1923), pp. 133–5, raises the question whether the song was actually sung by a eunuch. He notes that singing eunuchs were known in England, but that whether they appeared on the English stage is more doubtful, and concludes that Cloten may be referring, in a characteristically coarse way, to a counter-tenor. *amend* (F 2) F 'amed'. S.D. (i) (after Theob.) (ii) (F); Dyce and others postpone to follow 'fatherly' in l. 35, but cf. 1. 4. 25 n.

33–4. *late...early* Cf. *Tw.N.* 2. 3. 8–10 [Furn.].

39. *musics* Perh. (Her., after Delius) 'a Clotenism for "pieces of music"'; at any rate Han.'s 'music' is unnecessary—cf. *All's*, 3. 7. 40 [Evans].

43. *out* (Rowe; F 2 'ou't') F 'on't', which Sisson (*Readings*) retains, glossing 'more time must elapse which will still bear the impress of his memory'—a most frigid conceit. For the same corruption, cf. *Tw.N.* 3. 4. 205; *Wint.* 4. 4. 160.

47. *solicits* (F 2) F 'solicity', more prob. caught from 'orderly' than (Sisson, *Readings*) a graphic misreading. The sing., which Thiselton suggests, would also be poss., but O.E.D. records the word only in the plural (first here). Also poss. is 'soliciting' (Collier).

51. *that* Catches up 'as if' in l. 49; cf. Abbott, §285.

53. S.D. (Rowe); om. F.

59. *his...us* Best taken as a parenthesis: 'since he has previously been good to us'.

63. S.D. (after Camb.) F 'Exeunt'.

65. S.D. (Theob.)

67–8. *'Tis...admittance* The idea, though not the wording, is proverbial; cf. Tilley, M 1050.

69. *Diana's rangers* see G. 'ranger'. In several passages in Sh. (*All's*, 4. 3. 208; *Rom*. 1. 1. 208; *Tim*. 4. 3. 388), the name 'Dian(a)' is mentioned in close proximity to the idea of seduction by gold. I suspect an unconscious association with the name 'Danae'.

71. *true man* F 'True-man' (also in l. 72), indicating the stress in such phrases which survives only in 'mad-man'. Specially common where the meaning is 'honest man' as opposed to 'thief'.

75. *understand the case* know how best to conduct my suit.

76. S.D.s (F).

77. *more?* (Rowe) F 'more.'.

81. *ready* see G.

84. *good name* reputation.

85. *what...good* what seems good to me (which may, of course, not be a good report of Cloten). S.D. (i) (after Cap.) (ii) (F). The exit is not absolutely certain, but there seems no good reason for her to remain, and there are a number of omitted exits and entries in this play.

86. *fairest sister.* (Cap., with colon; K., Neilson and Hill, Al.) F 'fairest, Sister', which many edd. have accepted, with Theob.'s strengthening of the comma to

a colon, and with a comma after 'sister'. But it is too awkward to be plausible.

94. *say...silent* According to the prov., 'silence gives consent' (Tilley, S446).

96. *equal discourtesy* discourtesy equal (Abbott, §419a).

97. *one...knowing* Ironical.

101–2. *Fools...do* Much disputed. Warb.'s 'cure' for 'are', suggested by l. 104, has met with some favour. I think Im. means 'I may be a fool to refuse you, but that does not mean I am mad' (with no concealed innuendo that he is a fool). Clot., ever ready to take offence (as at l. 53), assumes that any reference to 'fools' must be directed against him. Im. then pretends to accept the charge that she has referred to him, but turns it off by an admission of madness.

106. *verbal* It is easiest, with Deighton and others, to take this clause as referring to Clot., with 'verbal' = 'talkative' (O.E.D., citing); but even if it refers to Im., there is no need for a nonce-meaning, 'plain-spoken'; though Im. has not used many words, she has gone beyond what she would have liked (cf. ll. 94–5)— the dignified silence appropriate to a lady faced with unwanted attentions.

109–10. *charity...myself* (K.) F 'Charitie...my selfe,'. Most edd. since Cap. treat 'to...myself' as parenthetical, but F gives better sense, 'I am so near to lacking Christian charity as to be forced to accuse myself of hating you'. This softens the paradox, naked in Cap.'s punct., of saying that hatred is only a sign that she is *near* to lacking charity.

112. *father.* (Cap.; Rowe with semi-colon) F 'Father,'.

118–19. *On...beggary* 'in the case of whose marriage no other result is depending except the rearing of brats in beggary' (Deighton). O.E.D.'s 'body of

dependants' for 'dependency' fits the context less well;
and Deighton is confirmed by Q. Elizabeth's speech of
12 Nov. 1586, *ap.* Hol. (1808 ed.), IV, 933, 'that there
were no more dependencie vpon vs but mine owne life
were onelie in danger'.

121. *consequence...crown* 'all that follows from
the fact that you are heir to the crown' (Dowd.). *foil*
see G.; Han.'s 'soil' is unnecessary.

122. *it* (Pope) F 'it;': prob. an error, but perh.
corresponding to a dash, with impatient anacoluthon—
cf. l. 124.

124. *pantler*— (Staunton). Prob. the best equivalent of F's semi-colon.

128. *envy*, (F2) F 'Enuie.'.

128–9. *if...virtues* if the offices each of you held
corresponded to your respective virtues. As Delius and
others have seen, 'your' is a genuine plural.

129. *virtues*, (F) Edd. since Pope usu. omit the
comma, but 'to be styled' goes more naturally with
'dignified...envy' than with 'if...virtues'.

131. *south fog* Hyphenated in F and by most edd.
But such hyphens are common in F where there is no
question of a compound according to modern usage.
Edd. give many parallels for the unwholesomeness of
the south wind: cf. 4. 2. 349, *Cor.* 1. 4. 30, Ovid,
Met. 1, 65–6 (Golding quoted by Dowd.), *Batman
vppon Bartholome* (1582), XI, 3 (quoted by Furn.).

133. *meanest* (F2) F 'mean'ſt', but 'meaneſt' in
l. 150.

136. S.D. (F).

137. *garment* (F2) F 'Garments'.

139. *sprited* Cf. 'ghosted' in *Ant.* 2. 6. 13
[Steev.].

144. *king's* Pope 'king', but the double possessive
was, and is, common; cf. *K.J.* 2. 1. 65.

145. *am* (Dyce, F4 with comma). F 'am.', which

Nos. vainly defends by drawing a distinction between confidence and certainty.

146. *kissed* F 'kiſs'd', with an effective pause. Pope regularized to 'kissed' (='kisséd' of this edn).

149. *I hope so* Wyatt notes that mod. usage would require 'I hope not'; so also *Wint*. 4. 4. 254. S.D. (after Han.).

153-4. *and...me* Ironically: 'with her usual charity, she will put the worst construction on everything I do' [Deighton, substantially]. The irony would be less broad if 'hope' had the neutral sense 'expect', as in *Ant*. 2. 1. 38.

154. *you*, (F 3) F 'your'.

155. S.D. F 'Exit'.

156. S.D. F 'Exit'.

2. 4

S.D. *Loc*. (Camb.) *Entry* (F).

3. *means* see G., and cf. *M.V.* 4.1.81, 'use no farther means'.

6. *feared* 'mixed with fear' (Schmidt). Tyrwhitt 'seared', but 'Post. does not believe that his hopes are altogether seared or blasted' (Crosby *ap*. Furn.). *hopes* (F 2) F 'hope'.

14. *Or* Many take as='ere', i.e. rather than, but the ordinary sense is perfectly apt: he will do the one, or he will have to do the other [Delius]. *look upon* face; cf. *M.N.D.* 3. 2. 69.

18. *legions* (Theob.) F 'Legion', but cf. 3. 7. 4; the slip is more likely to be F's than Sh.'s.

20-6. *Our...world* According to Hol., Cym. was unwilling to break with the Romans 'because the youth of the Britaine nation should not be depriued of the benefit to be trained and brought vp among the Romans, whereby they might learne both to behaue

themselues like ciuill men, and to atteine to the knowledge of feats of warre' (Boswell-Stone, p. 8, who also
notes a reference to 'lacke of skill' from Hol.'s account
of the Britons at the time of Caesar's invasion).

24. *mingled* (F 2) F 'wing-led'. The error, with a
hyphenated form giving the semblance of a meaning,
looks more like a slightly sophisticated transcriber's than
a compositor's. Defences of F are fatuous. Discipline
has been added to the courage they always had, whereas
F (and likewise Cartwright's conj. 'winged') would
imply the reverse order. *courage* (Dyce) F 'courages',
but F is very careless with final *s* in this play; see
Note on the Copy, p. 127.

25. *approvers* see G.

25–6. *such...world* i.e. men whose reputation is
increasing. It seems that 'mend upon' is a variant of
'gain upon'='win favour with' (O.E.D. 9d);
Donne, *Sermons* (ed. Potter and Simpson), 11, 12, 284,
writes that the Christian sacraments have 'gain'd upon
the whole world'.

26. S.D. (F).

27. *The...land* 'you must have been conveyed by
coursers as fleet as the fleetest stags' (Deighton).

28. *of...corners* 'from every quarter' (Wyatt).

30. *your answer* the answer you received.

32. *one* (Steev.) F 'one of', which is metrically
harsh, and does not fit in with Post.'s rejoinder. Jach.
says she is the *very* fairest (cf. 1. 6. 164 n.) not just one
of the fairest. *upon—* (Ingleby) F 'vpon'. For absence
of punct. to indicate an interruption, cf. Simpson,
p. 98.

34. *Look...casement* Cf. *Tim.* 4. 3. 116–17 [Mal.].
through (Rowe) F 'thorough'; there seems to be no
significance in the alternation of sp. in Qq, F.

35. *letters* Freq. for a single letter, e.g. *1 H. IV*, 4.
1. 13.

36. *tenour* For F's sp. 'tenure', cf. A. W. Pollard (ed.), *Sh.'s Hand in Sir Thomas More* (1923), p. 137.

37. sp.-pref. Philario (Cap.) F 'Poſt.'. The correction gives Post. time to glance at the letter, which he would certainly not delay doing. *Briton* F 'Britaine'; cf. 1. 6. 60 n.

39. *All...yet* Post.'s comment on the letter, after which he turns to Jach.

41–2. *have...should have* The irregularity shows Jach. 'playing a cat-and-mouse game' (Nos.): he is not prepared at this stage either to assert or deny that he has lost. Collier's 'had' for 'have' (anticipated by D'Urfey) makes the claim to have won explicit too soon.

47. *not* (F2) F 'note'.

51. *knowledge* see G.

55. *you,* (F2) F 'you'.

57. *you* (F2) F 'yon'.

59–60. *gains...mine* gains one of us the other's sword. The addition of 'loses' is logically redundant, but produces a balanced phrase.

60. *leaves* (Rowe) F 'leaue', scarcely to be defended as a plur. by proximity [Furn.].

68. *watching* see G.

73–4. *strive...value* It was doubtful whether the workmanship or the intrinsic value was the greater. An echo, as Thiselton notes, of the familiar Ovidian tag, 'materiam superabat opus' (*Met.* II, 5).

76. *was out on't* (anon. conj. *ap.* Camb.) F 'on't was—'. This excellent correction restores metre and avoids an unconvincing interruption in mid-sentence; Jach.'s speech appears to be working up to a natural close. The omission of one of the indistinguishable words 'out on't' could easily lead to a transposition giving more appearance of sense.

83. *likely* see G. But Han.'s 'lively' is attractive;

cf. the confusion of 'likelihood' and 'livelihood' (whichever is right) at *R. III*, 3. 4. 55.

84. *nature; dumb*, (Cap. after Han.) F 'Nature dumbe,', whence Warb. 'nature, dumb;'. The choice is a subtle one, but 'outwent her, though dumb' seems to be more pointed than 'another nature, though a dumb one'. F can convey the meaning of Cap.'s punct. if it embodies 'strong internal and weak, or indeed non-existent, external punctuation' (P. Alexander, *Proc. of the Brit. Acad.* xxxi (1945), 77).

91. *Depending...brands* see G.

95. S.D. (Camb.).

95–6. *can | Be pale* Cap., most edd., 'can,', but F's punct. is acceptable, esp. if 'if...pale' = '*so that I can see whether* you can retain your normal colour, unflushed by anger'—still a normal colloquial use of 'if' (comparable to that in *R. III*, 1. 2. 175). Others take 'pale' to refer to the pallor of dismay that Jach. hopes to induce, but 'can' is against this.

100. *that.* (Rowe, with semi-colon) F 'that'.

105. *you,* (Collier) F 'you?', which may be a clue to the method of delivery; but over-punctuation is common in this text; cf. 3. 4. 137.

106. S.D. (J.).

111. *be* let them be.

115. *probable* see G.

116. *one her women* (F; Al., Sisson) F 2 'one of her women' Collier 'one her woman'. Cf. *Ant.* 1. 3. 36, 'none our parts', *Wint.* 2. 3. 35, 'each his needless heavings', Franz, §352, though the construction is harsher with 'one'. *One...corrupted* In the Boccaccio story, the villain achieves his entry by bribing a poor woman who was much in the house of the heroine [Dowd.].

128. *this. She* (K., Rowe with semi-colon) F 'this: fhe', which could be taken as introductory to an

explanation, 'she...dearly', but more likely marks an emphatic pause (cf. Simpson, p. 67), 'this' being the ring [Furn.].

132. *of.* (F) Rowe+most edd., 'of—', taken to= 'by one convinced of' with 'her virtue' to follow. But the phrase makes good sense if interpreted 'of [=about] one whom we are persuaded to think well of' (Ingleby). Cf. *Tw. N.* 2. 3. 155–6, 'the best persuaded of himself'.

135. *the* (Rowe) F 'her', prob. from l. 134 [Mal.]. Cap. thought F's reading conveyed 'a very delicate compliment', but surely it would be very precious so to praise the mole.

142–3. *Spare...swearing* Arranged by Han.; 'never...million' one line in F.

142. *turns* For the sb., cf. *Ant.* 2. 5. 59, and for the vb., *Oth.* 4. 1. 253–5.

143. *sworn.* (F) Rowe, most edd., 'sworn—', but we already know what he is swearing, and he need say no more.

149. *I'll...something* Cf. *Lr.* 2. 4. 283–5 [Ingleby]. *something.* (F) Again, Rowe and edd. 'something—'. The *meaning* indeed is incomplete, but dashes are best reserved to indicate *sentences* that are incomplete or interrupted. S.D. F 'Exit'. *besides* see G.

151. *pervert* see G.

152. S.D. F 'Exeunt'.

2. 5

S.D. *Entry* (Theob.) F 'Enter Poſthumus'. Most edd. since Cap. arbitrarily add a *Loc.* such as 'Another room in Philario's house'. For convenience, I retain the usual scene-numeration rather than, more logically, continue 2. 4 with Nos.

1–2. *Is...half-workers?* Edd. quote similar sentiments from Milton, *P.L.* x, 888–95; Ariosto, *Orlando*

Furioso, XXVII, st. 120 (in Harington's trn, st. 97) [Steev.]; Lodge, *Rosalynde* (ed. W. W. Greg), p. 38; Marston, *Fawne*, Act 4 (*Plays*, ed. H. Harvey Wood, II, 201) [Nos.].

5. *stamped* Cf. *Meas.* 2. 4. 46 [Mal.].

12. *Might...her* One line in Pope; divided after 'Saturn' in F.

13. *As...snow* Tilley, I 1, 'As chaste as ice (snow)', cites no pre-Sh. instance.

15. *at first* right away; cf. 1. 4. 101.

16. *full-acorned* It is, I am told, true that a diet of acorns strengthens the procreative powers of wild boars. *German one* (Rowe) F 'Iarmen on'; cf. *2 H. IV*, 2. 1. 144 n.

20. *me—* (Pope) F 'me,'. *motion* see G.

25. *changes of prides* varying extravagances; cf. O.E.D. 'pride', 7, 'ostentatious adornment'. Schmidt glosses 'one excess changed for another'.

26. *nice* Either 'wanton' or simply 'over-fastidious, pernickety'.

27. *man may name* (S. Walker conj.) F 'name'. Any supplement must be conjectural, but 'man may' could easily have dropped out by similarity before 'name', and 'man' neatly balances 'hell'. Even easier, but not quite convincing, is Vaughan's 'name may name'. Also poss. is Dyce's conj. 'have a name', for which Ingleby quotes *Mac.* 4. 3. 60. Since ll. 28–9 are metrically irregular in F, Nos., following a suggestion by Dowd., here retains F, and transfers 'Why, hers' to complete the line. But then 'In...vice' becomes a very lumbering alexandrine (which Dowd. proposed to avoid by deleting 'but'); and 'all faults that name... knows' is not a happy expression.

28–9. *Why...vice* Divided by Cap.; one line in F.

30. *still* (J.) F 'ſtill;'.

32. *I'll...them* So Claudio in a similar situation;

cf. *Ado*, 4. 1. 55 [Clarke]. On. gives the special gloss
'denounce' for 'write against' in both passages, but
with no support from O.E.D. Nos. (on l. 16; = 2. 4.
168 in his edn) notes the mention of Dian in both
passages.

33. *skill* see G., and cf. *Wint.* 4. 4. 152; this seems
the obvious meaning, though O.E.D.'s last ex. is *c.* 1550.

35. S.D. F 'Exit'.

3. 1

S.D. *Loc.* (Camb.) *Entry* (F).

On the patriotic behaviour of the Queen and (more
especially) Cloten in this scene, often thought to be
inconsistent with the rest of the play, see W. D. Smith,
Studies in Philology, XLIX (1952), 185–94, who argues
that Cloten is as boorish as elsewhere, and R. Behrens,
N. & Q. CCI (1956), 379–80, who notes that the
Queen and Cloten must be the aggressors here, to
prepare for the final reconciliation.

5. *uncle* So in Fabian. Hol. quotes this version, but
himself makes him his great-uncle.

6. *less* Perh. a 'less'–'more' confusion (cf. 1. 4.
22 n.), but it makes good sense taken literally—Cass.'s
fame derives as much from the praise of Caesar as from
his own feats [Dowd.].

10. *to kill the marvel* to make it cease being a marvel
(when it becomes the rule and not the exception)
[Vaughan].

11–14. *There...noses* I retain F's lineation. Edd.,
after Pope, divide 'Ere...Britain is (Pope) | A world...
pay'. But 'By...pay' is quite a good headless line.
Nos. prints as prose, to agree with Clot.'s other speeches
in the scene, but the verse-rhythms are dominant.

12–13. *a world | By itself* A common idea, stem-
ming, as Theob. noted, from Virgil's 'penitus toto

divisos orbe Britannos' (*Ecl.* 1, 66); cf. Boswell-Stone, p. 10, and New Arden (1956) note on *R. II*, 2. 1. 45.

14. *our own noses* Instead of Roman ones; cf. l. 37 [Ingleby].

19. *ribbed and paled in* F 'ribb'd, and pal'd in'. Most edd., since Rowe, treat the endings as syllabic, but perh. the irregularity, with a pause after 'park', is more attractive.

20. *rocks* (Theob. conj., in Nichols, *Lit. Illustrations of the 18th Cent.*, II, 629) F 'Oakes'.

23–4. *brag...overcame* Referred to also in *A.Y.L.* 5. 2. 30–1, *2 H. IV*, 4. 3. 41.

30. *Cassibelan* In Hol., his brother Nennius.

37. *crooked noses* Cf. *2 H. IV*, 4. 3. 40–1, 'the hook-nosed fellow of Rome'.

42–3. *put...pocket* C. B. Young points out Browning's echo of this in the last line of *Master Hugues of Saxe-Gotha*.

48–9. *stretch...world* For 'the idea of fame or worth stretching beyond the confines of the world...in a Roman context', cf. *Ant.* 5. 2. 79–86; *Cor.* 5. 6. 126–7 (Nos.). For 'the sides o'th'world' [or, 'earth'], cf. *Ant.* 1. 2. 193, *Wint.* 4. 4. 475 [Dowd.].

49. *colour* see G. There may be a pun on 'collar', carried on in 'yoke' [Nos.].

52. *be. We do* (Mal.) F 'be, we do.'. The simplest change seems best, though it implies a perverse mis-punctuation in F. See Furn. for other proposals.

62. *hath...servants* Cf. *Ant.* 3. 12. 5, 'Which had superfluous kings for messengers'.

68–9. *Thy...him* Cf. Hol., 'This man (as some write) was brought vp at Rome, and there made knight by Augustus Cesar, vnder whome he serued in the warres' (Boswell-Stone, p. 7; the verb 'knighted' is used on p. 8).

70. *which...utterance* which I must defend to the

death, now that he seeks to take it back. *he to seek* the fact that he seeks; cf. *Tim.* 4. 3. 267–8, 'I to bear this...is some burden' [Deighton]; 3. 5. 76 n. below. The presence of the impersonal verb 'behoves' makes this example unusual, but the construction itself is well-established; cf. Malory, *Works* (ed. Vinaver), p. 322, l. 3, 'thou to love that lovyth nat the is but grete foly'.

71. *perfect* see G.

72–3. *the Pannonians...arms* For this reason, Hol. writes, Augustus 'left off for a time the warres of Britain' (Boswell-Stone, p. 8). Hol. places this in the reign of Theomantius (Tenantius).

84. S.D. F 'Exeunt'.

3. 2

S.D. *Entry* (F). There is no need for a change of place.

2. *monster's her accuser* (Cap.) F (+Collier, Al., Sisson) 'Monſters her accuſe'—where 'accuse' looks like a miscorrection, 'Monsters' being taken as a plur. sb.

3–4. *what...ear!* Cf. *Oth.* 2. 3. 349.

5. *As...handed* as skilled in administering the 'poison' of false accusation as in poisoning by sleight of hand (an Italian accomplishment). *poisonous tongued* As 'poisonous' goes also with 'handed', it is best not to hyphenate with Dyce [Dowd.].

9. *take in* see G.

10. *to* see G.

12. *Upon* As in mod. colloq. 'on top of'.

13. *her blood?* i.e. shed her blood?

17. *comes to* Cf. 5. 3. 17, *H. VIII*, 2. 3. 42. S.D. (Rowe) *The letter* (Rowe) F 'The Letter.', with ital. for quotation beginning only in l. 18. The ital. justify Rowe's S.D., though, as Mal. noted, the words do not

occur in 3. 4. 21–31, which is in prose. From the
spectator's point of view, Pis. is reading, and that is all
that matters.

21. *fedary* F 'Fœdarie'; see G. and *Wint*. 2. 1.
90 n.

22. S.D. (F). After l. 23 in Singer and others, but
cf. 1. 4. 25 n.

23. *am ignorant* i.e., must profess ignorance.

26. *Leonatus?* Camb. 'Leonatus!', but though F
question-marks often stand for exclamation-marks, a
question is natural here.

27. *astronomer* see G.

31–4. *content—*. . .*love—*   F '*content;*. . .*Loue,*'.
Recognized as a parenthesis by Theob.

31. *yet not* *sc.* content.

34. *it* . . .*love* 'grief for absence keeps love in health
and vigour' (J.).

36. *of counsel* to keep secrets.

40. S.D. (Rowe) F prints the letter, except for the
signature, in italics.

42. *would* Cap. 'would not', which the sense
requires. But this is the sort of place where Sh. often
muddles his negatives, writing as if he had said, not
'as', but 'but' (which Pope reads).

46. *love* (Cap.) F '*Loue.*'. The interpretation of
'your POSTHUMUS' as the signature is Tyrwhitt's,
though he enclosed 'increasing in love' in commas.
Thiselton retains F, treating 'your. . .love' as 'your
advancement or prosperity in love', as object of
'wishes'.

56. *beyond beyond* (Ritson) F 'beyond, beyond'.
thick see G.

59. *by th'way* 'as we go' (Deighton).

62–3. *gap*. . .*in time* Cf. *Ant*. 1. 5. 5.

63–4. *from*. . .*And* A colloquial irregularity for
which Mal. (though himself misinterpreting) cited

Cor. 2. 1. 241, 'From where he should begin and end'.

64. *get* (F2) F 'ger'.

65. *or ere begot* 'before the act is done, for which excuse will be necessary' (Mal.).

67. *score...ride* (F2) F 'ſtore...rid'.

68. *'Twixt...hour* between one hour and the next; cf. 3. 4. 42, ''twixt clock and clock' [Elze] *'twixt... sun* between sunrise and sunset; cf. *R. II,* 4. 1. 55, with New Arden (1956) note.

70. *execution* (F2) F 'Excution'.

71. *riding wagers* races with wagers on them.

73. *i'...behalf* instead of a clock.

77. *you're* Cf. *Tp.* 1. 2. 367, 'thou'rt best'. The past tense is usual, but the pres., even unabbreviated, is occasionally found; cf. Wapull, *The Tyde Taryeth No Man* (1576), f. 4ᵛ l. 1, 'you are best'; Dekker, *1 Honest Whore,* 2. 1. 224, 3. 1. 54, 'y'are best'; Beaumont and Fletcher, *Maid's Tragedy,* 2. 1. 18, 'you're best' (where Mason cited the present passage). On the construction, cf. Abbott, §230.

78. *before me* what is immediately ahead, the road to Milford. This does not conflict with the statement that 'what ensues'—the remoter prospect—is obscure. (So, substantially, Mal.) *man.* (K.; colon in Camb.) *Nor...here,* (Pope) F '(Man) nor...heere;'. *here, nor* (F2) F 'heere, not'. *Nor here, nor here* neither on this side nor on that.

82. S.D. F 'Exeunt'.

3. 3

S.D. *Loc.* (Camb.) *Entry* (F).

2. *Stoop* (Han.) F 'Sleepe', prob. from 'stope', misread 'slepe'.

6. *turbans* F 'Turbonds'. 'The idea of a *giant* was,

among the readers of romances, . . . always confounded
with that of a Saracen' (J.).

9. *prouder livers* those who live more splendidly.

13. *place* 'position...literally and metaphorically'
(Deighton).

15. *courts,* Vaughan, perh. rightly, deletes the
comma.

16. *This* For the use = 'any particular service'
(Mal.), to 'make it instance an object cited by way of
general observation', Clarke compares *Mac.* 1. 7. 10,
'this even-handed justice'.

17. *allowèd* F 'allowed' Rowe 'allow'd'. But the
line seems to run at least as well with syllabic ending,
slur of 'To' and a feminine ending.

20. *sharded* see G. On the alternative view,
accepted by O.E.D., that it = 'living in dung' cf. *Mac.* 3.
2. 42 n., and Tilley, B 221 'The beetle flies over many
a sweet flower and lights in a cowshard'.

20–21. *beetle...eagle* H. W. Crundell, *N. & Q.*
CLXVIII (1935), 312, pointed out the allusion to Æsop's
fable of the beetle and the eagle (quoted by Baldwin, 1,
635, in Camerarius's version), with its moral, not to
despise the weak. Cf. Lyly, *Euphues and his England*, II,
215, l. 21, with Bond's note.

22. *check* see G.

23. *bauble* (Rowe) F 'Babe'. If Rowe is right, the
MS. prob. had 'bable'. The correction is supported by
3. 1. 27, 3. 2. 20—'*Cym.* is peculiarly a play of
reminiscences' (Verity). Han.'s 'bribe' is also poss.
Mal. thought 'babe' = 'puppet' could stand, and F is
perh. supported by a passage in Nashe which deals with
trifling returns, 'the Vsurer snatcheth vp the Gentleman, gyues him Rattles and Babies for his ouer-rackt
rent' (II, 98, ll. 22–3).

25. *gain the cap* receive the salute. *them* (Rowe) F
'him', prob. by confusion with 'him' preceding and

'his' following. This seems more prob. than that the
confusion is Sh.'s, or that 'Such gain'='let such a one
gain' [Thiselton].

26. *keeps...uncrossed* keeps his account un-
cancelled.

28. *know* (F2) F 'knowes'.

33. *travelling abed* 'the imagined travel of one who
lies motionless' (Dowd., comparing *Son.* 27. 3, 'then
begins a journey in my head').

34. *prison, or* Pope, most edd., 'prison for'. But F
is defended by Hunter (cited by Furn.), Thiselton and
Nos. That the debtor 'not *dares* to stride a limit'
suggests that he is in sanctuary, or in the 'liberties'
outside a prison, rather than *in* prison. The transition
from a place to a person does not seem to me unnatural
in late Sh.; and there has already been a departure
from complete symmetry in 'A cell of ignorance,
travelling abed'.

37. *December,* (Han.) F 'December?' F over-
punctuates, and the clause more aptly goes with what
follows.

40. *beastly-subtle* (anon. conj. *ap.* Camb.) F
'beaſtly; ſubtle'. The compound gives a better balance
with 'Like...wolf'. The point is that such qualities as
they have are only those of the beasts. F's semi-colon
could be a misinterpretation of the comma that is sometimes found where a compound adj. is intended; cf.
R. II (Qq.), 1. 3. 43, 'daring, hardy'; 5. 3. 43, 'foole,
hardie'; *H. VIII*, 5. 3. 173, 'Brother; loue'. With the
whole phrase cf. *Ven.* 675, 'The fox which lives by
subtlety' [Nos. p. lxviii]; *H. VIII*, 1. 1. 158–60.

44. *freely* Ironical: that is the only sort of freedom
they have.

46. *felt them knowingly* Cf. *Lr.* 4. 6. 152, 'I see it
feelingly'.

47–9. *As...falling* Cf. Bacon, *Essays*, 'Of Great

Place', 'The standing is slippery, and the regress is either a downfall, or at least an eclipse' [J.D.W.].

51. *which* The aptest antecedent, as Vaughan saw, is 'pain': 'the labour perishes without attaining fame and honour' (Dowd.).

63–4. *Shook...weather* Cf. *Tim.* 4. 3. 264–7 [Steev.].

71. *at* Cf. 'at peace', 'at liberty' [Dowd.].

78. One line in Cap. Divided after 'state' in F. S.D. (after Theob.) F 'Exeunt'.

82. One line in Rowe. Divided after 'mine' in F. *meanly,* (Staunton) F 'meanely'. The comma enables 'I'...bow' to be, more appropriately, taken with 'their...palaces'.

83. *cave wherein they bow,* (Warb.) F 'Caue, whereon the Bowe'.

86. *Polydore* (Rowe) F 'Paladour', here only.

87. *who* F2 'corrects' to 'whom'.

96. *in...figure* 'as graphically as his brother' (Her.).

97–8. *shows...conceiving* 'exhibits his own conception of things much more than merely gives life to what I say' (Dowd.).

103. *reft'st* F 'refts', avoiding an unpronounceable combination; cf. *Tim.* 5. 1. 181 n.

105. *her* 'i.e. to the grave of Euriphile; or to the grave of "their mother, as they suppose it to be"' (Mal.).

106. *Morgan* (Rowe) F 'Mergan', but 'Morgan' at 5. 5. 332. As 'Margan' also occurs in Hol. (Boswell-Stone, p. 17), the inconsistency may be Sh.'s.

107. S.D. F 'Exit'.

3. 4

S.D. *Loc*. (Camb.) *Entry* (F).

3. *have* As if 'had longing' had preceded, rather than with ellipse of 'longed'. *now*. (Han.) F 'now:' Rowe (+others) 'now—', supposing an aposiopesis.

7. *perplexed* see G.

15. *out-craftied* see G.

21. S.D. F 'Imogen reads' (centred).

22. *lie* (Rowe) F 'lyes', perh. rightly.

24. *grief* Can mean simply 'injury', but Granville-Barker (*Prefaces to Shakespeare, Second Series* (1930), p. 336, n.) thinks that Post. may be credited with the 'touch of...nobility' involved in the more emotional sense.

33–4. *slander...sword* Cf. *Wint.* 2. 3. 86–7, 'slander, Whose sting is sharper than the sword's' [Dowd.].

36. *belie* see G. A nonce-use, though On. joins with it the participial adj. in *Lucr.* 1533, but intelligible in the context; cf. O.E.D. 'be-', 6.

42. *'twixt clock and clock* from hour to hour; cf. 3. 2. 68 n.

46. *thy* Apostrophe to Posthumus [Cap.].

49. *favour's* (Rowe) F 'fauours'.

50. *Whose...painting* 'made by art; the creature, not of nature, but of painting' (J.); cf. 4. 2. 83–4 [Collier, though he rejected the reading].

52. *richer than* too rich; Abbott, §390 n., refers to a similar idiom in Greek. *hang...walls* like discarded clothing or armour, as in *Meas.* 1. 2. 163 [Steev.]; *Troil.* 3. 3. 151–3 [Nos.].

55. *revolt* see G.

58. *heard like* (Vaughan) F 'heard, like'. The comma obscures the sense, 'when they were heard to speak like'. The reference is to his false professions of

love for Dido. Delius interpreted correctly, though retaining the comma.

61–4. *So...fail* For the general idea cf. *H.V*, 2. 2. 138–40 (cited by Upton in support of his 'fall' for 'fail').

62. *leaven* Perh. with I Corinthians, v. 6, in mind (cited by Upton; see previous note). *proper* see G.

77–8. *so...that* Cf. 1. 1. 65 n.

79. *afore't* (Rowe) F 'a-foot'.

80. *obedient...scabbard* 'as ready to receive the sword as the sheathe itself is' (Deighton).

88–90. *That...suits* Arranged by Ingleby; two lines in F, divided after 'king'. Most edd. follow Cap. in making 'Stands...woe' a short line, followed by 'And...up' as one line, but this involves inserting 'thou' before 'that', with Cap.

90. *make* (Cap.) F 'makes'.

92–3. *no...rareness* 'no common act, but an impulse such as ordinary women would not have yielded to' (Deighton).

92. *passage* see G.

94. *disedged* Cf. *Ham.* 3. 2. 248–9 'take off mine edge' [Steev.]; Chapman, *Hero and Leander*, III, 5, 'Love's edge is taken off'.

95. *tirest* see G.

102. *out first* (J. conj.) F 'firſt'; cf. *Bugbears* (in *Early Plays from the Italian*, ed. R. W. Bond), 2. 4. 37, 'I shall watche my eyes oute' [Steev.]. Han.'s 'blind first' is also possible.

109. *To be unbent* only to unbend your bow again; J.'s 'to have thy bow unbent' misses the exact point, which is that he has made all preparations, bent his bow, only to make them useless.

124. *courtezan.* (Cap.) F 'Curtezan?' Theob. 'curtezan—'. With the question-mark, it would be difficult not to make Pis.'s 'No' a reply, which it obviously is not.

131. *court*— (Pope) F 'Court.'.

133. *harsh, feeble* (J.C.M.) F 'harſh'. An epithet opposed to 'harsh' as 'simple' to 'noble' is required, and 'feeble', with which cf. *2 H. IV*, 3. 2. 170, 'most forcible Feeble', could easily have dropped out by homoeoteleuton before 'noble'.

136. *Where then?* This apparent contradiction to what follows is acceptable 'considering it as a question apart, and the others as afterthoughts' (Cap.).

137. *Day, night,* (Theob.) F 'Day? Night?', with characteristic overpunctuation.

138. *but* except.

139. *of it, but not in't* 'a page of the world's great volume, but, as it were, a page torn from it' (Dowd.).

145. *Dark* 'impenetrable to the search of others' (J.).

148. *Pretty...view* 'affording a fair prospect of turning out happily' (Cap.). More plausible than to take 'full of view'='with opportunities of examining your affairs with your own eyes' (J.). *haply* (Pope) F 'happily', as often.

158. *it* its.

160. *weasel* Cf. *1 H. IV*, 2. 3. 80 [Dowd.].

162. *the harder heart* Prob., as most edd. agree, a parenthetical reference to Post.'s cruelty which has brought Im. to this pass. Others, after Rolfe, treat it as a self-rebuke. An application to Im., either 'the danger of your heart becoming harder' (Wyatt), or 'she must also harden her heart' (Nos.), is less prob.; the definite article is against it.

166. *made...angry* i.e. aroused her jealousy. Cf. *Cor.* 4. 2. 53, 'In anger, Juno-like'. Her anger against the Trojans is prominent in the *Æneid*.

168–9. *one....this,* (Rowe) F 'one,...this.'.

171. *in their serving* served by them.

174. *his service* employment as his servant.

175–6. *happy*—...*know*...*music*— (Indicated as parenthesis by Theob.; comma after 'know' om. Ingleby) F 'happy;...know,...Muſicke,'. Construction and meaning are uncertain; 'tell...happy' = 'tell him your accomplishments' (notably singing: cf. 4. 2. 48); and I take 'which...music' as elliptical, 'your accomplishments, when he comes to be acquainted with them, will test whether he has an ear for music' [based on Ingleby]. None of the proposed emendations for 'will', e.g. 'you'll' (Han.), 'we'll' (Mal. conj.), rings true.

178. *Your means* 'as for your subsistence' (Mal.).

182. *even* see G.

184. *soldier to* 'firmly and constantly devoted to' (Schmidt, citing also *Per.* 4. 1. 8).

185. *prince's* Not only masc. in Sh.'s Eng.

186. *short* 'hasty' (Dowd.).

188. *Your carriage* carrying you away.

194. S.D. (J.C.M.) F 'Exeunt'.

3. 5

S.D. *Loc.* (Cap.) *Entry* (F).

2. *wrote* (Neilson and Hill)...*hence;* (Cap.) F 'wrote,...hence,' Pope 'wrote;...hence,', so that 'am sorry' may have an expressed subject. But the lack of this is less objectionable than the awkwardness of 'My...wrote' as an isolated sentence. J.D.W., however, would read 'I'm' (anon. conj. *ap.* Camb.) for 'am'.

7. *So* 'very good' (Deighton). A polite way of declining to discuss what Cym. has just said.

9. *and you* Having addressed the queen, Luc. finally turns to Cym. again (scarcely, as anon. *ap.* Camb, Delius, and Sisson think, to Cloten).

17. S.D. (after Mal.) F 'Exit Lucius, &c.'.

22. *It fits...ripely* it is high time.

32. *looks us* (J.) F 'looke vs' F 2 'lookes as'. See G. 'look'.

35. *too slight in sufferance* 'too lax in allowing such behaviour' (Wyatt). S.D. (after Cap.) F om.

37–8. *cure...do* The stock 'doloris medicus tempus' (cf. Tilley, T 325) was current in such school-books as Culmann's *Sententiae Pueriles* [Anders].

40. *strokes* (F 2) F 'ſtroke;'.

41. S.D. (Camb. after Cap.) F 'Enter a Meſſenger'.

44. *loud'st of* (Cap.) F 'lowd of' Rowe 'loudest'. F has been defended by Thiselton, citing *Troil*. 3. 3. 241, 'even to my full of view', but the possessive there makes the expression easier, and as the sense here is clearly superlative, it seems best to emend.

51. *to blame* F 'too blame', cf. 1. 6. 76 n.

52. *fear* Placed here by Rowe; at beginning of l. 53 in F.

53. S.D. F 'Exit'.

56. S.D. Placed here by Cap.; F, after 'days', 'Exit'.

66. S.D. (Pope) F 'Enter Cloten'.

69. S.D. (S. Walker) The aside is not perhaps absolutely necessary, but the Queen is not likely to be quite so outspoken even to her son.

70. *forestall...day* 'prevent him from ever seeing another day' (Mal.). S.D. F 'Exit Qu.'.

71. *her.* (J.C.M.) F 'her:'. *For* because. I take this to be the correlative of 'therefore' in l. 75, and have slightly modified the usual punctuation to bring out the construction.

72. *that* Takes up the causal sense of 'For'; cf. Abbott, §285.

73. *than lady, ladies, woman* 'than any lady, than all ladies, than all womankind' (J.). Cf. *All's*, 2. 3. 196 [Tollet].

73–4. *from...hath* Cf. *Tp.* 3. 1. 46–8 [Seward, *ap.* Furn., who suggests the note may come from Theob.].

76. *Disdaining* the fact that she disdains; cf. 3. 1. 70 n., 5. 5. 344 n.

81. *Shall* Placed here by Theob.; at end of l. 80 in F. S.D. (F).

82. *pandar!* (Cap.) F 'Pandar,'.

92. *nearer* i.e. 'nearer to the point' (Hudson) rather than literally.

100. *this paper* Described at 5. 5. 279 as a 'feigned letter'. Sh. does not expect us to consider too curiously what it 'really' is; all we need to know is given at l. 131.

101. S.D. (Mal.).

102. S.D. (Rowe).

105. S.D. (Theob.). *write to* S. Walker 'write', perh. rightly.

112. *industry* assiduity.

113. *do,...it* (Theob.) F 'do...it,'.

130. S.D. F 'Exit'.

131–2. *I...anon* Edd. have conjectured what this is, but prob. it is only a characterizing touch.

141. *insultment* (F 2) F 'infulment'. Baldwin (II, 160) thinks that Sh. has in mind the etymology of the word (which is not found elsewhere): 'Cloten intended literally to leap [*insultare*] on the dead body of Posthumus.'

144. *foot* Cf. 4. 1. 18.

146. S.D. (Cap.) F 'Enter Pifanio'.

154. *voluntary* 'not by necessity...with an allusion to the *mutes* in Turkish harems, who were, if not dumb by nature, made so by having their tongues cut out... cf. *Tw.N.* 1. 2. 61' (Deighton, after Delius).

155. *duteous and true,* (S. Walker, followed by K., Al.) F 'dutious, and true'. But the sense of 'true preferment' is not obvious, though Furn. suggests 'solid and substantial', in contrast to what he might

hope from Imogen and Posthumus. In favour of the correction, J.D.W. notes that 'be true' in l. 157 looks like a repetition of the earlier injunction.

157. S.D. F 'Exit'.

158. *my* Collier 'thy', plausibly. If F is right, the loss must be that of Pis.'s honour or even his soul. With 'thy', the meaning would be, 'it would be to your loss if I were true, for falsehood to you is truth, just as truth to you is falsehood'.

159. *be* (F, Delius) Rowe, most edd., 'be,'.

160. *him...true* A surprising description of Post. at this point. Hence Han.'s 'her' for 'him' (which J.D.W. prefers), and the anon. conj. (*ap.* Camb.) 'Him', i.e. God. But Post., though misled, can still be regarded as a true master to Pis., especially when the contrast is with Cloten [so Furn., after Mal.].

162. *fool's speed* Cf. Tilley, F518, 'Fool's haste is no speed' (cited by Thiselton on l. 80).

163. *labour...meed.* Cf. Tilley, L1, 'He has his labor for his pains'. S.D. F 'Exit'.

3.6

S.D. *Loc.* (Camb.) *Entry* (after Rowe) F 'Enter Imogen alone'

7. *Foundations* see G. The audience can scarcely be expected to grasp the second sense until she adds 'such...relieved'.

13. *sorer* 'a greater, or heavier, crime' (J.).

16. *but even before* only a moment ago; cf. *K.J.* 3. 1. 233, 'And even before this truce, but new before' [Vaughan].

24. *Take or lend* Prob. 'take my money or give me food' (cf. l. 47)—both of which could be carried out by dumb show, without the need of speech. The context

does not support the view that she is inviting them to take her life. Prob. 'lend'='give'.

27. *Such a foe* that's the sort of foe I pray for. S.D. (i) (after Rowe) F 'Exit'; (ii) (F). F begins a new scene at this point.

30. *our match* At 3. 3. 74–5.

31. *The...die* i.e., men would no longer labour; cf. the common fig. use of 'sweat'=toil.

34–5. *flint...down* Opposed also in *Oth.* 1. 3. 230–1.

36. *keep'st thyself* i.e. it 'has no one to look after it' (Deighton); cf. *A.Y.L.* 4. 3. 81 [Evans].

38. *browse* The choice of a word more commonly used of animals may be deliberate (as it certainly is in *Ant.* 1. 4. 66); cf. 3. 3. 39–44 [Nos.].

39. S.D. (Dyce).

43. *earthly paragon* So in *Gent.* 2. 4. 144 [Steev.].

44. S.D. (J.C.M.) F 'Enter Imogen'.

51. *As...parted* The metrical irregularity is acceptable with 'a very timid pause after "meal"' (Furn.).

52. *Money, youth?* (Rowe) F 'Money? Youth.'.

61. *embarked* Im. can scarcely mean that she expected to find her kinsman already departed. Thiselton's interpretation 'was to embark', as if in *oratio obliqua*, is plausible,—a spectator would not analyse it, but would not be held up by it—and makes Han.'s 'embarks' (anticipated by D'Urfey) unnecessary.

63. *in* into; cf. Abbott, §159.

69. *but be* 'ere I should fail to be' (Dowd.). This sense of 'but', though very common, has confused some edd. *groom in honesty;* (F, with colon) Tyrwhitt, most edd. 'groom. In honesty,'. But 'in honesty'='in an honourable way' (Wyatt) gives perfectly good sense, whereas the sense Tyrwhitt requires, 'in plain truth', is not recorded. For the opposite type of groom,

Ingleby cites *Wint.* 4. 4. 151, 'you wooed me the false way'.

70. *I'ld* (J., after Han. 'I would') F 'I do'. F has been defended by Wyatt and Furn. as = 'as I habitually buy', but an error of 'I do' for 'Ide' is more likely. There is no need to read 'I'ld bid' with Han.: the sense is 'I am bidding for you on the terms I should actually offer if it were a real bargain'; or 'I only offer a price which I should be prepared to give if you were to be bought' (Deighton).

70–1. *I'll...brother* I shall console myself for his being a man by loving him as my brother. F's comma after 'man' conveys this better than the heavier punctuation of most edd. since Pope, which makes 'I'll love...brother' a principal clause.

74–5. *friends?* | —*If* (J.C.M.) F 'Friends? | If' Rowe 'friends, | If'. I follow Furn.'s suggestion that Im. answers her own question with an unexpressed 'yes', which I represent by a dash. Sisson also retains the question-mark.

75. S.D. (Theob.; Rowe had made the whole speech aside).

76–7. *had...less* I should have been less of a prize (in the nautical sense); the figure is carried on in 'ballasting'.

79. *I;* (Steev.) F 'I,', leaving the attachment of 'whate'er it be' uncertain.

80. S.D. (Rowe).

85. *That...multitudes* i.e. 'obsequious adoration' (Theob.)—the worthless gift of fickle multitudes.

88. *Leonatus'* The apostrophe, not in F, seems necessary, whether it is taken to represent 'is' [Mal.], which would be unparalleled, or the possessive, with 'false' = 'falsehood' (cf. Rowe's first ed., 'Leonatus's').

93. One line in Pope; divided after 'owl' in F.

95. S.D. F 'Exeunt'.

3. 7

This scene, which Pope relegated to the foot of the page, is, as Daniel said, 'out of place' in terms of any objective time-scheme, as Cloten's arrival in Wales (4. 1) can only be a day or two after that of Imogen and Pisanio, and the landing of the Romans only a few days later still; but there is no reason to think that it is not where Sh. meant it to be. Eccles placed it at the end of Act 2, having already transferred 3. 1 to follow 2. 3. But in its present position it serves to remind us that the Roman army is on its way.

S.D. *Loc.* (Rowe; Dyce) *Entry* (F).

9. *commends* (Warb. *ap.* Theob.) F (+recent edd.) 'commands'—a very late instance of the form, if it is what Sh. wrote. Nos. cites *Roister Doister*, 1. 3. 126, which post-dates O.E.D.'s latest example. Still later is Middleton, *Your Five Gallants*, 1. 2. 15.

14. *supplyant* see G. The sp. is that of Cap. (F 'ſuppliant') to distinguish this sense, with which cf. *Ham.* 1. 3. 9, 'suppliance'.

16. S.D. F 'Exeunt'.

4. 1

S.D. *Loc.* (Camb.) *Entry* (F).

5. *saving reverence* see G. An apology for the pun on 'fitness'.

6. *fitness* see G. *workman.* (J.; Theob. with semi-colon) F 'workman,'.

11. *the advantage of the time* A vague phrase, perh.='superior opportunities of social intercourse' (Dowd.).

12. *general services* 'military services rendered in common with others' (Deighton).

13. *single opposition* single combats [Cap., comparing *1 H. IV*, 1. 3. 99]. *imperceiverant* (Dyce,

Remarks) F 'imperſeuerant'. 'Perceiverance'='per-ception', is quite common from *c.* 1440. Attempts to link with 'persevere' are pointless.

17. *her* (Warb. *ap.* Han.) F 'thy', caught from 'thy garments'. Mal. and others retain 'thy' as suitable to 'so fantastick a character as Cloten', but, as Dyce remarks, his obsession is revenge on Imogen for the insult at 2. 3. 133–6.

18. *haply* F 'happily', as often.

20. *power of* 'control over' (Deighton, citing *Ham.* 2. 2. 27).

22. *Fortune* (F) Han. 'Fortune,', but 'let Fortune put' is perfectly good sense.

22–3. *This...meeting-place* Cf. *Tim.* 5. 3. 1, 'By all description this should be the place'.

24. S.D. F 'Exit'.

4. 2

S.D. *Loc.* (Camb.) *Entry* (F).

1. S.D. (Cap.).

2. S.D. (Theob.).

5. *dust...alike* Tilley, A 119, cites various versions of the Erasmian adage, 'omnia idem pulvis'; cf. l. 247 below.

16. *Stealing so poorly* 'making no greater theft than that' (Deighton). *thee,...it,* (Dowd.) F 'thee:... it,'. Most edd. punctuate more heavily, but a mere parenthesis seems intended.

17. *How much* Prob., as Mal. thought, a mere grammatical variant on the following 'as much'. (J. conj. 'As' here.) Dowd. ingeniously but unconvincingly glossed 'Whatever the quantity may be', seeing a con-trast between quantity, in which love for his father might be greater, and weight (of passion). J.D.W., accepting the heavier punctuation after l. 16, proposes

'How...quantity?', with 'the weight...father' as the answer.

22. *Love's...reason* Cf. Tilley, L517, 'Love is without reason'.

24. S.D. (Cap.).

26–7. *"Cowards..."Nature* Gnomic inverted commas. Cf. *Meas.* 2. 4. 185 n., and, for full discussion of the practice, G. K. Hunter, *Library*, 5th ser. VI (1951–2), 171–88. For the idea involved, see Horace, *Odes*, IV. iv. 29 ff. (noted by S. Walker); cf. Baldwin, II, 511.

28–9. *who...me* 'that this boy of whom we know nothing should be loved more than me is surely miraculous' (Deighton, citing *Lr.* I. I. 223, 'that monsters it', for 'miracle' as a vb.,); '*who* this should be' carries a further sense of 'I wonder who he is'. For the mixture of 'that' and 'who', cf. a present-day kindred example, 'how this letter ever reached me is incredible' (heard in a lecture, 1958).

31. S.D. (S. Walker < Cap.). *So please you, sir* i.e., at your service; F indicates the turning to Belarius by a dash after 'health'.

32. S.D. (J.). One line in Rowe; divided after 'creatures' in F. *heard!* (Rowe) F 'heard:'—not poss. in a mod. text, but intelligible, since the next lines go on to specify the lies; cf. Simpson, p. 78.

35. *breeds* F2 'breed', but the collective sense of 'seas' helps out the singular verb; cf. *Wint.* 4. 4. 487, where F has 'hides', though this edition silently alters to F2's 'hide'.

38. S.D. (Dyce). *stir him* 'move him to tell his story' (J.); or perh. less precisely, 'rouse him from his depression' [C. B. Young].

41. *hereafter* (Rowe) F 'heereafter,'.

46. S.D. (after Theob.) F 'Exit', after 'you'; placed here by Cap.

47. *This...had* Conflation of (i) it appears he hath had, (ii) he appears to have had (Abbott, §411).

49. *he* (Cap.) F '*Arui*. He'. The combination of two successive speeches headed '*Arui*.' in F with the metrical irregularity suggests that something may have been lost. *in characters* Placed in a separate line by Globe, but this can scarcely have been Sh.'s intention, though there may have been corruption (see this note, init.). Cf. Fletcher, *Elder Brother*, 4. 1. 15, 'to cut his meat in characters' [Steev.]; Jonson, *Volpone*, 2. 1. 81–3, 'the meat was cut | So like his character, and so laid, as he | Must easily reade the cypher' [Dowd.].

57. *him* (Pope) F 'them', prob. under the influence of 'both'. Some retain 'them', but to regard grief and patience as rooted in their external manifestations, the smile and the sigh, is intolerable.

58. *Grow patience* (Rowe) F 'Grow patient'. Theob. added a comma after 'Grow', but the meaning is prob. 'let patience grow'. The MS prob., as Thiselton suggests, read 'patienc'; cf. *MSH*. 111.

59. *stinking elder* Hyphenated in F., but no such compound is recorded and unnecessary hyphens are common in this play. The evil repute of the elder was partly due to the tradition that Judas hanged himself on it; cf. *L.L.L.* 5. 2. 603–4 [Ellacombe *ap.* Furn.].

60. *perishing* see G. Grief was held to dry up the blood; cf. *M.N.D.* 3. 2. 97 n., *J.C.* 2. 1. 289–90 n. *with* Han. 'from'; but 'untwine...with' is poss. for 'no longer twine his...root with the vine' (Mal.).

61. S.D. (F).

64. *partly* slightly; so *R. III*, 4. 2. 40, *Ham.* 2. 1. 15, 'in part'.

66. *saw* For the tense (=mod. 'have seen') cf. Abbott, §347, 4. 2. 191, 4. 3. 36 [Wyatt]; *R. III*, 5. 3. 277.

70. *Let...him* leave me to deal with him. This menacing sense is common; cf. *Tit.* 1. 1. 449, 4. 3. 113. S.D. (after Rowe) F om.

71. *villain mountaineers* (Theob., retaining hyphen) F 'villaine-Mountainers'. This sp. is not elsewhere in Sh., as Dyce notes, though cf. such forms as 'pioner'.

74. *a slave* I think Guid. merely retorts the charge on Clot.: 'you are a slave too' [Deighton]. Mason and others interpret 'that abusive word *slave*', indicating 'slave' or 'a slave' as a quotation (cf. l. 89).

80. *thee.* (Han.) F 'thee?'

82. *grandfather.* (F 2, with colon) F 'Grand-father?'.

83. *which...thee* The proverb 'the tailor makes the man' is not recorded in Tilley, T 17, before Sh., but this passage and *Lr.* 2. 2. 60 imply it; cf. also J. Day, *Isle of Guls* (Sh. Assoc. Facs., 1936), A 4, 'Had hee not beene of my fathers owne making, I should ha condemnd his taylor for an exceeding botcher'.

89. *Cloten...name* even if your name is 'Cloten, thou double villain' [Delius]. This is more pointed than 'let your name be Cloten, you double villain'.

90. *Toad...Adder...Spider* All venomous creatures; cf. *R. III*, 1. 2. 19 [Dowd.], where the Q reporter substitutes 'adders' for Sh.'s less conventional 'wolves'.

92. *mere confusion* see G.

96. *Die the death* 'seems to be a solemn phrase for death inflicted by law' (J., cited by O.E.D.). It is Biblical in origin: O.E.D.'s first quotation is from Coverdale's version of Judges, xiii. 22.

100. S.D. (i) after Cap. (ii) Cap. F 'Fight and Exeunt. | Enter Belarius and Aruiragus'.

101. *company's* F 'Companie's' Globe 'companies', with some support from l. 69, but the sing. occurs at l. 129.

103. *I cannot tell* A common expression of puzzlement, not to be taken so literally as to conflict with the statement of certainty that follows.

108. *make good time* 'acquit himself well' (Schmidt).

109. *scarce made up.* Cf. *R. III*, 1. 1. 21, 'scarce half made up' [Ingleby]. Perh. Bel. adds 'I mean, to man' to make clear that he is not, as in the *R. III* passage, referring to any specific deformity. The total effect is something like 'When he was scarce made up— I mean to manhood (though I admit you might say he is "scarce made up" even now)'.

111–12. *cease* (Herr, *Scattered Notes on the Text of Sh.* (1879), p. 140) F 'cauſe'. The easiest solution is to suppose this corruption of a rare sb. (cf. *Ham.* 3. 3. 15 where Q2 has 'cesse' and F 'cease'). It is not certain, and *Ham.* 2. 2. 101–3 suggests that play on 'defect', 'cause', would be Sh., but defences of F are forced; for details, see Furn. The variety of the solutions proposed casts doubt on them all; it is poss., as Camb. suggests, that Sh. merely got into a tangle about opposites.

112. S.D. (Cap., at end of line) F, after 'Feare', 'Enter Guiderius', with 'But... Brother' as new line. *see,* (Theob.) F 'ſee'.

121. *take...in* see G.

122. *thank* (Steev.) F 'thanks'.

128–9. *himself, ...law?* (J., without comma) F 'himſelfe? ...Law.'.

129. *For* because.

132. *humour* (Theob.) F 'Honor'. The same error occurs in *Wiv.* (F) 1. 3. 82 [Theob.]; for a non-Sh. instance, see *N. & Q.* CCIII (1958), 64.

134. *not* Placed here by Cap.; at beginning of l. 135 in F.

145. *ordinance* (Pope). F 'Ord'nance', which looks like a transcriber's licence.

154. *reck* F 'reake'. S.D. F 'Exit'.

157. *So* As a conj., this usually means 'provided that' (so Deighton glosses). But perh. the sense is rather 'in order that the revenge should have pursued me alone, as it would then have done'. F has a colon after 'done't', which would make it poss. to take 'So. . . me' as a principal clause, with past tense for conditional. But that seems less probable.

160. *possible strength* 'strength such as we could possibly possess' (Dowd.). *through* see G. 'seek through'. Vaughan's 'three' (thre > thro) is ingenious.

167. *him.* (Rowe, with semi-colon) F 'him,'.

168. *let. . .blood* 'kill as many Clotens as would fill a parish' (J.).

169. S.D. F 'Exit'.   170. *how* (Pope) F 'thou'.

177. *instinct* Always stressed on the second syllable by Sh.

180. *wildly grows* grows wild. For other cases where Sh. has an adv. in '-ly' contrary to mod. usage, cf. Abbott, §23; *Troil.* 3. 3. 256.

183. S.D. (Pope) F 'Enter Guidereus'.

184. *Cloten's clotpole* Cf. 1. 2, initial S.D. n. (p. 140).

186. S.D. (F). *ingenious* (Rowe) F 'ingenuous'; interchange between the two words was frequent in the 17th century, but, as Clarke notes, 'ingenuous' is not elsewhere found in Sh., though some edd. have introduced it at *L.L.L.* 4. 2. 81 (see note there). Nos. thinks 'the adj. seems to imply that the instrument was a mechanical one', and notes that such were known in Henry VIII's reign. Hunter had suggested an Aeolian harp, but then how would Cadwal 'give it motion'? Sh. prob. intends no more than to quiet any doubts as to how the form of music he used—a 'consort of viols' (Nos.), or whatever—was available.

191. *did not speak* Cf. 4. 2. 66 n.

193. *lamenting toys* 'lamentations over trifles' (Deighton).

194. *apes* O.E.D. cites for sense 'fools', but the lit. sense, as Nos. notes, is acceptable.

195. S.D. (F, with 'Enter' for 'Re-enter').

200. *leaping time...crutch* Sh.'s choice of these contrasting words may have been influenced by the recollection of Vaux's poem which he had used in *Ham.* 5. 1. 61 ff. (see n. there), 'For age with stelying steppes, | Hath clawed me with his crowch: |And lusty life away she leapes, | As there had been none such'.

204-5. *what...in* 'on what kind of a coast your sluggish hulk might best find harbour' (Deighton). *crare* (Sympson) F 'care'. See G.

206. *Might* (F2) F 'Might'ſt', prob. by anticipation of 'eaſileſt', or of 'might'ſt' in l. 207.

207. *I* i.e. what I know is [Tyrwhitt].

211. *as...at* as if laughing at Death's sting (which in fact he is). Cf. I Corinthians, xv. 55 [J.D.W.]. Most edd. add a comma after 'dart', but F brings out more clearly that 'death's...at' is a single phrase.

212-13. *floor,...leagued;* (Most edd., substantially) F 'floore: ...leagu'd,'.

214. *clouted* see G. and O.E.D. 'clout-shoe'. This meaning is more appropriate here than 'patched', though the word is used of shoes in that sense as well.

218. *to thee* (F, most edd.). I find this transition to direct address harsh, and incline to accept Cap.'s 'there', though the metre of the line can be saved by taking 'fairest' as a monosyllable.

218-19. *With...lasts* Cf. *Per.* 4. 1. 17-18 [Steev.].

221. *face,* (Rowe) F 'face.'.

223. *whom...slander* 'the relative is attracted to a subsequent implied object' (Abbott, §246).

224. *ruddock* (Han.) F 'Raddocke'; O.E.D. records sp. with 'i' and 'e', but 'a' only here. For this

fable about the redbreast, familiar from *The Babes in the Wood*, Steev. cited T. Lupton, *A Thousand Notable Things* (1579).

228–9. *besides,* (Theob.) ...*corse.* (Cap.) F 'befides.... Coarse—'. As the sentence is complete, though the speech may be interrupted, the dash is inappropriate. For another dash that may be the result of tinkering, cf. 2. 4. 76 n.

229. *winter-ground* Not found elsewhere. If Cap.'s punctuation is correct, it is presumably a verb, meaning 'protect from the winter' [Steev.]. With F's punctuation we might, as Nos. suggests, interpret, 'to winter-ground thy corse ⟨shall be itself a flower⟩', but this sort of sense, as he recognizes, would be more easily conveyed by 'To winter ground' (F 4). Nos.'s objection to Theob., that 'the ruddock could hardly bring moss *in addition* to flowers when there are no flowers' is sophistical. It is quite natural to say, 'he will bring flowers (when there are flowers) and besides, he will bring moss (when there are no flowers)'. J.D.W. favours Douce's 'winter-green' = 'cover with green in winter'.

234. *shall's* Cf. 5. 5. 228, *Per.* 4. 5. 7 n.

235–42. *though...then* R. Noble, *Sh.'s Use of Song* (1923), p. 137, thinks that singers were not available, and that Sh. 'was compelled to make excuse in the context for the lack of singing'. But it would be a most clumsy excuse, whereas taken at its face value the dialogue has an attractive air of spontaneity and naïveté. Nos., p. 223, treats as a poss. explanation 'the breaking of an actor's voice', but surely the princes' parts are conceived throughout for adult actors.

237. *our* (Pope) F 'to our', the 'to' prob. caught from l. 236 [Mal.].

243. *Great...less* Cf. Tilley, G 446, 'The greater grief (sorrow) drives out the less'; *Lr.* 3. 4. 8–9, etc.

246–7. *though...dust* Cf. 4. 2. 5 n.

248. *angel of the world* 'divinely sent messenger from God to man' (Deighton). As 'the power that keeps peace and order in the world' (J.), 'reverence' has a claim to obedience.

254. S.D. (after Cap.) F om.

255. *to th'east* Dowd. cites Browne, *Hydrotaphia*, ch. 3, for this as the custom among 'the Megarians and Phoenicians'. Sh. prob. introduces it as the reverse of Christian practice 'to suit the pre-Christian period of his play' (Wyatt).

262. *Golden* A favourite term of praise in Sh., with suggestions of the golden age, as well as of a splendid position in society.

267. *reed...oak* Cf. the Aesopian fable (Baldwin, I, 626–7) of the reed which survives by yielding when the oak is overthrown [H. Green, *Sh. and the Emblem Writers* (1870), pp. 314–16]; the difference between these traditional opposites now means nothing to Fidele.

275. *Consign* see G. for J.'s gloss, accepted by O.E.D.; a contextual sense not exactly paralleled; 'this' for 'thee' (J. conj.) would permit the more normal sense, 'submit to'. Han. read 'thee' for 'this' in l. 269, and J.D.W. suggests that both were originally set up 'thee', and the wrong one corrected.

276. *exorciser* see G. For this use, Mason cited 'exorcist' in *J.C.* 2. 1. 323.

281. S.D. (F, with 'Enter' for 'Re-enter').

282. One line in Pope; two, divided after 'obsequies', in F.

283. *'bout midnight* Cf. *Ham.* 4. 7. 143–4, *M.V.* 5. 1. 12–13, *Sh. Survey*, 10 (1957), 21–3 [J.D.W.].

285. *Upon their faces* Puzzling, as the audience in the theatre can hardly ignore the fact that Clot. is supposed to be headless. Perh. the meaning is vague, 'on the front of their bodies' (Deighton).   J.D.W.

thinks that 'upon their faces' refers to the flowers, that
l. 284 represents Sh.'s first draft, and that the second
draft would have run,

> The herbs that have cold dew upon their faces
> Are strewings fitt'st for graves—

had 'on them' and 'o'th'night' been deleted as he
intended.

290. *is* (Pope) F 'are'. S.D. (after Cap.) F
'Exeunt'.

291. S.D. In F, 'Imogen awakes', centred above
this line, with no sp.-prefix.

295. S.D. (Camb. after Rowe).

298. *For so* I think the sequence of thought is: 'I
thought I was a cave-keeper. This has proved to be a
dream. Therefore I have grounds for hoping this is a
dream too' [Eccles, Vaughan].

301. *fumes* see G., and, for the physiological background, *Tp.* 5. 1. 66–8 [Dowd.], *Mac.* 1. 7. 65–7
[Steev.], with note in this edn.

310–11. *His...face* Cf. *Ham.* 3. 4. 56–8 [H.
Coleridge, *ap.* Furn.].

313. *madded Hecuba* In Seneca's *Troades*, esp.
994–1008. Ovid, *Met.* XIII, which Baldwin cites
(II, 193), does not contain curses. Cf. *Ham.* 2. 2.
505 ff. Verity notes the frequency of 'Hamlet touches'
in this speech.

316. *Hath* A double irregularity; 'Thou...with
...Cloten' is treated as a plural subject (Franz, §675a),
and 'hath' used for 'have' (Abbott, §334). Each of
these in isolation is common, and I see no special
difficulty about the combination, though most edd.
accept Pope's 'Hast'.

323. *be?* (Cap.) F 'be,'.

329. *Cloten's* (Pope) F 'Cloten', which Vaughan
retains, and which may be defensible with the possessive

of 'Pisanio's' carrying over. Both Beaumont and Fletcher folios have 'my honour, or my friend' at *The Little French Lawyer*, 1. 1. 93, where Seward emended to 'friend's'. For less violent examples cf. Franz, §684c.

332. S.D. (i) Globe, (ii) Camb. F 'Enter Lucius, Captaines, and a Soothſayer'.

333. *To them* in addition to them. The dialogue is already in full swing when we begin to hear it. The anon. conj. *ap.* Camb. that these words have strayed from the preceding S.D. is superficially attractive, but these words as part of a S.D. are 'rarely found in either manuscript or printed plays' as distinct from 'plots' (W. W. Greg, *The Sh. First Folio*, 1955, p. 173). The closest Sh. parallel would be the initial S.D. of *Cor.* 1. 4, 'to them a Messenger', but there the messenger's entry is immediately recognized, 'Yonder comes news', whereas here no notice is taken of the soothsayer for thirteen lines.

336. *are here* F 2's 'are' has been popular, and 'here' could have crept in from l. 335, but as the repetition is not offensive to sense or metre it is safer not to emend.

337. *confiners* see G; 'confines' more often = 'district' than 'borders' in Sh. [Schmidt].

341. *Siena's* F '*Syenna*'s'. A duke of Siena occurs in Beaumont and Fletcher, *Women Pleased* [Dowd.].

347. *fast* For this form of the past tense see Abbott, §341.

351. *abuse* make unreliable; a natural transference from the diviner to his art.

356. *Or dead* F's comma after this gives a false suggestion, by modern conventions, that 'on him' goes only with 'sleeping' and not also with 'dead'. Vaughan punctuated 'page, ... sleeping,'.

364. *did* i.e. painted; 'do' is common for various

types of representation in art: cf. 2. 4. 73, *Tw. N.* 1. 5. 239 [Steev.], *Wint.* 5. 2. 98.

366. *wreck* F 'wracke', as frequently. *How came't? Who is't?* Steev. 'How came it? Who is it?' But this achieves regular metre at the cost of a very jog-trot movement. Irregularity in these abrupt questions is not out of place.

373. *Try...never* Here too, irregularity is not ineffective, and no supplement is convincing: the easiest would be Pope's 'serve them'.

377. *Richard du Champ* Perh. in friendly allusion to Richard Field, Sh.'s fellow-townsman, and the printer of *Ven.* and *Lucr.* (R. J. Kane, *Sh. Quart.* IV (1953), 206, who notes that 'R. [or 'Ricardo'] del Campo' appears in the imprint of his Spanish books). S.D. (Rowe).

379. *Say you?* Cf. 2. 1. 23 n.

391. *pickaxes* 'her fingers' (J.).

392. *wild wood-leaves* Camb. conj. 'wild-wood leaves', and O.E.D. cites under 'wildwood' = 'forest of natural growth,...uncultivated or unfrequented wood'. But there is nothing obviously wrong with F, which recent edd. have retained.

398. *My friends* Separate line in Pope; with l. 399 in F.

402. *arm* see G. *he is* (F 2) F 'hee's'. This time, there seems no special point in the irregularity.

405. S.D. F 'Exeunt'.

4. 3

S.D. Loc. (Cap.) *Entry* (Camb.) F 'Enter Cymbeline, Lords, and Piſanio'.

1. *bring* (F 2) F 'hring'. S.D. (after Dyce).

2. *with* 'caused by' (Deighton).

3. *A madness* Pope 'Madness', perh. rightly.

4. *touch* see G.

21. *will*=he will; cf. Abbott, §400. *troublesome*
A stronger word than in modern Eng., as Deighton
notes, citing *2 H. IV*, 4. 5. 186; B.C.P., Baptism
Service, 'this troublesome world'.

22. *jealousy* see G. S.D. (J.).

27. *queen!* (Theob.) F 'Queen,', which Nos.
retains, thinking that 'for the counsel' may mean 'for
lack of the counsel', and citing 3. 6. 17 and *H. V*, 1. 2.
114. But this would be very harsh.

28. *amazed with matter* 'confounded by a variety
of business' (Steev., citing *K.J.* 4. 3. 140).

29. *affront no less* face an army no smaller.

33. *as it seeks us* i.e. 'with spirit' (Cap.).

35. S.D. (after Camb.) F 'Exeunt'.

36. *heard* Cf. 4. 2. 66 n. *letter* Perh., as Mal.
thought, 'letter of the alphabet' (figurative and
hyperbolical) rather than 'epistle', which does not go
readily with 'heard', though Thiselton quotes a
modern (1901) example; or perh. a mixture of 'heard
no news' and 'had no letter' [Her.].

40. *betid* (Han.) F 'betide', cf. O.E.D., and *R. II*
(Q2, etc.), 5. 1. 42, *Tp.* (F 2–4), 1. 2. 31; similarly
R. II (Qq), 5. 5. 79, 'bestride'.

44. *to...king* so that 'the king shall remark my
valour' (J.).

46. S.D. F 'Exit'.

4. 4

S.D. *Loc.* (Dyce) *Entry* (F).

2–3. *find we...adventure?* (F 2) F 'we finde...
Aduenture.'.

7. *During their use* while they have use for
us.

8. *us* (F 2) F 'v.'.

14. *Drawn on* see G. Perh. 'with an idea of the lingering nature of such a death' (Deighton).

17. *the* (Rowe) F 'their' (from l. 18).

20. *upon our note* on observing us; cf. 4. 3. 44.

26. *Who...breeding* who experience the lack of proper education that is the result of my exile (which they share).

27. *certainty* 'certain continuance' (Vaughan); they know they cannot escape from it. *hard* (F 2) F 'heard'.

29. *But to be* A positive counterpart to 'hopeless', such as 'destined', is understood.

33. *o'ergrown* i.e., with a beard; cf. 5. 3. 17 [Dyce, *Remarks*].

35. *is't* F 2 (+most edd.), 'is it', but a pause after 'thither' is tolerable.

37. *hot* lustful. So traditionally, cf. *Oth.* 3. 3. 405 [Delius].

46. *therefore due* 'which my disobedience and loss of blessing makes only my due' (Vaughan).

53. S.D. (Han.).

54. S.D. F 'Exeunt'.

5. 1

S.D. *Loc.* (Dyce) *Entry* (F; 'with...handkerchief' Rowe).

1. *wished* (Pope) F 'am wiſht', which would imply that he still retained the wish. The source of the error is not obvious—it might be a false start in the MS. (Sisson, *Readings*), though it is hard to see what it could have started. If it were metrically happier, Kellner's 'once [<ame] wished' (*Anglica, Untersuchungen...Alois Brandl...überreicht* (1925), II, 168) might be worth considering.

2. *You married ones* For the address to the audience,

cf. the more indirect 'side-glance' pointed out in *Wint.*
1. 2. 192–3 n. [J.D.W.].

9. *put on* see G.; but it could also mean 'put on this
fault (like a garment)'.

14. *each elder worse* 'the last deed is certainly not
the oldest, but Sh. calls the deed of an elder man an
elder deed' (J.). Clarke compares 'elder [=later] days'
in *R. II*, 2. 3. 43, where the metaphorical context eases
the expression.

15. *dread it* Theob. 'dreaded', but though 'it' is
rather vague, it is intelligible as='this accumulation'
(Deighton). *doers'* (Theob.) F 'dooers'.

16. *But...own* i.e., but you have chosen to take
Imogen to yourselves, and it is presumptuous of me to
speculate on what *might* have been. *best* J.D.W. finds
J.'s conj. 'blest' attractive.

20. *mistress; peace* Staunton's ingenious 'mistress-
piece' (a rare formation after 'masterpiece'; see O.E.D.)
does not ring true.

32–3. *begin* (Theob.) | *The fashion—* (Evans) F
'begin, | The fashion'.

33. S.D. F 'Exit'.

5. 2

S.D. *Loc.* (Camb.) *Entry* (after Cap.) F 'Enter
Lucius, Iachimo, and the Romane Army at one doore;
and the Britaine Army at another: Leonatus Poſthumus
following like a poore Souldier. They march ouer, and
goe out. Then enter againe in Skirmiſh Iachimo and
Poſthumus: he vanquiſheth and diſarmeth Iachimo,
and then leaues him'. Note that Post. has fulfilled the
intention announced in 5. 1. 22–4. Dyce and Camb.
give Imogen an entry here, perhaps to emphasize her
fidelity to Lucius.

2–6. *I...profession* 'The thought seems to have

been imitated in *Philaster* [4. 3. 106–7]: "The gods take part against me; could this boor Have held me thus else?"' [Steev.].

4. *or* otherwise.

10. S.D.s F, with 'Exit'.

13. S.D. F, with 'Enter...Exeunt...enter... and' for 'Re-enter (Dyce)...go out...re-enter (Dyce)...with (Deighton)'.

18. S.D. F 'Exeunt'.

5. 3

S.D. *Loc.* (Cap.) *Entry* (Pope); F 'Britaine' for 'British'.

2. *fliers?* Most edd. follow F 3 in substituting a full-stop for the question-mark, but the tone is interrogative. *I did* Craig (*ap.* Furn.), to avoid repetition, conj. 'Ay' [sp. 'I'].

3–58. *No blame...bane* This is the one passage in the play which closely follows Holinshed: see Introduction, p. xv.

10–11. *some falling...fear* Not, strictly, a third object to 'struck down', as Deighton notes, though not clearly distinguished in its syntax.

slightly Vaughan, Dowd., add a comma, so that (as Delius had already suggested) both 'mortally' and 'slightly' should go with 'touched'. But in this rapid narrative, 'struck down mortally' and 'struck down... slightly touched' make a natural enough pair.

12. *dead men* F 'deadmen'; cf. 2. 3. 71 n. *hurt behind* 'A sign of cowardice' (Nos., citing *Mac.* 5. 8. 46, 'Had he his hurts before?').

16–17. *deserved...to* 'deserved of [his country] the support it had given him during the life which his white beard showed him to have lived' (Deighton, after Grant White).

21–2. *fit...shame* 'so delicate of complexion as to

deserve masks to protect them from the sun, or rather I should say, fairer than those by which masks are worn for that purpose, or to prevent impertinent curiosity' (Deighton).

24. *harts* (Theob.) F 'hearts'. *our* Thirlby's 'her' is elegant, and 'our' could have been caught from the beginning of the line.

28. *But...frown* 'only by looking back with a bold frown of defiance' (Clarke). *These three* The vb. to which this is subject does not come until l. 34, 'gilded'.

30. *are the file* 'practically constitute the whole troop' (On.). The more technical sense, referring to the depth of a formation in line, is prob. not involved.

34–5. *looks;...renewed*, (F) Many edd. after Cap. have unnecessarily transposed the punctuation.

35. *Part...renewed* Edd. who alter the punct. (see previous note) treat 'renewed' as parallel to 'gilded', and interpret 'renewed in part the sense of shame, in part the spirit of courage' (Dowd.) But Dowd. also notes that with Vaughan's conj. 'looks.'— and the same applies to F's punct.—the meaning is 'Shame renewed some, and courage some'. I think this is preferable. For this meaning of 'part...part', cf. Latin 'partim...partim'.

35–6. *turned...example* who had become cowards only by imitation.

37. *Damned...beginners* 'doubly accursed in those who set the example' (Deighton); perh. with a glance at the primal sin of Satan [J.D.W.].

38. *they* the three heroes.

40. *chaser* pursuing body imaged as a single horse; cf. G. 'stop' [J.D.W.].

42. *stooped* (Rowe) F 'ſtopt'.

43. *they* (Theob.) F 'the'.

44. *fragments...voyages* i.e., something to fall back on in the last resort.

46–8. *wound!* (Cap.) ...*before,* (F 2) *some dying,*
(Camb.) F 'wound,...before...dying;'. The central
problem is the construction of 'Some...some...some'.
I take them to be the subject of 'Are now' in l. 49. This
means that 'slain' and 'dying' cannot be literal, but =
'some who feigned death' (Dowd.), or is simply a bold
hyperbole: cf. *Mac.* 5. 2. 4–5 [J.D.W.]. The alternative interpretation, deleting the comma after 'wound',
and treating 'Some...wave' as its object, turns a
heroic recovery into a shambles; cf. Sisson's paraphrase
(*Readings*), 'In the confusion they strike indiscrimi-
nately at dead bodies, at dying men, and some of these
their own friends struck down in a previous assault'.
Deighton treats 'some' as subject in each case, but
'slain', 'dying', and 'their friends' as object. I do not
think this is English.

47–8. *some their friends | O'erborne* Poss. as 'some
friends of theirs [i.e. of those just mentioned] who had
been o'erborne'. But the phrase is awkward, and I
suggest 'O'erbore', i.e. 'some whom their friends
o'erbore', the transcriber or compositor having failed to
follow the construction and corrected 'O'erbore' on the
assumption that it was meant to be a pa. pple.

53. *do not* Suspected, in view of what follows;
hence Theob. 'do but', Ingleby, 'do you...it?'. But
'Post. first bids him not wonder, then tells him in
another mode of reproach, that wonder is all that he
was made for' (J.).

55–6. *Will...one* 'Do you want to make up
rhymes about it, and bring ridicule on the deed by
hawking them around? Here is a specimen for you.'
I take 'it' to be the exploit, as described in verse, and
'for a mock'ry' to refer to the ludicrous effect of a crude
broadsheet ballad, not to any satiric intervention on the
composer's part; though Post.'s own rhymes which
follow are satiric. I withdraw my suggestion (*ap.* Nos.)

that 'rhyme' ('Rime', with a capital, in F) is a noun; 'one' can easily refer to the implied mention of 'rhymes'. Pope, while relegating the whole of ll. 55–63, 'Will...rhyme', to the margin, read 'rhymes' at l. 55.

57. *old man* F 'Oldman'; cf. 2. 3. 71 n. *twice a boy* Cf. Tilley, M 570, *Ham.* 2. 2. 389 [Delius].

60–2. *Who...too* I shan't have to put up with his (unwanted) friendship for long, for if he runs true to type 'he'll quickly fly my friendship'.

63. *put...rhyme* driven me to rhyming too. S.D. F 'Exit'.

64. *Still going?* not stopped running yet? *This is* Prob. pronounced 'this'; cf. Abbott, §461. *noble misery* wretched state of one who is called 'noble'.

68. *in...charmed* my wretchedness causing me to live a charmed life.

74. *being* since he (Death) is [Cap.]. This is the simplest way of taking a much-discussed and emended line. To find Death, Post. must return to the side of Death's enemies, which is now the Roman.

78. *touch my shoulder* i.e., in token of arrest; cf. *Err.* 4. 2. 37, 'shoulder-clapper' [Rolfe], *A.Y.L.* 4. 1. 46 [Evans].

81. *either* one or the other.

83. S.D. (F; 'British' added by Theob.).

91. *dog!* (Theob.) F 'dog,', which Nos. retains, 'not a dog, not even a leg, of Rome'. But for the climax to work, would not the leg have to be a *dog's* leg, which it clearly is not?

92. *leg* Daniel conj. 'lag', comparing Rowe's 'lag' for 'leg' in *Tim.* 3. 6. 79. But 'in the case of fliers the leg may well represent the man' (Dowd., comparing *Dick of Devonshire* (*M.S.R.*), 734, 'Not soe much as the leg of a Spanyard left').

94. S.D. (F, to 'Gaoler'; 'then all go', after

Theob.). Whether there is a genuine exit here for
Post. and his gaoler is in dispute. Their immediate re-
entry is anomalous (cf. C. M. Haines, *R.E.S.* 1 (1925),
449–51); and J. C. Adams, *The Globe Playhouse*
(1942), pp. 336–7 (followed by Nos.), rejects the
editorial location for 5. 4: 'If in fact a new scene does
begin here (which may be doubted), the heading should
read: "*Britain*: An open place near the British camp".'
Adams also argues (p. 339) that Post. is chained (5. 4. 1)
to one of the stage posts because he 'must be forward on
the platform in the orbit of a descent from the heavens'.
In view of the scene-division and new entry (itself
inaccurate, since there are two gaolers), I think it
unwise to be dogmatic, and therefore follow the usual
editorial tradition. Localization is in any case secondary
on the Jacobean stage; the main point is that Post. is a
prisoner, whether in prison or not; and a specific out-
of-door location in a reader's edition is perhaps an
inappropriately naturalistic translation of a setting that
is essentially unlocalized. Certainly a modern producer
can introduce a prison without falsity to Sh.'s dramatic
intentions.

5. 4

S.D. *Loc.* (Camb.) *Entry* (Rowe) F 'Enter
Posthumus, and Gaoler'; F's prefixes in ll. 1 and 2 are
'*Gao.*' and '*2. Gao.*'.

1. One line in Rowe; two, divided after 'stol'n', in
F. *You...stol'n* 'alludes to the custom of putting a lock
on a horse's leg, when he is turned to pasture' (J.); cf.
2 Return from Parnassus (ed. J. B. Leishman), 264–5,
'clap a locke on their feete, and turne them to commons'
[Thiselton].

2. S.D. (after Rowe); F om.

10. *The penitent instrument* the instrument, which

is repentance; not, as some edd. take it, with an *explicit* reference to death—this only follows in 'Then free for ever'.

13. *repent*, (F) Pope, most edd., 'repent?', but the run of the passage does not demand a strict parallelism with l. 11.

15. *constrained*. (Rowe, with semi-colon) F 'con-ftrain'd,'. *satisfy* see G.

16. *main part* A. Walker, *ap.* Nos., 'mainport', glossing, 'if atonement consists of the small tribute of my liberty'. It is not fatal that this legal term, = 'small tribute', is rare, and not recorded before 1664, but the word-order does not seem to me compatible with treating 'of' as = 'constituted by'. F is acceptable as interpreted by Grant White, 'if expiation is the main part, the most important requisite, to my freedom of conscience'.

17. *stricter* The usual meaning gives good sense, with 'my all' a surprise ending; perh. quasi-proverbial, cf. *Troublesome Reign of King John* (Sh. Classics), 1. 5. 133, 'Now will I take no more but all they have'. To interpret 'restricted' weakens the conceit. It is true that continued life would be 'stricter' to Post. than death [Her.], but I do not think that is what is meant.

18. *vile* F 'vilde'; cf. 1. 1. 143 n.

20. *sixth* F 'fixt', as often.

21. *abatement* see G. This commercial sense, not recorded in O.E.D. before 1624, seems clearly present here; cf. mod. 'rebate'; so Tieck, 'Abzug'.

23–4. *coined it…stamp* Frequent in Sh. (normally for physical parentage); cf. 2. 5. 5 n.

25. *for the figure's sake* Cf. Marlowe, *Hero and Leander*, 1, 265, 'Base bullion for the stamp's sake we allow' [Deighton].

26. *You rather mine*, (Han.) F '(You rather) mine'. *being yours* Perh. simply 'because "you coined it"'

(l. 23)' (Wyatt); or, with more specific reference to 'for the figure's sake', 'because I am made in your image' [Delius, Ingleby].

28. *bonds* Perh. 'with triple play on the word: in reference to the legal instrument so called, to the iron shackles on the speaker's limbs, and to the sense in which the poet uses "bond" as that whereon the term of "life" is held [cf. *Mac.* 3. 2. 49, already cited by Steev.]' (Clarke). Similarly, 'cold' may play on the lit. sense, applicable to fetters, and fig. 'depressing'. That there is a specif. legal sense, 'without force' [Thiselton, Dowd.], is not established.

29. S.D. (i) after Rowe, (ii) F (with 'followes' for 'follow').

30–113. On the Vision, see Prefatory Note.

30–92. *No...fly* The line division is that of Theob. F treats as a set of fourteeners, though usually dividing after the fourth foot.

31. *mortal flies* Cf. *Lr.* 4. 1. 38, 'As flies to wanton boys are we to the gods' [Delius].

32. *with Juno chide* R. K. Root cites Chapman's translation of *Iliad*, v, 893 [=888 in Chapman, ed. A. Nicoll (1957)], 'Though I correct her still and chide', where Jupiter is speaking to Mars of Juno (*Classical Mythology in Sh.* (1903), p. 84).

36. *saw?* (F4) F 'ſaw:'.

39–40. *as...art* Cf. Psalm lxviii. 5, 'He is a father of the fatherless' [J.D.W.].

42. *earth-vexing* 'plaguing the life of man' (Schmidt).

50. *he deserved* F 'he d ſeru'd'.

55–7. *be...dignity* (Rowe, with comma after 'be') F 'bee?...dignitie.'.

60. *Leonati* The plur. used adjectivally with 'seat'; cf. Abbott, §22.

67. *geck* F 'geeke'.

69. *came* S. Walker 'come', plausibly; apart from the sense, the 'came...twain' assonance is unpleasing.

81. *look* (F2) F 'looke, | looke', which Dowd. alone retains, suggesting an elision of the second syllable of 'window' before 'ope'.

92. S.D. (F). The method of staging is, of course, a matter of conjecture. For one reconstruction, see J. C. Adams, *The Globe Playhouse* (1942), pp. 336–40.

101. *Whom...cross* Jupiter borrows from Christianity; cf. Hebrews, xii. 6, 'whom the Lord loveth he chasteneth', *Oth.* 5. 2. 21 n.

102. *delighted* delighted in.

113. S.D. (F).

115. *sulphurous* The thunderbolt of l. 92 S.D. may actually have caused a smell; on such effects in the Eliz. and Jac. theatre, cf. Adams, *The Globe Playhouse*, pp. 121–3.

116–17. *ascension...fields* i.e., in contrast to the sulphurous descent, 'the odour is sweeter than that of our flowery fields of Elysium' (Dowd., after Wyatt).

122. S.D. (Camb. after Cap.) F 'Vaniſh'.

123. S.D. (Theob.).

128. *greatness'* (Rowe, without apostrophe) F 'Greatneſſe,'. *favour* (Camb.) F 'Fauour;'. Other edd. make clear that 'dream' is indic. by reading 'wretches, [comma in F]...favour,'.

137. S.D. (F).

146. *either both, or nothing* If the text is sound, I suspect there should be a comma after 'either' (as Thiselton suggested, though he preferred 'either both' ='either of the two', comparing 'either which' in *Ham.* 4. 7. 13), giving three alternatives, 'one or other (of dream and madness)' (cf. 5. 3. 81), 'both' and 'nothing'; with the same idea, Cap. read 'either, or both'. Hertzberg's 'either of both' is also possible.

147–8. *Or...untie* 'senseless speaking' corresponds to 'such...brain not', and 'a speaking...untie' to 'a dream', which ordinary intelligence cannot interpret [Dowd.]. This is more plausible than J.'s tentative paraphrase, 'a speech without consciousness, as in a dream, or a speech unintelligible, as in madness'.

150. S.D. (Cap.) F 'Enter Gaoler'; cf. note to initial S.D.; the prefix continues to be 'Gao.'. The presence of a second gaoler is not strictly necessary here, and Al. and Sisson follow F, but it seems prob. that Sh.'s final intention would have been the same here as at the beginning of the scene.

153. *Hanging* see G.

157–170. *But...follows* The whole speech is simply an elaboration of the proverb 'Death pays all debts' (Tilley, D 148, citing).

157. *reckoning* settling of accounts; takes up 'shot' from l. 156.

159. *are as* (Collier conj.) F 'are'—a common type of error; the correction makes the sentence run more smoothly.

162–3. *sorry...much* For the play in 'paid'= 'subdued by liquor' [Steev.], of which O.E.D. gives only one instance (1638), cf. Dekker, *2 Honest Whore* (*c.* 1605), 4. 3. 51–3, '*Lod.* Y'are paid? *2 Vint.* Yes Sir. *Math.* So shall some of vs be anon, I feare.'; Fletcher, *Wit Without Money*, 5. 3. 3, 'Thou wert cruelly paid'.

164. *heavier...light* Cf. the proverbs, 'A heavy purse makes a light heart' and 'A light purse makes a heavy heart' (Tilley, P655, 659; cited in Muir's Arden (1952) note on *Lr.* 4. 6. 148).

165. *drawn* see G. *Of* (Globe) F 'Oh, of', by anticipation of the next clause.

166. *penny cord* Cf. *H. V*, 3. 6. 47 [Furn.].

167–8. *debitor-and-creditor* Hyphenated by Delius. See G.; and cf. *Oth.* 1. 1. 31.

169. *sir* (F2) F 'Sis'.

173. *a man...to* 'if there were a man who was destined to' (Abbott, §367).

178. *Your* Genuinely personal, rather than generic— cf. *Ham*. 1. 5. 167, 'your philosophy'—as Vaughan takes it.

179. *pictured* In the traditional death's head, or skull.

180. *take* (Heath) F 'to take', more likely caught from 'to know' than an example of the construction noted in Abbott, §416, final quotation.

182. *jump* see G., and cf. *Mac*. 1. 7. 7 [J.].

184. *on* (J.C.M. *ap*. Nos.) F 'one', which='on' at 5. 5. 134, 311, and elsewhere. The sentence runs more naturally than with the rather formal 'one' as object.

185–7. *none...them* Embroiders on the proverb, Tilley, S206, 'Who so blind as he that will not see?'

190. S.D. (F).

195. *I'll...then* 'Post. of course means he is to be liberated by death, but the hangman takes, or pretends to take, his words literally' (Deighton).

197. S.D. (after Camb.) F om. F2 'Exeunt'.

200–2. *for...wills* A non sequitur typical of Sh.'s common folk. This clause modifies 'verier knaves', i.e., 'there are worse than he, Roman though he is'. But he turns aside to comment that even some of the Romans die unwillingly, as if their stoicism rather than their villainy had been his reason for mentioning them in the first place.

205–6. *my...in't* Generally taken to mean 'if my wish were fulfilled I should hope for preferment to a better office' (Wyatt). But it is not clear how this hope is in the wish he has expressed, and I think he may mean 'it is a pious wish that will stand me in good stead in the next world'. There could, as J.D.W.

suggests, also be a quibble on 'preferment' = 'preference' (as in *Shr.* 2. 1. 93), 'my wish expresses a preference'.

204. *gallowses* This plur. not elsewhere in Sh., though 'a gallows' is frequent. O.E.D. does not strongly support Rolfe's view that it is 'intended as a vulgar plural'.

206. S.D. F2 'Exit' F 'Exeunt'.

5. 5

S.D. *Loc.* (Rowe) *Entry* (Cap.) F 'Enter Cymbeline...Piſanio, and Lords'.

5. *targes* Monosyllabic; cf. *Ant.* 2. 6. 39 n.

10. *poor looks* Strictly, 'it was not the poor look which was promised; that was visible' (Warb.), but that is no reason for emending in late Sh. He promised nothing *beyond* what appeared on the surface.

13. S.D. (Rowe).

14. *liver, heart, and brain* Described as 'these sovereign thrones' in *Tw. N.* 1. 1. 37. The seats, respectively, of passions, affections, and reason [Dowd.].

20. *knights o'th'battle* 'Knighthood conferred on the field of battle was specially honourable' (Dowd., after Delius, citing *K.J.* 1. 1. 53–4; cf. also *Tit.* 1. 1. 196).

22. *estates* see G. S.D. (F).

23. *There's...faces* Cf. *Ant.* 5. 1. 50 [Mal.], *R. II,* 2. 2. 75 [Deighton].

41. *but...dying* For examples of the dictum that 'dying men speak truth', cf. Tilley, M 514. Here, of course, there is no reference to prophetic inspiration, but only to not lying.

47. *delicate* see G.

54. *O'ercome...time* No metrical supplement commends itself irresistibly. An unobtrusive one is Jarvis's 'and so' for 'and'.

58. *shameless-desperate* Hyphenated by Cap.

64. *heard* (F 3) F 'heare'.

68. *in thy feeling* by feeling it. S.D. (Camb. after Cap.) F 'Enter Lucius, Iachimo, and other Roman priſoners, Leonatus behind, and Imogen'.

69 ff. For the spirit of this dialogue, cf. Henry and Mountjoy in *H. V*, 4. 7. 67 ff. [J.D.W.].

70. *razed* F 'rac'd'; cf. *Per.* 1. 1. 17 n.

72–3. *That...captives* Cf. *Tit.* 1. 1. 126, 'T'appease their groaning shadows that are gone' [K., p. 1332].

74. *estate* i.e., of your souls [Dowd.].

75. *chance of war* Many quotations on its uncertainty in Tilley, C223.

86. *duteous, diligent* S. Walker 'duteous-diligent', plausibly.

87. *tender...occasions* 'nicely sensible of his [i.e. his master's] wants' (Schmidt); cf. *Wint.* 2. 3. 128, 133.

95. *I...why* i.e., I do not know any reason for saying it, but say it I do. Vaughan and Dowd. less convincingly join with 'art mine own', = 'in some mysterious way'. *wherefore* Rowe 'nor wherefore', but cf. *M.N.D.* 3. 2. 272 and *R.J.* 2. 2. 62 for the stress 'wheréfore', and, for the exact form of expression, Jonson, *Every Man Out of his Humour*, 2. 4. 144, 'And asking, why? wherefore?'.

96. *Ne'er...master* i.e., it is not his plea that has saved you.

103. *a thing* the ring on Jachimo's finger.

106–7. *Briefly...boys* Cf. Tilley, L526, *Lr.* 3. 6. 19–20, 'he's mad that trusts in...a boy's love'; and the situation in *Tw. N.* 3. 4 [Verity].

107. *truth* loyalty.

108. *perplexed* see G.; an emotionally stronger word than in mod. Eng.—cf. *Oth.* 5. 2. 348 and F. P. Wilson, *Proc. Brit. Acad.* XXVII (1941), 173.

118. *youth,* (F2)...*page;* (Theob.) F 'youth:...
Page'.

119. S.D. (Theob.).

121. *resembles—* (Steev., with semi-colon, after J.,
with full stop) ...*lad* (Han.) F 'refembles...Lad:'.
I do not find this poss. even as a late-Sh. ellipse for
'does not resemble more closely ⟨than he resembles⟩
that etc.' [Wyatt]. Perh., as S. Walker thought, a
whole line is lost, and the original ran 'Not more
resembles ⟨... | than he resembles⟩ that'.

124. *forbear;* (Steev.; F2 with comma) F 'for-
beare'.

126. *saw* (Rowe) F 'fee', perh. caught from l. 127,
but perh. the archaic pa. tense, which is found in Sh.
Qq in *M.N.D.* 4. 1. 171 (see note), and *L.L.L.* 4. 1.
68, 69, as well as in the F text of *H. VIII*, 1. 3. 12
(prob. Fletcher), and in other passages of Fletcher.
But it would be awkwardly ambiguous here.

127. S.D. (Rowe).

129. S.D. (Theob.).

130. S.D. (Rowe).

134. *On,* (F3) F 'One'; cf. 5. 4. 184 n.

136. S.D. (Cap.).

139. *Thou'lt...unspoken* 'you wish to torture me
for leaving [i.e. if I leave] unspoken' (Abbott, §356).

142. *Torments* (Ritson) F 'Which torments'. The
correction makes the line run much better, and a transcriber might easily fill in the grammatical ellipse,
perh. influenced, as Nos. suggests, by l. 140.

148. *and* and whom.

149. *remember—* (Pope) F 'remember.'.

150. *strength;* (Theob.; F4 with comma) F
'ftrength'.

151. *while Nature will* the rest of your natural life.

164. *shrine* O.E.D. 5¶b, noting that the usual
gloss is 'image', treats this, with *Lucr.* 194, *M.V.* 2. 7.

40—cf. also *Rom*. 1. 5. 94 with note—as 'merely some-what strained figurative applications of sense 5', i.e. 'temple', of which, however, no instance earlier than 1629 is cited. The choice of a specific literal sense is perh. arbitrary; in all these passages the underlying idea is that something divine is embodied in something physical.

165. *brief* This prob. refers both to the hastiness of Nature's workmanship [Warb.] and the 'fleeting existence' (Deighton) of her products. This contrasts both with the immortality of the gods and the relative permanence of their statues. *Nature;* (Rowe) F 'Nature.'.

166. *shop* see G.

167. *hook of wiving* For the metaphor cf. *Meas*. 2. 2. 180–1, *Ant*. 2. 5. 10–15 [Dowd.].

177. *cracked* F 'crak'd'; a variant form.

178. *unspeaking sots* i.e., as having been unable to find comparable terms to describe our loves.

186. *hers and mine* Parallels in Abbott, §238; cf. 5. 5. 230.

189–90. *carbuncle...wheel* Cf. *Ant*. 4. 8. 28–9, with note.

196–7. *Italian...Britain* On the popular theory 'that northern climates had a deleterious effect on the human mind and tended to make men dull-witted', cf. Z. S. Fink, *Modern Language Quarterly*, 11 (1941), 67 ff.

197. *operate* (F 2) F 'operare'.

198. *vilely* F 'vildely'; cf. 1. 1. 143 n.

200. *simular* O.E.D. glosses 'counterfeited'; perh. rather 'plausible'—so Furn., who notes that the tokens were genuine, and that Post. only 'drew wrong inferences from true premisses'. Sh. has the sb. in *Lr* 3. 2. 54, = 'one who simulates'.

205. *got it* (F 2) F 'got'.

209. S.D. (Camb. after Rowe).

212. *due* 'applicable' [Dowd.].

216–17. *amend...they* For 'the thought that a great crime or sin makes slighter sins look less hideous, or even beautiful by comparison', Dowd. cites *K.J.* 4. 3. 51–6; so *3 H. VI*, 5. 5. 53–5.

221. *she herself* virtue herself.

225. *Be 'villain'* (J.C.M.) F 'Be villany', which can be made to give the same meaning, 'let the term "villainy" hereafter signify some degree of criminality much less than it used to mean' (Vaughan). But the correction is slight, presupposing 'villanie'<'villaine', and also improves the metre.

228. *Shall's* Cf. 4. 2. 234 n.

229. *There...part* 'play your part there; *i.e.* by lying on the ground' (Deighton). S.D. (after Rowe).

230. *Mine and your* Cf. 5. 5. 186 n.

233. *comes* Rowe, many edd., 'come', but cf. Abbott, §335.

234–5. *If...joy* Cf., at the corresponding point in the action, *Per.* 5. 1. 196–8 [Ingleby].

238. *tune* see G. There is prob. a suggestion also that what she says is characteristic of her, but this is hardly strong enough to warrant Furn.'s gloss, 'character, temper, disposition'.

239. *Lady* As separate line Mal.; with l. 240 in F.

240. *stones of sulphur* thunderstones; cf. *Oth.* 3. 3. 331.

243. *still.* Pope, most edd., 'still?', unnecessarily.

245. *Pisanio* (F 2) F 'Pasanio'.

252. *vile* F 'vilde'; cf. 1. 1. 143 n.

254. *of more danger* i.e., to do greater harm.

255. *cease* see G. This sense, though recorded in O.E.D. to the end of the 17th c., was unfamiliar enough for F 2 to emend to 'seize', which is a more

obvious word with 'power' as object, and is sometimes spelt 'cease' at this period (O.E.D.). But as the main point is the cessation of activity, there is no doubt which word Sh. intended.

260. *is, sure,* (Theob.) F 'is ſure', which Nos. retains, unconvincingly interpreting 'sure' as an adj. on the analogy of 4. 2. 107, 'very Cloten', 5. 5. 358, 'true Guiderius'.

261. *from* (Rowe) F 'fro', accepted by O.E.D. here, but cf. *Rom.* 4. 1. 75, where F substitutes 'fro' for Q2's 'from'. The *Rom.* compositor was the inexperienced E (see C. Hinman, *Studies in Bibliography*, IX, 1957), not, as here, B.

262. *lock* (Dowd. conj.) F 'Rocke'. O.E.D.'s quotations, e.g., 'If the devil catches us at this lock, he will throw us flat' (Fuller, 1646), amply justify this emendation, and no defence of 'rock' is plausible. (For the specific phrase, *'upon a lock'*, see Dowd.'s Additional Note.) Misreading of 'l' as 'r' is not easy, as Sisson notes (*Readings*); but, whatever the cause, the corruption can be paralleled in both directions: *1 H. VI,* 4. 4. 16, 'Regions' (Rowe 'legions'); *Edw. III* (in *Sh. Apocrypha*), 4. 9. 40, 'loyall' (Cap. 'royal').

263. S.D. (Mal.).

265. *mak'st...dullard* treat me as a fool (by leaving me out); cf. *Lr.* 2. 1. 76.

266. S.D. (Rowe).

267. S.D. (Pope).

268. *motive* cause; not restricted, as in mod. Eng., to something that the agent has in mind.

270. *mother's* (F3) F 'Mothers'.

279. *feignèd...master's* Cf. 3. 5. 100 n.

284. *unchaste purpose* The audience will not ask how Pis. knows this; it is unnecessary to assume that he eavesdrops at 3. 5. 131–46.

290. *again* i.e. 'in contradiction to what you have affirmed' (Vaughan); cf. *M.N.D.* 1.1.181, 'that "fair" again unsay'.

292. *incivil* Not elsewhere in Sh.; Cap.'s 'uncivil' (anticipated by D'Urfey) may be right.

297. *sorrow* F2 'fory', which most edd. accept, perh. rightly. But there is some evidence for the existence of 'I am sorrow' on the analogy of 'I am woe' (O.E.D. 'woe', C1; Abbott, §230). It occurs in Webster, *White Devil* (Q1), 5.1.44, and in *Lr.* (Q1), 4.6.262 (noted by Dowd.), though caution is suggested by the fact that F there, perh. authoritatively, substitutes 'forry': certainly the addition of 'only' there makes 'sorrow' harsher, but the Webster passage also has an adverb, 'inly'.

299–300. *That...lord* Divided by Pope; one line in F.

305. *Had...for* ever deserved by honourable wounds; cf. *Troil.* G. 'scar'. S.D. (Theob.).

306. *soldier:* (F, Nos.) Most edd. follow F4 in reducing the colon to a comma, and this, with the comma (not in F) after 'Why', implies the construction 'Why...wilt thou'. F is preferable, with 'Why' = 'What's this?'.

310. *thou* He continues to address Belarius.

311. *But...prove* if I do not prove. Some edd. obscure the construction by strengthening F's comma at the end of l. 310 to a semi-colon; better to drop it, as I follow Clarke in doing. *on's* (F2) F 'one's'; cf. 5.4.184 n.

313. *For...part* Goes closely with 'dangerous' [Delius]; cf. Abbott, §419a.

315. *then; by leave,* (J.C.M. < Cap. 'then.—By leave;') F 'then, by leaue'. Pope and most edd. give the stronger stop after 'leave', but it is more natural to take 'Have...then' by itself = 'here goes', with 'by

leave' introductory to what follows. Cap. (followed by Sisson) transferred 'by leave' to l. 316, perh. rightly. (Cap. filled out l. 315, as he had left it, by reading 'Ay, and our good is his'.)

317–18. *What...traitor* Divided by Cap.; one line in F.

319. *Assumed this age* 'become so aged in appearance' (Deighton); 'assumed' does not imply that he is not really old, but that 'to Cym. he must appear as quite another person' (Schmidt).

323. *confiscate* This stress (on the second syllable) was normal up to mid-19th cent. (see O.E.D.), though Sh. also has 'cónfiscate'. *all*, (F) Dowd., with some plausibility, 'all'; cf. *R. III*, 1. 1. 157, 'all so much'.

334–6. *Your...did* 'My whole offence..., the punishment which that (fancied) offence incurred, and all the treason of which I was (i.e. seemed) guilty, had their birth in your caprice; beyond suffering in consequence of that caprice, I did no harm' (Deighton).

334. *mere* (Tyrwhitt) F 'neere'. The correction (see G.) is prob. if not certain. Nos. prints the unplausible compound 'ne'er-offence'='what was never an offence', comparing other adjectival uses of adverbs and, for the sense, 3. 3. 65, 'My fault being nothing'.

335. *treason;* (Pope, with colon) F 'Treafon'.

337. *such and so* i.e., princes and gentle (by chiasmus) [Delius].

339. *as* Placed here by J.; at beginning of l. 340 in F.

344. *Beaten* the fact that I was beaten; cf. Abbott, §413, and 1. 6. 96, 3. 5. 76.

345–7. *Their...them* 'the more keenly you felt the loss...the better was my purpose in stealing them answered' (Deighton).

351. *like* (F2) F 'liks'.

352. *inlay...stars.* Cf. *Rom.* 3. 2. 22–3, 'Take him

and cut him out in little stars, | And he will make the
face of heaven so fine' [Steev.].

352–4. *Thou . . . tell'st* 'thy tears give testimony to the
sincerity of thy relation, and I have the less reason to be
incredulous, because the actions which you have done
within my knowledge are more incredible than the
story which you relate' (J.).

359–60. *Arviragus, . . . son;* (Rowe) F 'Aruiragus.
. . . Son,'.

365. *of wonder* wonderful; cf. *Tp.* 1. 2. 10, 'god of
power'.

367. *end . . . donation,* (Han.) F 'end, . . . donation'.

368. *what am I?* (Han.) F 'what am I.'. Dyce's
'what, am I' is also possible.

371. *orbs* see G., and cf. *Ant.* 3. 13. 146, *K.J.*
5. 7. 74, *M.N.D.* 2. 1. 153.

378. *ye* (Rowe) F 'we', which might be defended
(so, tentatively, Mal.) as meaning 'when we were
brothers and sister', were it not that the specific
correctness of her word 'brothers' is the point.

382. *fierce* O.E.D. gives no fully appropriate sense;
perh. the dialect meaning, 5 b, 'brisk, lively', is the
closest. Nos.'s 'drastic' fits the context, and is perh.
supported by three passages in Jonson, *Poetaster*, 5. 3.
129 (cited by O.E.D. 5, 'ardent'); *Sejanus*, 5. 1. 542;
Alchemist, 4. 1. 39. Herford and Simpson gloss 'rash',
but the word seems to have a more general intensifying
force.

383–4. *which . . . in* which deserve to be elaborately discriminated.

386. *brothers* (Rowe) F 'Brother'.

387. *whither? These* (Theob.) F 'whether thefe?'.

388. *your three motives* the motives of the three of
you; cf. *All's,* 1. 3. 160, 'both our mothers' [Delius],
Tim. 4. 2. 28 [Clarke], Franz, §324.

392. *inter'gatories* (Tyrwhitt, comparing *M.V.* 5.

1. 299, where Q sp. 'intergotories') F 'Interrogatories'.

395. *me, her master,* (Rowe) F 'Mé: her Maſter'.

397. *severally in all* 'in all, and individually in
each' (Dowd.).

399. S.D. (Rowe).

403-4. *My...service* Divided by Pope; one line
in F.

405. *forlorn* Prob. just 'lost'; the association
suggested by On. (and already mentioned as poss. by
Dowd.) with 'forlorn hope' is questionable; Furn.'s
'poor in appearance' is too contextual. *so* (F2) F 'no'.

412. S.D. (Steev. after Han.).

421. *freeness* see G. Not elsewhere in Sh., but this
use of 'free' is common, notably in *Timon* (cf. Introd.
in this ed., pp. xxxv–xxxvii).

431. *from sense* unintelligible. Whether the primary
meaning of 'sense' here is 'meaning' (which the
'containing' lacks) or 'intelligence' (which it eludes;
cf. 5. 4. 148), I am not sure.

435. S.D. (Cap.) F 'Reades', centred above, and
with no sp.-pref.

444. *Leo-natus* (Cap.) F '*Leonatus*'.

445. S.D. (Theob.).

446. *mollis aer* The connection of 'mulier' with
'mollis' (not, as some edd. say, also that with 'aer'),
goes back to Varro, according to Lactantius (Aldis
Wright, *N. & Q.*, 7th ser. II (1886), 85), cf. Isidore,
Etymologiae, XI, ii. 18, and is still regarded as probable
(Walde-Hofmann, *Lateinisches Etymologisches Wörter-
buch*, vol. ii, 3rd ed., 1954). The earliest Eng. citation
for the whole etymology, noted by F. C. B. Terry,
N. & Q., 7th ser. IV (1887), 105, is in Caxton's *Game of
the Chess*, III, v (ed. Axon (1883), p. 123), who
follows the French of de Vignay (the etymology is not
in the Latin original). Nearer Sh.'s time, Aldis Wright

found it in H. Stephen [i.e. Henri Estienne], *A World
of Wonders* (1607).

447. S.D. (Sisson; l. 448 Cap.).

448. If the Soothsayer has turned to Post., the
audience will not be worried by the oddity of 'who'
not referring to 'wife'. But Cap.'s 'thy' for 'this'
certainly eases the passage.

463. *Whom* As if a trans. verb were to follow.
There is no need, with Keightley, to read 'hand on'
for 'hand'; the omission of such prepositions is common, as Mal. noted, giving examples. *hers* i.e., Cloten.

468. *this yet* (F 3) F (+K., Al.) 'yet this', which
it would be hard to parallel. For transpositions by
Compositor B in *1 H. IV*, see Alice Walker, *Studies in
Bibliography*, vi (1953 for 1954), 53, though none
listed there result in such an odd word-order as F
offers here. The surviving uncorrected frag. of *Ant.* has
'the of full Tide' at 3. 2. 49 (E. E. Willoughby, *The
Printing of the First Folio* (1932), p. 63). Though this
was caught, a comparable error may well have escaped
here.

484. S.D. F 'Exeunt'.

GLOSSARY

Note. Where a pun or quibble is intended, the meanings are distinguished as (*a*) and (*b*). Notes such as 'here only', 'first here', refer to what O.E.D. records.

ABATE, depreciate, lower the price of; 1. 4. 66

ABATEMENT (see note); 5.4.21

ABIDE, (i) endure; 1. 1. 89; (ii) wait for; 2. 4. 4; (iii) face; 3. 4. 184

ABODE, temporary remaining; 1. 6. 52

ABROAD, (i) outside; 1. 2. 3; (ii) about; 4. 2. 101

ABSOLUTE, certain, positive; 4. 2. 106

ABUSE, (i) deceive; 1. 4. 113; 1. 6. 130; 3. 4. 121; 4. 2. 351 (see note); (ii) misuse; 3. 4. 103; (iii) insult; 2. 3. 149

ACCESSIBLE, practicable, affording access; 3. 2. 82

ACCIDENT, occurrence; 4. 2. 192; 5. 4. 99

ACCOMMODATED, favoured; 5. 3. 32

ACE, (*a*) throw of one at dice, (*b*) quibble on 'ass'; cf. *M.N.D.* 5. 1. 307–10; 2. 3. 2

ACQUITTANCE, written discharge of an account (fig.); 5. 4. 170

ACT, action; 1. 5. 22

ACTION, suit at law; 2. 3. 151

ADJOURN, postpone; 5. 4. 78

ADMIRATION, (i) wonder; 1. 6. 37; (ii) mod. sense, 'wonder mingled with reverence'; 1. 4. 5; 4. 2. 232

ADVANTAGE (see note); 4. 1. 11

ADVENTURE (vb.), venture; 1. 6. 171; 3. 4. 154

ADVICE, reflection; 1. 1. 156

AFFECT, (*a*) aspire to, (*b*) love; 5. 5. 38

AFFIANCE, confidence (cf. *H.V*, 2. 2. 127); 1. 6. 162

AFFIRMATION, confirmation (here only Sh.); 1. 4. 57

AFFRONT (sb.), attack; 5. 3. 87

AFFRONT (vb.), face; 4. 3. 29

AFRIC, Africa; 1. 1. 167

AFTER (prep.), according to, in accordance with; 1. 1. 71, 152; 2. 3. 4; 4. 2. 119, 334

AFTER-EYE, follow with one's eye (here only); 1. 3. 16

AGAIN (see note); 5. 5. 290

AJAX, a Greek leader before Troy, here as the type of a warrior; 4. 2. 252

ALLAYMENT, means of abatement (here and *Troil.* 4. 4. 8 only); 1. 5. 22

ALLOW, approve; 3. 3. 17

AMAZE, bewilder; 4. 3. 28

AMEND, (i) correct; 2. 3. 31; (ii) cure; 4. 2. 12; (iii) make (appear) better (by comparison); 5. 5. 216

ANCHOR, fix one's thoughts; 5. 5. 393

ANDIRON, fire-dog; 2. 4. 88

ANNOY, harm; 4. 3. 34

ANON, presently; 3. 5. 132; 5. 3. 40

ANSWER (sb.), retaliation (cf. On.); 4. 2. 161; 5. 3. 79

ANSWER (vb.), (i) render account, pay for (abs. and trans.); 1. 4. 156, 162; 3. 5. 42; (ii) (trans. or with 'to'), correspond (to); 3. 4. 171; 4. 2. 192; 5. 5. 449; (iii) act in corresponding manner to; 5. 3. 91

APE, (i) imitator; 2. 2. 31; (ii) (see note); 4. 2. 194

APPARENT, evident; 2. 4. 56

APPEAR, be manifest; 1. 4. 160

APPREHEND, understand, take (in a certain way); 3. 3. 17

APPROBATION, proof; 1. 4. 123

APPROVE, prove; 4. 2. 382; 5. 5. 245

APPROVER, one who has put someone to the test; 2. 4. 25

ARABIAN BIRD, the phoenix, myth. bird of whom only one at a time existed, in Arabia; here, fig. a unique person; 1. 6. 17

ARCH, 'vaulted arch', the sky; 1. 6. 32

ARM, take up, carry, in the arms (here only); 4. 2. 402

ARREARAGES, arrears; 2. 4. 13

ARTICLES, clauses of a contract; 1. 4. 156

As, (i) that; 1. 1. 20; (ii) as if; 4. 2. 50, 210; 5. 2. 16; 5. 5. 180, 423; (iii) 'as being', because he is; 4. 2. 250

ASSUME (see note); 5. 5. 319

ASSURED, (a) certain; (b) betrothed; 1. 6. 72

ASTRONOMER, astrologer; 3. 2. 27

ATONE, reconcile; 1. 4. 37

ATTEMPTABLE, open to attempts (on her honour) (here only); 1. 4. 59

ATTEND, (i) follow; 2. 3. 62; (ii) wait on, or at, be in attendance on; 1. 2. 37; 1. 3. 40; 2. 3. 37; 3. 6. 83; (iii) listen to; 1. 6. 141; (iv) guard; 1. 6. 196; (v) (abs.) dance attendance, be present; 3. 3. 22, 77; (vi) wait for; 4. 2. 334; 5. 4. 38

AUDIT, statement of accounts; 5. 4. 27

AVER, assert the existence of; 5. 5. 203

AVOID, depart; 1. 1. 125

AZURED, sky-blue; 4. 2. 222

AZURE-LACED, streaked with blue veins; 2. 2. 22

BACK, mount on the back of; 5. 5. 427

BACKSIDE (see note); 1. 2. 11

BALLASTING, freight (fig.); 3. 6. 77

BARE (adj.), beggarly; 3. 5. 119

BARE (vb.), open; 2. 2. 49

BASE, boys' game, in which a player who leaves his 'base' is chased, and, if caught, made prisoner; 'prisoner's base'; 5. 3. 20

BASILISK, fabulous serpent, said to kill by breath or look, also called cockatrice; 2. 4. 107

BATE, aphetic form of 'abate'; qualify (a too extreme statement); 3. 2. 54

BATTERY, assault (fig.); 1. 4. 21

BAUBLE, (i) mere toy; 3. 1. 27; (ii) worthless thing; 3. 2. 20; 3. 3. 23

BAY, pursue barking; 5. 5. 223

BEAR, (i) 'bear down' (see note); 2. 1. 51; (ii) 'bear in hand', pretend; 5. 5. 43

BEASTLY, like animals; 5. 3. 27

BECOME, grace; 2. 2. 15; 5. 5. 406

BEGGARY, contemptible meanness; 1. 6. 114

BEHALF, 'i'...behalf', for the benefit of, i.e. (here) as a substitute for; 3. 2. 73

BEING, place of abode; 1.5.54

BELIE, fill with lies (here only); 3. 4. 36

BENT, inclination; 1. 1. 13

BESEEMING, guise (here only); 5. 5. 409

BESIDES, beyond; 2. 4. 149

BETIDE, happen; 4. 3. 40

BIDE, abide; 3. 4. 129, 136

BIG OF, pregnant with (here only with 'of'); 1. 1. 39

BLAZON, proclaim; 4. 2. 170

BLOOD, (i) blood considered as seat of emotion; 4. 2. 174; 4. 4. 53; hence (ii) mood, disposition; 1. 1. 1; (iii) (a) physical blood, (b) (ii); 1. 1. 128; (iv) offspring; 5. 5. 331

BOILED STUFF, fig., women with venereal disease (allusion to sweating-tub treatment); 1. 6. 124

BOLD, (i) confident; 2. 4. 2; (ii) 'make bold', presume to think; 5. 5. 89

BOLT, (i) arrow (fig.); 4. 2. 300; (ii) fetter (fig.); 5. 4. 10, 197

BOND, (i) fetter; 1. 1. 117 (fig.); 5. 5. 402; (ii) sealed deed or contract; 3. 2. 37; 5. 5. 207 (fig.); (iii) obligation; 5. 1. 7; (iv) (see note); 5. 4. 28

BONDAGE, binding force; 2. 4. 111

BORE, small hole, 'bores of hearing'=ears; 3. 2. 57

BOTTOM, penetrate to the utmost depth; 3. 4. 116

BOUND, (i) under obligation; 1. 4. 25; 1. 5. 73; 2. 3. 44; 3. 5. 49; (ii) (a) (i), (b) linked fast, bound by affection; 4. 2. 46; (iii) 'dare be bound'=feel certain; 4. 3. 18

Bow, make stoop; 3. 3. 3.

BRAIN, think (nonce-use in antithesis with 'tongue'); 5. 4. 146

BRAND, torch; 2. 4. 91

BRAVELY, finely; 2. 2. 15; 2. 4. 73

BRAVERY, defiant posture; 3. 1. 18

BRAWN, muscle of arm or leg; 4. 2. 311

BREATHING, blowing (of the wind); 1. 3. 36

BREED, strain; 4. 2. 25

BREEDING, (i) education; 4. 4. 26; (ii) (see note); 5. 3. 17

BRIEFLY, quickly; 5. 5. 106

BROGUE, rough, heavy shoe of untanned hide, worn in wild parts of Ireland and the Scottish highlands; 4. 2. 214

BROKEN, bankrupt; 5. 4. 19

BUG, object of terror; 5. 3. 51

BY-DEPENDENCES, additional or secondary circumstances; 5 5. 390

By-peeping, peeping sidelong (here only); 1. 1. 107

Calf's-gut, fiddlestring; 2. 3. 30

Cambria, Wales; 3. 2. 43; 5. 5. 17

Can, (i) know; 4. 2. 394; (ii) may (be); 4. 2. 404

Cap, doffing of cap; 3. 3. 25

Capitol, temple on the Capitoline hill; 1. 6. 105

Capon, (a) castrated cock, (b) dull, stupid fellow; 2. 1. 21

Carbuncle, a red precious stone; 5. 5. 189

Carl, churl; 5. 2. 4

Case, encase (in mask); 5. 3. 22

Cassibelan, uncle of Cymbeline (see Boswell-Stone, p. 7, n. 1), the Lat. Cassivelaunus, leader of resistance in S.E. Britain to Julius Caesar's second invasion, 54 b.c.; 3. 1. 30, 40

Casual, subject to accident; 1. 4. 90

Cave, live in a cave (first here; one other ex., 19th c.); 4. 2. 138

Cease, bring to a stop, arrest; 5. 5. 255

Century, series of one hundred; 4. 2. 393

Cere up, wrap in a cere-cloth (see note); 1. 1. 116

Chaliced, cup-shaped; 2. 3. 22

Chance, (i) opportunity (of good fortune); 1. 5. 68; 5. 4. 132; (ii) occurrence; 4. 3. 35; 5. 3. 51

Change, change colour; 1. 6. 11

Characters, (i) handwriting; 3. 2. 28; (ii) letters of the alphabet; 4. 2. 49

Charge, lie heavy on; 3. 4. 42

Charm, (i) compel as by a magic spell; 1. 6. 116; (ii) lay a magic spell on; 4. 2. 277; (iii) protect as by a magic spell; 5. 3. 68

Charming, having the power of a magic charm; 1. 3. 35; 5. 3. 32

Check (sb.), rebuke; 3. 3. 22

Cheer, (i) frame of mind, 'what cheer'=how goes it with you?; 3. 4. 39; (ii) hospitable entertainment, so, here, food; 3. 6. 66

Cherubin, cherub (Sh.'s usual form); 2. 4. 88

Chimney, fireplace; 2. 4. 80

Chimney-piece, work of art (here prob. tapestry) over fireplace (here first); 2. 4. 81

Cinque-spotted, having five spots (here only, exc. Coleridge, prob. imitating); 2. 2. 38

Circumstances, details; 2. 4. 61

Circumstantial, detailed; 5. 5. 383

Citizen, city-bred, hence, effeminate (here only); 4. 2. 8

Civil, civilized; 3. 6. 23

Clean, entirely; 3. 6. 20

Clip, (i) surround; 2. 3. 134; (ii) (a) (i), (b) embrace; 5. 5. 450

Cloak-bag, portmanteau; 3. 4. 170

Close (adj.), (i) secret; 1. 6. 138; (ii) shut up; 3. 5. 46; (iii) secretive; 3. 5. 86

CLOSET, private room; 1. 5. 84

CLOTH, livery distinctive of retainer; 2. 3. 123

CLOTPOLL, thick wooden skull (like 'clodpole', not pre-Sh.); 4. 2. 184

CLOUTED, studded with nails; 4. 2. 214

CLOY, (i) clog; 4. 4. 19; (ii) claw (here only, but also variant sp. of 'cly'=seize, steal); 5. 4. 118

COGNIZANCE, token; 2. 4. 127

COINER, minter of false money, so, fig., adulterer; 2. 5. 5

COLD, (i) cool, calm; 2. 3. 2; (ii) dispirited, gloomy; 2. 3. 3; (iii) spiritless; 3. 1. 74; (iv) chaste; 5. 5. 181; (v) (see note); 5. 4. 28

COLLECTION (OF), inference (from); 5. 5. 432

COLOUR, (i) banner (fig.); 1. 4. 19; (ii) arguable ground; 3. 1. 49

COLT, have sexual intercourse with (cf. 2. 5. 17); 2. 4. 133

COME, (i) 'come off', come away; 1. 4. 150; (ii) 'come from horse', dismount; 3. 4. 1

COMFORT, joy; 5. 5. 403

COMMAND (sb.), habit of commanding; 3. 4. 155

COMMAND (vb.), demand with authority; 1. 5. 8

COMMEND, (i) recommend; 1. 4. 127; (ii) commit, entrust; 2. 2. 8; 3. 7. 9

COMMENDATION, recommendation; 1. 4. 153

COMMISSION, mandate; 3. 7. 10, 14

COMMON MEN, commoners; 3. 7, 2

COMMON-KISSING, kissing all alike (here only); 3. 4. 164

COMPANION (contempt.), fellow; 2. 1. 25

COMPANY (sb.), companion; 4. 2. 69

COMPANY (vb.), accompany; 5. 5. 408

COMPARATIVE (see note); 2. 3. 129

COMPARE, abs., be selected for comparison; 1. 1. 22

COMPLAINING, lamentation; 4. 2. 375

CONCEIVING, conception; 2. 3. 98

CONCLUSION, experiment; 1. 5. 18

CONDITION, character; 5. 5. 165

CONDUCT, escort; 3. 5. 8; 4. 2. 340

CONFECTION, compounded preparation of drugs; 1. 5. 15

CONFINE, state in set terms; 5. 4. 110

CONFINER, inhabitant (second of two exx.); 4. 2. 337

CONFOUND, destroy; 1. 4. 49

CONFUSION, (i) discomfiture; 3. 1. 64; 4. 2. 92; (ii) disorder; 5. 3. 41

CONSCIENCE, inward knowledge, internal conviction; 1. 6. 115; 2. 2. 36; 3. 4. 46

CONSEQUENCE (see note); 2. 3. 121

CONSIDER, (i) remunerate; 2. 3. 29; (ii) 'consider of', think out, plan; 3. 4. 112

CONSIGN (TO), submit to the same terms (with); 4. 2. 275

CONSPIRED, in conspiracy; 4. 2. 315

CONSTRAIN, impose by compulsion; 5. 4. 15

CONSTRUCTION, interpretation; 5. 5. 433, 443

CONSUMMATION, death, end; 4. 2. 280

CONTAINING, contents; 5. 5. 430

CONTENT (refl.), set one's mind at rest; 1. 5. 26

CONVERSATION, intercourse; 1. 4. 102

CONVEY, euphem. for 'steal'; 1. 1. 63

CONVINCE, overcome; 1. 4. 94

CORDIAL (sb.), restorative medicine; 5. 5. 247

CORDIAL (adj.); restorative; 1. 5. 64; 4. 2. 327

CORNER, direction, quarter from which the wind blows; 2. 4. 28; 3. 4. 37

COUNSEL, (i) legal adviser; 1. 4. 164; (ii) secret thoughts, secrets; 3. 2. 36

COUNSELLOR, confidant; 3. 2. 57

COUNT (vb.), account; 3. 2. 15

COUNTER, round piece of metal used in calculations; 5. 4. 169

COUNTERCHANGE, exchange, reciprocation; 5. 5. 396

COUNTRY, of one's own country; 1. 4. 55; 4. 4. 51

COURT, assembly of the court; 3. 5. 50

COURTESY, courtly manners; 4. 4. 28

COURTLY, befitting the court; 3. 5. 72

COVENANT, (i) article, clause of a contract; 1. 4. 142; (ii) written contract or agreement; 1. 4. 163; 2. 4. 50

CRACK, utter boastingly; 5. 5. 177

CRACKED, broken down; 4. 4. 50

CRARE, small trading vessel; 4. 2. 205

CRAVEN, make cowardly; 3. 4. 78

CREDIT, trust, belief; 1. 6. 156, 158

CREEK, winding part of rivulet; 4. 2. 151

CREEP (see note); 1. 4. 23

CRESCENT, growing; 1. 4. 2

CROSS, thwart; 3. 5. 163

CUNNING, skill; 5. 5. 205

CURIOUS, (i) anxious; 1. 6. 190; (ii) exquisitely wrought; 5. 5. 361

CURTAIL, diminish; 2. 1. 11

CUTTER, sculptor; 2. 4. 83

CYDNUS, river in Cilicia, flowing into the Mediterranean, upon which Antony first saw Cleopatra (*Ant.* 2. 2. 186–7); 2. 4. 71

CYMBELINE, name only derived from the historical Cunobellinus, king of most of S.E. Britain from *post* 12 B.C. to *ante* A.D. 43, Claudius's first invasion of Britain, and capture of Colchester (Camulodunum); relations with Rome friendly; *passim*

CYTHEREA, Venus, name from Cythera in Cyprus, one of the chief places of her worship (again *Shr.* Ind. 2. 51; *Wint.* 4. 4. 122); 2. 2. 14

DALMATIANS, the people inhabiting the part of Jugo-Slavia along the coast; 3. 7. 3.

DANGER, harm; 5. 5. 254

DARK, concealed; 3. 4. 145

DAY, victory; 5. 5. 75

DEAR, grievous; 5. 5. 345

DEARLY, (i) with love; 1. 6. 13; (ii) finely; 2. 2. 18

DEBITOR-AND-CREDITOR, account book; 5. 4. 167–8

DECAY, destroy; 1. 5. 56

DEEM, judge; 5. 4. 57

DEEP, serious, weighty; 2. 3. 91

DEFENCE, something that defends; 3. 4. 79

DEFINITE, decided; 1. 6. 42

DELICATE, (i) delightful; 2. 4. 136; (ii) ingenious; 5. 5. 47

DELIGHTED, delightful; 5. 4. 102

DELIVERANCE, delivery, bringing forth of a child; 5. 5. 370

DEMESNE, region; 3. 3. 70

DENIAL, refusal; 2. 3. 48

DENY, refuse; 5. 5. 90

DEPEND, (i) lean; 2. 4. 91; (ii) remain in suspense; 4. 3. 23

DEPENDENCY, that which is dependent (abstr. for concr.) (see also note); 2. 3. 118

DEROGATE, act in a way derogatory to one's rank (with quibble, see note); 2. 1. 42, 45

DEROGATION, impairing of one's dignity; 2. 1. 41

DESERT, action meriting reward; 1. 5. 73

DESERVE, win; 3. 3. 54

DESIRE, request; 1. 6. 52; 3. 4. 174

DESPITE, scorn; 1. 6. 134

DEVICE, design; 1. 6. 188

DIAN(A), Diana, goddess of the moon, on earth a virgin huntress, type of chastity; 1. 6. 132; 2. 3. 69; etc.; so, of a woman as the perfect model of chastity; 2. 5. 7

DIET, feed (fig.); 3. 4. 181

DIETER, regulator of diet; 4. 2. 51

DIFFERING (see note); 3. 6. 85

DIRECTLY, (i) simply; 1. 6. 21; (ii) unambiguously; 1. 4. 157; (iii) straightforwardly; 3. 5. 113

DISCOVER, disclose; 1. 6. 97; 3. 5. 96; 5. 5. 277

DISEDGE (intrans.), lose the edge of appetite (first here); 3. 4. 94

DISMISSION, rejection ('dismissal' is 19th c.); 2. 3. 52

DISPATCH, (i) carry out promptly; 1. 3. 39; (abs.) 1. 5. 3; (ii) kill (with an implication of speed); 3. 4. 96

DISTEMPER, ailment; 3. 4. 192

DISTIL, extract the essence (here, scent-giving) of; 1. 5. 13

DISTINCTION, discrimination; 5. 5. 384

DIVORCE, separation; 1. 4. 19

DOOM, judge; 5. 5. 420

DOUBLE, twice as great; 1. 6. 120

DOUBLET, close-fitting upper garment of males (14th–18th c.); 3. 4. 170

DOUBT, fear; 1. 6. 94

DRAM, $\frac{1}{16}$ oz. avoird., $\frac{1}{8}$ fluid oz.; hence, very small quantity; 1. 4. 134; 3. 4. 191; (fig.) 3. 5. 90

DRAW, (i) collect together (to make an army; see 'head'); 3. 5. 25; (ii) 'draw on',

DRAW (*cont.*)
bring about; 4. 4. 14; (iii) 'draw of', empty of; 5. 4. 165

DROP, spot of colour; 2. 2. 38

DRUG-DAMNED, damnable for its use of poison (here only); 3. 4. 15

DUCAT, silver coin of Italy, worth about 3s. 6d.; 1. 4. 126, 149

DULL, (i) heavy (of sleep); 2. 2. 31; (ii) without lustre; 2. 4. 41; (iii) not sharp-witted; 5. 5. 197

DUTY, (i) (see note); 1. 1. 87; (ii) reverential act of service; 2. 3. 50; 3. 5. 32, 48

EASY, compliant; 2. 4. 47

EGLANTINE, sweet-briar; 4. 2. 223

ELDER, (i) older; 3. 6. 44; (ii) (see note); 5. 1. 14

ELECT, select; 3. 4. 110

ELECTION, choice; 1. 2. 25; 1. 6. 174

ELYSIUM, place of abode after death of those favoured by the gods; 5. 4. 97

EMBRACE, (i) accept; 1. 4. 155; (ii) welcome; 3. 4. 177

EMPERY, empire; 1. 6. 119

ENCHAFE, rouse to anger; 4. 2. 174

ENCOUNTER, (i) meet; 1. 3. 32; (ii) attack (fig.); 1. 6. 111

END, purpose; 3. 5. 64; 5. 5. 57, 347

ENFORCE, (i) violate; 4. 1. 16; (ii) extort by force; 4. 3. 11; 5. 5. 283

ENJOY, possess, use, with delight; here of, or includ-ing, sexual intercourse; 1. 4. 148; 1. 6. 90; 2. 1. 62; 2. 4. 126

ENLARGEMENT, freedom of action; 2. 3. 120

ENTERTAIN, (i) receive as guest; 1. 4. 26; (ii) employ as servant; 4. 2. 396

ENTERTAINMENT, reception; 1. 4. 153-4

ESTATE, (i) wealth; 1. 4. 108, 122; (ii) status, (high) rank; 5. 5. 22; (iii) state, condi-tion; 5. 5. 74

ESTEEM (sb.), worth; 5. 5. 253

ESTEEM (vb.), value; 1. 4. 77

EVEN (adv.), 'go even', agree; 1. 4. 42; (of time) just; 3. 6. 16

EVEN (vb.), keep pace with; 3. 4. 182

EVENT, outcome; 3. 5. 14

EVIDENT, indubitable, conclu-sive; 2. 4. 120

EVIL-EYED, malicious in dis-position; 1. 1. 72

EXACTLY, accurately, with complete truth to reality; 2. 4. 75

EXHIBITION, allowance for sup-port; 1. 6. 121

EXORCISER, one who can raise spirits (so always in Sh.); 4. 2. 276

EXTEND, (i) (see note); 1. 1. 25; (ii) magnify in repre-sentation; 1. 4. 20

EXTREMITY, extreme severity; 3. 4. 17

EYESTRING, muscles, nerves or tendons of the eye, sup-posed to break or crack at death or loss of sight; 1. 3. 17

FACT, (evil) deed; 3. 2. 17

FACTOR, agent; 1. 5. 28; 1. 6. 187

FAIL, fault; 3. 4. 64

FAITH, (i) ellipt. for 'in faith', truly; 1. 2. 7; 2. 3. 95; 4. 2. 294; ('good faith') 4. 2. 302; (ii) fidelity; 3. 4. 26

FALL, 'fall off', revolt; 3. 7. 6

FALSE (refl.), become corrupt; 2. 3. 69

FAN, winnow; so, fig., test; 1. 6. 176

FANE, temple; 4. 2. 242

FANGLED, given to finery; 5. 4. 134

FATHER, (i) beget; 4. 2. 26; (ii) act like a father to; 4. 2. 397

FAVOUR, (i) beauty; 1. 6. 41; (ii) countenance; 3. 4. 49; 4. 2. 104; 5. 5. 93

FEAR, fear for; 1. 4. 97

FEAT (adj.), dexterous; 5. 5. 88

FEAT (vb.) (see note); 1. 1. 49

FEATURE, shapeliness; 5. 5. 163

FEDARY, accomplice (Sh. only); 3. 2. 21

FETCH, (i) perform (a movement); 1. 1. 81; (ii) 'fetch in', close in on, surround; 4. 2. 141

FIERCE, ?drastic (see note); 5. 5. 382

FIGURE, (i) human form depicted; 2. 2. 26; (ii) human form stamped on coin; 5. 4. 25; (iii) acting of a part; 3. 3. 96

FIND, experience; 4. 4. 26

FINE, smartly dressed; 3. 3. 25

FINGER, play on a stringed instrument (with indelicate suggestion); 2. 3. 14

FINISH, die; 5. 5. 36, 412

FIT (adj.), (i) prepared; 3. 4. 169; (ii) suitable; 4. 1. 4

FIT (adv.), suitably; 4. 1. 2

FIT (vb.), (i) adapt, make suitable for a purpose; 3. 4. 193; 5. 5. 55; (ii) furnish; 5. 5. 21

FITMENT, something suitable (cf. *Per.* 4. 6. 6; no other exx. in comparable sense); 5. 5. 409

FITNESS, inclination (here sexual); 4. 1. 6

FLAT, level place; 3. 3. 11

FLATTERING, fawning; 1. 5. 27

FLY OUT, break forth; 3. 3. 90; 4. 4. 54

FOIL, foul, pollute; 2. 3. 121

FOOLERY, folly (here only of thought or speech rather than action); 3. 2. 73

FOOT, (i) kick; 3. 5. 144; (ii) seize (of a bird); 5. 4. 116

FOR (conj.), because; 3. 4. 52; 3. 5. 71; 4. 1. 5; 4. 2. 129

FOR (prep.), (i) for lack of; 3. 6. 17; (ii) as; 4. 4. 5, 6

FOR ALL, although; 5. 4. 200–1

FORBEAR, (i) withdraw; 1. 1. 68; (ii) let alone; 4. 2. 278

FORBEARANCE, abstention; 2. 3. 98; 2. 5. 10

'FORE, before; 3. 4. 173

FORE-END, early part (first here); 3. 3. 73

FORESAY, decree beforehand; 4. 2. 146

FORESPENT, previously bestowed; 2. 3. 59

FORESTALL, deprive by previous action; 3. 5. 70

FORETHINK, think out beforehand; 3. 4. 169

FORFEIT, thing forfeited for breach of contract; 5. 5. 208

FORFEITER, person penalised for breach of bond; 3. 2. 38

FORFEND, forbid; 5. 5. 287

FORWARDNESS, promptness; 4. 2. 342

FOUL, ugly; 1. 6. 37

FOUNDATION, (a) secure basis, (b) endowed establishment for charitable purposes; 3. 6. 7

FRAGMENT, scrap (of food); 5. 3. 44

FRAME, discipline; 2. 3. 46; 4. 2. 177

FRANCHISE, free exercise; 3. 1. 55

FRANKLIN, freeholder; 3. 2. 77

FRAUGHT (vb.), burden (fig.); 1. 1. 126

FREE (adj.), (i) unrestrained; 1. 6. 67; (ii) (a) leisure, (b) unfettered; 1. 6. 71

FREE (vb.), get rid of; 3. 6. 79

FREELY, without reserve, frankly; 5. 5. 119, 131

FREENESS, generosity; 5. 5. 421

FRETTED, elaborately carved; 2. 4. 88

FRIEND (sb.) (see note); 1. 4. 67

FRIEND (vb.), befriend; 2. 3. 47

FRIENDLY (adv.), as from a friend; 3. 5. 13

FROM, at variance with; 5. 5. 431

FROWN, 'in frown', defiantly; 5. 3. 28

FRUITFUL, promising good results; 5. 4. 55

FULL-HEARTED, full of courage and confidence; 5. 3. 7

FUME, fantasy; 4. 2. 301

FURNACE (vb.), exhale like blasts from a furnace; 1. 6. 65

FURNISH, equip; 1. 6. 16

GAIN, restore; 4. 2. 167

GALLIA, France; 1. 6. 200; 2. 4. 18, etc.

GALLIAN, French; 1. 6. 65

GECK, fool; 5. 4. 67

GENTLE, well-born; 4. 2. 39

GENTRY, nobility; 3. 7. 7; 5. 1. 18; 5. 2. 8

GIGLOT (adj.), wanton; 3. 1. 31

GILD, bring (bright) colour to; 5. 3. 34

GIVE, (i) 'give up', succumb; 2. 2. 46; (ii) 'give o'er', give up; 2. 3. 15

Go, (i) walk; 4. 2. 294; (ii) 'go before', be superior to; 1. 4. 70; 5. 2. 8

GOLDEN, precious, excellent; 4. 2. 262

GOOD-CONCEITED, well devised; 2. 3. 16

GORDIAN KNOT, knot tied by Gordias, king of Phrygia, for fastening the yoke of his wagon; the legend was that whoever unloosed it would gain the empire of Asia; Alexander the Great is said to have cut it with his sword; 2. 2. 34

GRACE (sb.), (i) sense of duty; 1. 1. 136; (ii) grace of God, i.e. redemption, salvation; 1. 1. 137; (iii) favour; 1. 4. 86; 5. 4. 79; (iv) that which wins favour; 4. 2. 27; (v) that which adorns; 5. 5. 132

GRACE (vb.), adorn; 5. 5. 406

GRANTED, acknowledged; 2. 1. 44

GRATIFY, requite; 2. 4. 7

GRAVE, serious-minded; 1. 1. 49

GREAT, see *morning*

GRIEF (see note); 3. 4. 24

GRIPE (sb.), grip, grasp; 1. 6. 105

GRIPE (vb.), seize hold; 3. 1. 39

GROOM, (i) servant; 2. 3. 127; (ii) bridegroom (not pre-Sh.); 3. 6. 69

GROUND, (i) 'give ground', (*a*) retreat, recede (fig. from fencing); (*b*) bestow part of one's estate; 1. 2. 17–18

GROW, 'grow unto', become inseparably united to; 1. 3. 1

GUISE, custom; 5. 1. 32

HA, excl. of surprise, indignation, etc. (i) what?; 1. 1. 160; (ii) eh?; 2. 1. 11

HABIT(s), dress, clothes; 5. 1. 30; 5. 3. 86

HALTING, hesitation; 3. 5. 93

HAND-FAST (sb.), marriage contract; 1. 5. 78

HAND-IN-HAND, on the same level; 1. 4. 68

HANGING, (*a*) execution by hanging; (*b*) hanging up of meat; 5. 4. 153

HANGINGS, what hangs on a tree (i.e. fruit); 3. 3. 63

HAPPY, skilful, accomplished; 3. 4. 175

HARDIMENT, bold exploit; 5. 4. 75

HARDNESS, (i) hardship; 3. 6. 21; (ii) difficulty; 5. 5. 431

HAREBELL, wild hyacinth (*scilla nutans*); 4. 2. 222

HARSH, rude, rough; 3. 4. 133

HAVE, (i) 'have with you', I'll go with you; 4. 4. 50; (ii) 'have at it', I will begin, 'here goes'; 5. 5. 315

HAVING, property; 1. 2. 17

HAVIOUR, behaviour; 3. 4. 9

HEAD, (i) armed force (see also *draw* (i)); 3. 5. 25 ('draw to head'); 4. 2. 139 ('make ...head'); (ii) for 'mouth'; 5. 5. 157

HEART, 'for his heart', to save his life; 2. 1. 52

HEAVE, lift (without implication of great weight); 5. 5. 157

HEAVINESS, (i) dejection; 5. 2. 1; (ii) (*a*) weight, (*b*) (i) (cf. *Ant.* 4. 15. 33); 5. 4. 165

HECUBA, wife of Priam, king of Troy; 4. 2. 313

HELP (vb.), cure; 3. 6. 4

HERCULES, Lat. name of Greek myth. hero, Heracles, famed for his supernormal strength; 4. 2. 114, 311

HILDING (sb.), good-for-nothing fellow (not pre-Sh. of human being); 2. 3. 123

HIND, peasant; 5. 3. 77

HIRE, reward (used contemptuously); 2. 4. 129

HIS, its; 1. 6. 160

HOLD (sb.), stronghold; 3. 6. 18

HOLP, pa. tense of 'help'; 5. 5. 422

HOME (adv.), thoroughly; 3. 5. 93; 4. 2. 328

HONOUR, renown (as a soldier); 1. 1. 29

HOODWINK, blindfold (fig.); 5. 2. 16

HOOK, lit. fishhook, fig. snare; 5. 5. 167

HORSE-HAIR, used for fiddle-bows, so, fiddle-bow; 2. 3. 30

HOSE, Elizabethan close-fitting breeches, worn by men; 3. 4. 170

HOT, lustful; 4. 4. 37; 5. 5. 180

HOW, HOW NOW, (i) interj. of remonstrance, expostulation, surprise, etc.; 'what!, hallo!'; 1. 1. 114; 1. 1. 159 ('how now'); 3. 2. 11; 3. 5. 67 ('how now'); 4. 2. 312, etc.; (ii) 'how now', as a summons; 2. 3. 136; 3. 2. 24

HUMOUR, inclination; 1. 5. 81

HUNT, game; 3. 6. 89

ILL, evil; 5. 5. 159

IMPERCEIVERANT, undiscerning (see note); 4. 1. 13

IMPERIOUS, majestic; 4. 2. 35

IMPORTANCE, affair that concerns someone; 1. 4. 39

IMPORTANTLY, with important matter (first here); 4. 4. 19

IN, (i) on; 3. 6. 49; (ii) into; 3. 6. 63

INCIVIL, unmannerly; 5. 5. 292

INCONTINENCY, unchastity; 2. 4. 127

INFORM, inspire, imbue; 1. 1. 79

INGENIOUS, (i) skilfully contrived; 4. 2. 186; (ii) skilful at contriving; 5. 5. 215

INHERIT, possess; 3. 2. 61

INJURIOUS, insulting; 3. 1. 46

INSULTMENT, contemptuous triumph (see note); 3. 5. 141

INTELLIGENCE, communication; 4. 2. 347

INTEREST, (i) legal right; 1. 3. 30; (ii) concern; 4. 2. 365

INTER'GATORIES, questions put formally, to be answered as on oath (syncopated form of 'interrogatories'); 5. 5. 392

INWARD, heart; 3. 4. 6

IRREGULOUS, lawless (here only); 4. 2. 315

IT, its; 3. 4. 158

JACK, ball used as the mark to be aimed at in the game of bowls; 2. 1. 2

JACKANAPES, impertinent fellow; 2. 1. 3

JACK-SLAVE, low-bred fellow; 2. 1. 19

JAY, loose woman; 3. 4. 49

JEALOUSY, suspicion; 4. 3. 22

JET, strut, swagger, 3. 3. 5

JEWEL, piece of jewellery; 2. 4. 96

JOINT (vb.), unite; 5. 4. 142; 5. 5. 439

JOLLY, jovial; 1. 6. 66

JOURNAL, diurnal; 4. 2. 10

JOVIAL, (i) majestic as Jove's; 4. 2. 311; (ii) belonging to Jove ('Jovial star'=the planet Jupiter); 5. 4. 105

JUMP, hazard (Sh. only); 5. 4. 182

JUNO, wife of Jupiter, queen of the gods; 3. 4. 166; 4. 2. 50

JUSTICE, judge; 5. 5. 214

JUSTIFY, prove; 2. 4. 79

KEN, distance within range of vision; 3. 6. 6.

KISS, touch (the jack) with one's bowl; 2. 1. 2

KITCHEN-TRULL, kitchen-wench (here only); 5. 5. 177

KNOCK, make go by blows; 3. 5. 144

KNOW (intr.), be acquainted (here and *Ant.* 2. 6. 84 only); 1. 4. 33

KNOWING, knowledge; 1. 4. 27; 2. 3. 97

KNOWINGLY, from personal experience; 3. 3. 46

KNOWLEDGE (OF), sexual intimacy (with); 2. 4. 51, 79

LABEL, slip of paper; 5. 5. 430

LABOURSOME, elaborate; 3. 4. 165

LADY, wife; 1. 6. 159

LAME, render, make to appear, deformed (in comparison); 5. 5. 163

LANGUISH, (i) pine away; 1. 1. 156; (ii) 'languishing', lingering; 1. 5. 9; (iii) pass in languishing; 1. 6. 71

LAP, wrap; 5. 5. 360

LATE, lately; 1. 1. 6

LAWYER (TO), advocate (for); 2. 3. 74

LAY (sb.), wager; 1. 4. 146

LAY (vb.), stake; 1. 1. 174; 1. 4. 126

LEAGUED, united, folded (fig.); 4. 2. 213

LEAN, (i) 'lean unto', defer to; 1. 1. 78; (ii) (see note); 1. 5. 58

LEARN, teach; 1. 5. 12

LEAVE, cease (with inf. as obj.); 1. 3. 15; (abs.) 1. 4. 98; 2. 2. 4

LEAVEN, 'lay the leaven on', corrupt (fig. from sour dough); 3. 4. 62

LEND, give; 3. 6. 24

LESSEN (refl.), decrease in (apparent) size; 5. 5. 471

LET BLOOD, bleed, i.e. kill (fig. use of medical sense; cf. *J.C.* 3. 1. 153); 4. 2. 168

LETTERS, letter (sing.); 1. 6. 11

LIEGER, resident ambassador, so, more generally, representative agent; 1. 5. 80

LIGHTS, eyes; 2. 2. 21

LIKE (adj.), (i) the same; 4. 2. 237; (ii) likely; 2. 4. 36; 5. 3. 19

LIKE (adv.), (i) probably; 3. 4. 117; 5. 5. 259; (ii) 'like... as', as...as; 3. 3. 41

LIKE (vb.), 'so like you'=if you please; 2. 3. 54

LIKELY, apparently suitable (cf. 'like', adj. (ii), esp. 5. 3. 19); 2. 4. 83

LIMB-MEAL, limb from limb; 2. 4. 147

LINE (sb.), lineament; 4. 2. 104

LINE (vb.), fill with money (cf. Tilley, P 664); 2. 3. 67

LIVER, (i) one who lives in a certain way; 3. 3. 9; (ii) living person; 3. 4. 141

LOCK (i) (fig. from 'doorlock', O.E.D. 1), seal; 3. 2. 36; (ii) grip in wrestling; 5. 5. 262

LONG OF, owing to, because of; 5. 5. 271

LOOK (i) seem to; 3. 5. 32; (ii) refl. (with 'into'), win by one's looks; 5. 5. 94

LORD, husband; 5. 5. 227

LOVE, beloved; 5. 5. 161

LOVER, beloved; 5. 5. 172

LUCINA, the name given to Juno (=she who brings to light) as presiding over childbirth; 5. 4. 43

LUD'S TOWN, London; Lud, a legendary British king who improved London; Cymbeline's grandfather in legend. chrons. (see Boswell-Stone, p. 14); acc. to Hol. III, ix, reigned from 72 B.C.; 3. 1. 32; 4. 2. 99

MAD, madden (which O.E.D. does not record before 18th c.); 2. 2. 37; 4. 2. 313

MAKE, (i)=mod. 'be the making of'; 1. 4. 9; (ii) 'make up', complete; 4. 2. 109

MANHOOD, male (not female) condition; 3. 4. 193

MANNERED, 'truest mannered', of the most loyal character; 1. 6. 165

MANNERLY, politely; 3. 6. 91

MANSION, dwelling-place; 3. 4. 68 (fig.); 5. 4. 87

MARRY (orig. invocation of the Virgin Mary), (i) indeed, 'to be sure'; 1. 1. 76; (ii) to express indignant surprise; 5. 5. 287

MART (vb.), traffic; 1. 6. 150

MARTIAL, strong as Mars's; 4. 2. 310

MASTER (sb.), courtesy title, 'Sir'; 3. 6. 45

MASTER (vb.), furnish with a master (first here); 4. 2. 385; (ii) be a master to; 4. 2. 397

MASTERLESS, without an owner; 2. 4. 60

MATCH (sb.), (i) marriage; 1. 1. 12; (ii) contest; 1. 4. 144; (iii) bargain; 3. 6. 30

MATCH (vb.), provide with an equal adversary; 2. 1. 20

MATTER, (i) 'from the matter', off the point, irrelevantly (sb.¹ 25a); 1. 4. 15–16; (ii) business; 4. 3. 28; (iii) point; 5. 5. 169

MEAN (sb.), 'make means', make overtures; 2. 4. 3

MEAN (adj.), (i) low, humble in rank; 1. 6. 8; 2. 3. 116, 117; (ii) unimportant, everyday; 2. 2. 29; 3. 2. 50

MEAN (vb.), intend; 1. 5. 66

MEANLY, humbly; 3. 3. 82

MEAT, food in general; 3. 6. 49; 5. 4. 161

MEDICINABLE, fig., curative (commoner in Sh. than 'medicinal'); 3. 2. 33

MEDICINE, cure; 4. 2. 243

MERCURIAL, like Mercury's feet (i.e. nimble); 4. 2. 310

MERE, entire; 4. 2. 92; 5. 5. 334

MERELY, entirely; 5. 3. 11

MIGHT, could; 1. 1. 139

MINERAL, mineral poison; 5. 5. 50

MINION, darling; 2. 3. 41

MINISTER (vb.), supply; 1. 1. 45

MINUTE, 'by the minute', minute by minute; 5. 5. 51

MISTRESS, sweetheart; 1. 4. 56

MOCK, subject for mockery; 5. 4. 188

MODESTY, chastity; 3. 4. 153

MOE, more; 3. 1. 36, 62; 5. 3. 72

MOIETY, half; 1. 4. 107

MOLLIS AER (Lat.), tender air; 5. 5. 446

MONSIEUR (French) gentleman; 1. 6. 64

MONUMENT, effigy (common in Sh.); 2. 2. 32; 4. 2. 227

Morning, 'great morning', broad daylight; 4. 2. 61

Morrow, morning; 2. 3. 35, 86, 87; 3. 3. 7, etc.

Mortal, (i) deadly; 5. 3. 51; 5. 5. 235; (ii) human; 1. 6. 170 (see note); 5. 4. 99

Mortality, human life; 4. 1. 14

Motion, impulse; 2. 5. 20

Movable, piece of furniture; 2. 2. 29

Move, incite; 1. 1. 103; 1. 5. 70; 5. 5. 342

Mover, cause; 1. 5. 9

Mow, grimace; 1. 6. 40

Much, very; 2. 3. 104

Mulier (Lat.), woman or wife; 5. 5. 447

Mulmutius, a king of Britain (Boswell-Stone, p. 14); he made laws, later translated into Lat. by Gildas and into Engl. by Alfred; hero of a lost play of 1599 (Chambers, *Eliz. Stage*, ii, 170); 3. 1. 53, 57

Music, band of musicians; 2. 3. 11; 5. 4. 29 S.D.

Muster, enlist; 4. 4. 10

Natural, related by blood; 3. 3. 107

Naught, wicked; 5. 5. 271

Nearer (adv.), closer to the point; 3. 5. 92

Neat, (i) elegant; 1. 6. 43; (ii) dainty; 4. 2. 49

Neat-herd, cowherd; 1. 1. 149

Neptune, god of the sea; 3. 1. 19

Nerve, sinew; 3. 3. 94

New, recent; 2. 3. 41

Newness, fact of being recent; 4. 4. 9

New o'er, over again; 1. 6. 164

Nice (see note); 2. 5. 26

Niceness, coyness; 3. 4. 156

Nonpareil, one without an equal; 2. 5. 8

Nor...nor, neither...nor; 5. 5. 391

North, north wind; 1. 3. 36

Note, (i) reputation; 1. 4. 2; 1. 6. 22; 2. 3. 122; 3. 3. 58; 5. 3. 94; (ii) indication; 2. 2. 28; (iii) tune; 4. 2. 237; (iv) (see notes); 4. 3. 44; 4. 4. 20

Nothing, not at all; 1. 1. 86; 1. 4. 66; 2. 4. 94, 112; 4. 2. 104; 4. 3. 14; 4. 4. 15; 5. 5. 293

Nothing-gift, worthless gift (here only); 3. 6. 85

Numbered (see note); 1. 6. 35

Object, object of sight; 1. 6. 101

Occasion, (i) cause; 4. 2. 187, 196; (ii) need; 5. 5. 87

Odds, probability; 5. 2. 9

Odd's pittikins, dimin. of 'God's pity', God have mercy; 4. 2. 293

O'erbear, knock down; 5. 3. 48

O'erlaboured, tired by excessive labour; 2. 2. 11

Of, (i) from; 2. 4. 11; 2. 5. 9; (ii) over; 4. 1. 20; (iii) by; 4. 4. 22; 5. 5. 194

Offence, (a) attack, (b) coarse sense, mod. 'nuisance'; 2. 1. 27

Office, (i) (religious) service; 3. 3. 4; (ii) duty; 3. 5. 10; (iii) that which performs a function (cf. *Cor.* 1. 1. 141); 5. 5. 257

OFFICER, public functionary, here, hangman; 5. 4. 175

OFTEN, many times over; 5. 5. 415

ON, (i) of; 1. 1. 164; 1. 6. 92; 2. 1. 32; 4. 2. 198; 5. 4. 184; 5. 5. 311; (ii) about; 2. 4. 132

ONE, (with superl.) of all, above all; 1. 6. 164; 2. 4. 32

OPE, open; 2. 3. 24; 5. 4. 81

OPEN, reveal; 5. 5. 42, 58

OPPOSITION, combat; 4. 1. 13

OPPRESS, distress; 5. 4. 99

OR...OR, either...or; 1. 4. 82–3; 4. 4. 5

ORB, (i) star; 1. 6. 34; (ii) sphere (Ptol. astron.), fig.; 5. 5. 371

ORDINANCE, divine dispensation; 4. 2. 145

OR ERE, before; 1. 3. 33; 3. 2. 65; 5. 3. 50

ORISON, prayer; 1. 3. 32

OUT OF DOOR, external, visible (cf. *Wint.* 2. 1. 69, 'without-door' [Ingleby]); 1. 6. 15

OUTCRAFTY, overpower by craft (here only); 3. 4. 15

OUTGO, surpass; 2. 4. 84

OUTLUSTRE, outshine (first here; rare); 1. 4. 71

OUTPEER, surpass (first here; only one other ex. in O.E.D., from 19th c.); 3. 6. 86

OUTPRIZE, exceed in value (first here; rare); 1. 4. 80

OUTSELL, exceed in value (first here); 2. 4. 102; 3. 5. 75

OUTSTAND, outstay (first here in this sense); 1. 6. 206

OUTVENOM, be more poisonous than (here only); 3. 4. 35

OUTWARD (sb.), exterior; 1. 1. 23

OUTWARD (adj.) (see note); 1. 1. 9

OVERBUY, pay too much for; 1. 1. 146

OWE, own; 3. 1. 37

PACK, plot; 3. 5. 81

PAIN, labour; 3. 3. 50

PALE, 'pale in', enclose; 3. 1. 19

PANG (vb.), torture; 3. 4. 96

PANNONIANS, people inhabiting present-day Hungary; 3. 1. 72; 3. 7. 3

PANTLER, servant in charge of the pantry; 2. 3. 124

PART (sb.), (i) personal quality; 3. 5. 72; (ii) side; 5. 1. 25; (iii) part in a play; 5. 5. 229; (iv) (see note); 1. 1. 165

PART (vb.), depart; 3. 6. 51

PART...PART (see note), 5. 3. 35

PARTHIANS, warlike people to the S.E. of the Caspian; famed as archers on horseback for shooting arrows behind them when taking flight; hence, 'Parthian shot'; 1. 6. 20

PARTING, departing; 5. 4. 160

PARTISAN, long-shafted spear with a broad head (see *Ham.* G.); 4. 2. 401

PARTITION, distinction; 1. 6. 36

PARTNER (vb.), associate; 1. 6. 120

PASSABLE (see note); 1. 2. 8

PASSAGE, occurrence; 3. 4. 92

PAWN, (i) stake; 1. 4. 107; (ii) pledge; 1. 6. 193

PAY, (i) punish; 4. 2. 246; (ii) (see note); 5. 4. 163

PECULIAR, individual; 5. 5. 83

PEEVISH, refractory; 1. 6. 53

PENETRATE, (i) intr., affect the feeling; 2. 3. 12, 28; (ii) tr., affect the feelings of (with indelicate quibble); 2. 3. 13

PERFECT, well aware; 3. 1. 71; 4. 2. 118

PERISHING, destructive; 4. 2. 60

PERPLEXED, distressed; 5. 5. 108

PERSONATE, represent; 5. 5. 453

PERUSE, inspect; 1. 4. 6

PERVERT, turn aside; 2. 4. 151

PHILOMEL, Philomela, sister of the wife of Tereus (q.v.); ravished by Tereus, who cut out her tongue to prevent her telling; metamorphosed into a nightingale; 2. 2. 46

PHOEBUS, Apollo, sun-god, so, the sun; 2. 3. 20

PHYSIC, act as medicine to; 3. 2. 34

PINCH, pang; 1. 1. 130

PINCHING, nippingly cold; 3. 3. 38

PLAY, gamble; 1. 6. 123

POINT (sb.), (i) 'at point to', just about to; 3. 1. 30–1; 3. 6. 17; (ii) 'hard point', tight corner; 3. 4. 16

POINT (vb.), 'point forth', indicate; 5. 5. 453–4

POSSESS, be in possession; 1. 5. 48

POST, (i) convey at great speed; 2. 4. 27; (ii) go post-haste; 3. 4. 36

POWER, armed force; 3. 5. 24; 4. 3. 31

POX, lit. venereal disease; as an imprecation, 'plague'; 2. 1. 17

PRACTICE, trickery; 5. 5. 199

PRECIOUS, arrant; 4. 2. 83

PREFER, (i) commend, recommend; 1. 4. 63; 2. 3. 46; 4. 2. 388, 402; (ii) promote, win advancement for; 2. 3. 131; 5. 5. 326

PREFERMENT, promotion; 3. 5. 116; 5. 4. 205–6

PREGNANT, obvious; 4. 2. 325

PREPARATION, force equipped for battle; 4. 3. 29

PRESENT, immediate; 2. 4. 137

PRESENTLY, immediately; 2. 3. 138; 3. 2. 75; 4. 2. 166

PRESS (sb.), crowd; 2. 4. 72

PRETEND, allege falsely as a pretext; 2. 3. 113; 5. 5. 250

PRETTY, ingenious; 3. 4. 148

PRICE, value; 1. 1. 51

PRIDE (see note); 2. 5. 25

PRIEST, priestess, 1. 6. 132

PRINCE IT, behave like a prince; 3. 3. 85

PRIZE (see note); 3. 6. 76

PROBABLE, capable of proof; 2. 4. 115

PROBATION, proof; 5. 5. 362

PRONE, eager; 5. 4. 199

PROOF, (i) experience; 1. 6. 69; 3. 1. 75; 3. 3. 27; (ii) tested strength; 5. 5. 5

PROPER, (i) honest; 3. 4. 62; (ii) own; 4. 2. 97

PROVE, test; 1. 5. 38

PRUNE, preen; 5. 4. 118

PUDENCY, modesty (first here); 2. 5. 11

PUPPY, vain, empty-headed young man; 1. 2. 19

PURPOSE (TO), design, or intend (someone) (for); 1. 1. 5

PUT, (i) 'put to', set before; 1. 1. 43; (ii) stake, wager; 1. 4. 122; (iii) force, compel; 2. 3. 105; 5. 3. 63; (iv) 'put on', instigate; 5. 1. 9

PUTTOCK, bird of prey of the kite kind; 1. 1. 140

QUAKE, shiver; 2. 4. 5

QUALIFIED, endowed with good qualities; 1. 4. 58

QUALITY, good natural gifts; 1. 4. 22, 28

QUARRELOUS, quarrelsome; 3. 4. 160

QUARTERED, belonging to milit. quarters (this and one 19th c. ex. only in O.E.D.); 4. 4. 18

QUENCH, (i) cool down; 1. 5. 47; (ii) 'quenched of hope', with hope suppressed; 5. 5. 195-6

QUESTION, (i) interrogate; 1. 3. 2; (ii) abs., dispute; 2. 4. 52

QUICK-ANSWERED, ready with answers (here only); 3. 4. 159

RAMP, bold, vulgar woman; 1. 6. 133

RANGER, gamekeeper; here of Diana's attendant nymphs, vowed to chastity; 2. 3. 69

RANK, licentious; 2. 5. 24

RANSOM, means of expiation; 5. 3. 80

RAP, transport; 1. 6. 50

RARE, exquisite, fine; 1. 1. 135; 1. 4. 59; 1. 6. 16, 174, 188; 3. 4. 161

RARELY, exquisitely; 2. 4. 75

RARENESS, rarity; 3. 4. 93

RATHER, more readily; 5. 4. 26

RAVEN, feed voraciously on; 1. 6. 48

READY, (a) dressed, (b) prepared; 2. 3. 81

REASON (sb.), (i) way of reasoning; 4. 2. 22 (first occurrence); (ii) reasonableness; 4. 2. 22 (second occurrence)

REASON (vb.), 'reason of', talk sensibly about; 4. 2. 14

RECK, care; 4. 2. 154

RECOIL, degenerate; 1. 6. 127

REDEEM, save; 1. 5. 63

REFER, hand over; 1. 1. 6

REFLECT, bestow attention; 1. 6. 23

REFLECTION (see note); 1. 2. 29, 30

REFT, pa. tense of 'reave', deprived; 3. 3. 103

REINFORCE, obtain reinforcements (this and one 19th c. ex. only in O.E.D.); 5. 2. 18

REJOICE, feel joy at; 5. 5. 370

RELIGION, sense of religion; 1. 4. 136

RELISH, have a taste; 3. 2. 30

REMAIN, what remains; 3. 1. 84

REMAINDERS, those who remain; 1. 1. 129

REMEMBRANCER, one employed to remind (legal term); 1. 5. 77

RENDER (sb.), (i) account; 4. 4. 11; (ii) restitution; 5. 4. 17

RENDER (vb.), (i) state; 2. 4. 119; 5. 5. 135; (ii) describe; 3. 4. 151

RENOWN, good name (here only); 5. 5. 202

REPAIR, restore; 1. 1. 132

REPEAT, relate; 1. 6. 4

REPORT, reputation; 3. 3. 57

RESERVE, (i) keep safe; 1. 4. 130; (ii) make reservation of, except; 1. 1. 87

RESPECT (sb.), esteem; 2. 3. 135

RESTRAINT (see note); 1. 1. 74

RESTY, sluggish; 3. 6. 34

RETIRE (sb.), retreat; 5. 3. 40

REVERENCE, see *saving reverence*

REVOLT (sb.), (i) casting off of faithfulness; 1. 6. 111; 3. 4. 55; (ii) rebel; 4. 4. 6

RIB, enclose with a strong protection; 3. 1. 19

ROMISH, Roman (pejorative); 1. 6. 151

ROUSE, startle (an animal from its lair); 3. 3. 98

ROYALTY, royal character; 4. 2. 178

RUDDOCK, robin redbreast; 4. 2. 224

RUDE, rough; 4. 2. 174

RUNAGATE, (i) deserter; 1. 6. 136; (ii) runaway, vagabond; 4. 2. 62, 63

SAD, serious; 1. 6. 62

SADNESS, seriousness, gravity; 1. 6. 61

SAMPLE, example; 1. 1. 48

SAND, (i) sand-bank; 3. 1. 21; (ii) grain of sand; 5. 5. 120

SANGUINE, blood-red; 5. 5. 364

SATISFY, make atonement (from the technical religious sense); 5. 4. 15

SATURN, planet and god, thought of as cold, sluggish and gloomy; 2. 5. 12

SAUCY, impudent; 1. 6. 150

SAVAGE, (i) belonging to un-civilized creatures; 3. 6. 18; (ii) uncivilized; 3. 6. 23; 4. 2. 33

SAVING REVERENCE (OF), begging pardon (for); 4. 1. 5

SAY (see notes); 2. 1. 23; 4. 2. 379

SCANDAL, bring into disrepute; 3. 4. 60

SCORN, object of contempt; 5. 4. 67

SCRIPTURES, writing (with quibble on sacred books of a religion); 3. 4. 81

SCRUPLE, 'make scruple', express doubts; 5. 5. 182

SEAL, attest, confirm; 3. 6. 84; 5. 5. 482

SEARCH, seek for; 5. 5. 11

SEASON (sb.), (i) time; 2. 3. 48; 5. 5. 401; (ii) time of life; 3. 4. 173

SEASON (vb.), add relish to; 1. 6. 9

SEAT, (honoured) abode; 5. 4. 60

SECOND (sb.), supporter; 5. 3. 90

SECOND (vb.), (i) follow up; 5. 1. 14; (ii) support; 5. 2. 13 S.D.

SEE, see each other; 1. 1. 124

SEEK THROUGH, make a tho-rough search for; 4. 2. 160

SEEMING, (i) outward appear-ance; 1. 6. 170 (see note); 3. 4. 54; (ii) appearance of truth; 5. 5. 451

SELF, same ; 1. 6. 121

SELF-, of or by, etc., oneself; (i) 'self-figured', formed by oneself; 2. 3. 119; (ii) 'self-explication', explanation to oneself; 3. 4. 8; (iii) 'self-danger', danger to oneself; 3. 4. 147

SENSE, (i) senses (uninflected plur.); 1. 5. 37; 2. 2. 11, 32; (ii) one of the five senses, here, hearing; 3. 2. 58; (iii) intelligence; 5. 4. 148; (iv) (see note); 5. 5. 431

SENSELESS, (i) 'senseless of', insensitive to; 1. 1. 135; (ii) insentient; 1. 3. 7; 3. 2. 20; (iii) insensible, without hearing; 2. 3. 53 (first occurrence); (iv) devoid of intelligence; 2. 3. 53 (second occurrence); (v) ?meaningless (see note); 5. 4. 147

SET, (i) 'set on', incite; 1. 5. 73; (ii) 'set off', show to the best advantage; 1. 6. 169; 3. 3. 13; (iii) 'set up', instigate; 3. 4. 88; (iv) 'set forward', 'set on', start marching; 5. 5. 478, 483

SEVERAL, respective; 1. 5. 23

SEVERALLY, by each in a particular way; 5. 5. 397

SHADOW, shade of the dead; 5. 4. 97

SHAME, modesty; 5. 3. 22

SHAPE, be conducive; 5. 5. 346

SHARDED, provided with wing-cases (see note); 3. 3. 20

SHE, woman; 1. 3. 29; 1. 6. 39.

SHIFT, change (clothes); 1. 2. 1, 5

SHOP, store (fig.); 5. 5. 166

SHORT, make of no effect (O.E.D., as nonce-use, comparing 'shorten' in *Lr.* 4. 7. 9); 1. 6. 199

SHOT, what one owes at a tavern; 5. 4. 156

SHOULD, would; 1. 6. 44

SHOW, (i) appearance; 1. 5. 40; (ii) display (of love); 5. 5. 54; (iii) vision; 5. 5. 428

'SHREW, beshrew (aphetic form); ''shrew me', emphatic asseveration; 2. 3. 142

SHUFFLE, shift; 5. 5. 105

SIGN, (i) appearance (see note); 1. 2. 28; (ii) token; 3. 4. 126

SIGNIOR (Ital.), gentleman; 1. 4. 99

SILLY, simple; 5. 3. 86

SIMPLE, foolish (with quibble on 'of humble birth' as opp. of 'noble'); 3. 4. 133

SIMULAR (see note); 5. 5. 200

SINGULAR, unmatched; 3. 4. 122

SINK, make fall; 5. 5. 413

SINON, a Greek who, pretending to be a deserter, persuaded the Trojans to admit into Troy the wooden horse, filled with Greek warriors, who then sacked the city; 3. 4. 59

SIR, gentleman; 1. 6. 159, 174; 5. 5. 145

SIRE, be father of (first here; not again before 19th c.); 4. 2. 26

SIRRAH, form of address to inferiors; 3. 5. 107, 109

SKILL, 'greater skill', more reasonable; 2. 5. 33

SKY-PLANTED, fixed in the sky (here only); 5. 4. 96

SLANDER, evil repute; 1. 1. 71

SLAVE, wretch; 4. 2. 72, 74

SLEEPY, permitting sloth; 3. 5. 26

SLIGHT, (i) careless, easy-going (cf. 'slightly', *M.V.* 5. 1. 168); 3. 5. 35; (ii) insignificant; 5. 4. 64

SLIP, let go free; 4. 3. 22

SLIPPERY, easy to slip off; 2. 2. 34

SLUTTERY, sluttishness; 1. 6. 43

SMOKE, fumigate; 5. 5. 398

SNATCH, 'catch', hesitancy (here only); 4. 2. 105

SNUFF, wick of a candle; 1. 6. 86

SO, (i) it is well; 2. 3. 14; (ii) 'that's right'; 4. 2. 257; (iii) 'so, so', good (expressing approval) (not noted O.E.D.); 1. 5. 82

SOFT (as exclam.), wait, stop; 3. 4. 79; 4. 2. 70, 295, 353

SOLACE, enjoy oneself; 1. 6. 85

SOLDIER (see note); 3. 4. 184

SOMETHING, somewhat; 1. 1. 86; 1. 4. 69, 109; 1. 6. 190

SOMETIME, once; 4. 2. 354

SORE, causing suffering; 4. 1. 22

SORROW, 'I am sorrow', I am sorry (see note); 5. 5. 297

SOT, fool; 5. 5. 178

SOUR, embitter; 5. 5. 26

SOUTH FOG, fog brought by the south wind; 2. 3. 131

SPECTACLES, organs of vision; 1. 6. 36

SPEED, fare; 5. 4. 183

SPEND, (i) exhaust; 3. 6. 62; (ii) finish; 5. 4. 104

SPONGY, wet; 4. 2. 349

SPRING (fig.), youth; 1. 1. 46

SPRITED, haunted as by a spirit; 2. 3. 139

SPRITELY, spectral; 5. 5. 428

SPUR (sb.), root; 4. 2. 58

SPUR (vb.), urge on (in speech); 1. 6. 98

SQUIRE, man of the rank next below that of knight; 2. 3. 123

STAGGERS, giddiness; 5. 5. 233

STAIN (sb.), (i) blotch; 2. 4. 139; (ii) disgrace, with quibble on (i); 2. 4. 140

STAMP (sb.), (i) coin; 5. 4. 24; (ii) distinguishing mark; 5. 5. 366

STAMP (vb.), beget (fig.); 2. 5. 5

STAND (sb.), station taken up by hunter to shoot at game; 2. 3. 70; 3. 4. 109

STAND (vb.), (i) withstand; 1. 2. 13, 16; 5. 3. 60; (ii) remain firm; 2. 1. 61; (iii) 'stand for', support; 3. 5. 57; (iv) halt; 5. 3. 88

STARK, rigid in death; 4. 2. 209

STARVE, die from cold; 1. 4. 165

STATE, (i) magnificence, regal pomp; 3. 3. 78; (ii) person of highest rank; 3. 4. 37; (iii) status; 5. 5. 98

STATIST, statesman; 2. 4. 16

STAY, wait; 3. 6. 39

STEW, brothel; 1. 6. 151

STILL (adj.), quiet; 5. 4. 69

STILL (adv.), always; 1. 3. 12; 1. 4. 62 (or, even yet); 2. 3. 92

STIR (sb.), mental agitation; 1. 3. 12

STIR (vb.), move (to tell one's story); 4. 2. 38

STOMACH, appetite; 3. 6. 32; 5. 4. 2

STOMACHER, women's breast-covering (fig.); 3. 4. 84

STOMACH-QUALMED, feeling sick (here only); 3. 4. 191

STOOP, swoop (falconry); 5. 4. 116

STOP, sudden check in a horse's career; 5. 3. 40

STORY, give an account of; 1. 4. 31

STRAIGHT, immediately; 1. 4. 164

STRAIGHT-PIGHT, erect (here only); 5. 5. 164

STRAIN, (i) impulse; 3. 4. 93; (ii) natural disposition; 4. 2. 24

STRAIT, narrow; 5. 3. 7, 11

STRANGE, (i) belonging to another place; 1. 4. 88; (ii) foreign; 1. 6. 53

STRANGER, foreigner; 1. 4. 28; 1. 6. 58; 2. 1. 30, 32, 38; 2. 4. 126

STRIDE, overstep; 3. 3. 35

STUFF, (excellent) substance; 1. 1. 23

SUBJECTION, what belongs to being subject; 4. 3. 19

SUCCESSION, successors; 3. 1. 8; 3. 3. 102

SUFFER, (i) allow (freq.); 1. 1. 170; 4. 2. 143; (ii) admit of; 1. 4. 53

SUFFERANCE, toleration; 3. 5. 35

SUIT (sb.), amorous solicitation; 5. 5. 185

SUIT (vb.), clothe; 5. 1. 23

SUMMER (fig.), joyful; 3. 4. 12

SUPPLY, reinforcements; 4. 3. 25; (plur.) 5. 2. 16

SUPPLYANT, supplementary (here only); 3. 7. 14

SUPPLYMENT, continuance of supply (second of two exx.); 3. 4. 180

SUR-ADDITION, additional title or name (here only); 1. 1. 33

SURE, assuredly, for certain; 4. 2. 102; 5. 5. 260

SWATHING-CLOTHES, swaddling-clothes; 1. 1. 59

SWEET, sweetheart (here male, and contemptuously for 'husband'); 1. 5. 80

SWELLED (fig.), inflated, exaggerated; 5. 5. 162

SWERVE, err; 5. 4. 129

SYMPATHY, conformity (i.e. of my life and it); 5. 4. 150

SYNOD, assembly (of the gods); 5. 4. 89

TABLE (sb.), writing tablet; 3. 2. 39

TABLE (vb.), set down in a list; 1. 4. 6

TAINT, (i) corrupt; 3. 4. 26; 5. 4. 65; (ii) become corrupt (fig.); 1. 4. 135

TAKE, (i) 'take up', rebuke; 2. 1. 4; (ii) 'take in', overcome; 3. 2. 9; 4. 2. 121; (iii) 'take off', remove, destroy; 3. 4. 17; 5. 2. 2; 5. 4. 86; 5. 5. 47; (iv) accept; 5. 4. 27; (v) 'take on one(self)', profess; 5. 4. 180, 180–1

TALENT, natural gift; 1. 6. 79

TANLING, person tanned by the sun (first here; 19th c. exx. prob. echoes); 4. 4. 29

TARGE, light shield; 5. 5. 5

TARQUIN, Sicilius Tarquin, son of Tarquin Superbus, the ravisher of Lucretia; 2. 2. 12

TASTE, (i) have sexual experience with; 2. 4. 57; (ii) 'taste of', experience; 5. 5. 308, 403

TEMPER, mix; 5. 5. 250

TENANTIUS, the father of Cymbeline; 1. 1. 31; 5. 4. 73

TENDANCE, attention; 5. 5. 53

TENDER (sb.), presentation; 1. 6. 207

TENDER (adj.), (i) 'tender of', sensitive to; 3. 5. 40; (ii) considerate; 4. 2. 126; 5. 5. 87

TENDER (vb.), offer; 3. 4. 11; 3. 5. 31

TENT, roll of lint, to probe and cleanse wound (fig.); 3. 4. 116

TEREUS, king of Thrace, married to Procne; see *Philomel*; 2. 2. 45

TERMS, circumstances; 3. 1. 78

THANKINGS, thanks; 5. 5. 407

THERETO, in addition; 4. 4. 33

THERSITES, scurrilous Greek warrior, deformed and ugly, in the siege of Troy; see *Troil.* passim; 4. 2. 252

THICK (adj.), occurring in quick succession; 1. 6. 66

THICK (adv.), rapidly; 3. 2. 56

THREAT, threaten; 4. 2. 127

THRIFT, advantage; 5. 1. 15

THROUGHFARE, thoroughfare; 1. 2. 9

THROUGHLY, thoroughly; 2. 4. 12; 3. 6. 36

THUNDER-STONE, thunderbolt; 4. 2. 271

TICKLE, (i) please; 1. 1. 85; (ii) disturb by tickling; 4. 2. 210

TIED, bound by ties (of gratitude); 1. 6. 23

TIME, (i) time of life; 1. 1. 43; (ii) present state of affairs; 2. 4. 4; 4. 3. 21, 33; (iii) life-time, life; 3. 3. 73; (iv) 'good time', happy issue (see note); 4. 2. 108

TINCT, colour (not pre-Sh. in this sense); 2. 2. 23

TIRE, feed ravenously; 3. 4. 95

TITAN, sun-god, sun; 3. 4. 164

TITLE, 'in title', nominally; 1. 4. 87

TO, (i) for; 1. 4. 105; 1. 5. 66; (ii) compared with; 3. 2. 10

TOMBOY, wanton; 1. 6. 121

TONGUE, utter; 5. 4. 146

TOUCH (sb.), feeling (here, of pain); 1. 1. 135

TOUCH (vb.), wound; 4. 3. 4; 5. 3. 10

TOY, trifle; 4. 2. 193

TRIAL, test (of faith or virtue); 3. 6. 11

TRICK, knack; 3. 3. 86

TRIMS, fine attire; 3. 4. 165

TRIP, detect in an error; 5. 5. 35

TRIUMPH, public festivity; 4. 2. 193

TROTH, truth; 5. 5. 274; 'good troth', ellipt., in truth; 3. 6. 47

TROW?, do you think?; 1. 6. 46

TRUE, (i) loyal; 3. 5. 158, 160; 4. 3. 18, 42; 5. 5. 87; (ii) honest; 2. 3. 71, 72; 3. 4. 58

TRULY, faithfully; 1. 6. 209

TRUTH, fidelity; 3. 2. 7, 12; 5. 5. 107

TRY, test; 1. 5. 18, 21; 1. 6. 172

TUNE (sb.), tone, accent; 5. 5. 238

TUNE (vb.), attune, (fig.); 5. 5. 465

TWINNED, as like as twins (not pre-Sh. in any sense); 1. 6. 34

'TWIXT, (aphetic form) betwixt; 1. 6. 33; 3. 2. 68

TYRANNOUS, violent; 1. 3. 36

TYRANT, cruel, unjust person possessed of power; 1. 1. 84

UNCROSSED, with debts not crossed out (first here in this sense); 3. 3. 26

UNDERGO, (i) undertake; 1. 4. 140; 3. 5. 111; (ii) endure; 3. 2. 7

UNDER-PEEP, peep below (first here); 2. 2. 20

UNDERTAKE, (i) take in hand to deal with; 2. 1. 24; (ii) venture; 4. 2. 142

UNDONE, ruined; 4. 2. 123

UNFLEDGED (fig.), inexperienced (not pre-Sh.; always fig. in Sh.); 3. 3. 27

UNFOLD, (i) amplify; 1. 1. 26; (ii) display; 2. 3. 96; (iii) make a communication by uttering; 5. 5. 313

UNLAID, not exorcised (first here in this sense); 4. 2. 278

UNLEARNT, untaught; 4. 2. 178

UNLIKE, improbable; 5. 5. 354

UNPARAGONED, matchless; 1. 4. 79; 2. 2. 17

UNPAVED, without 'stones', i.e. (jocular) castrated (here only); 2. 3. 31

UNPEOPLE, strip bare (of persons); 1. 5. 79

UNPRIZABLE, inestimable (not pre-Sh.); 1. 4. 89

UNSPEAKING, incapable of effective speech; 5. 5. 178

UNSUNNED, untouched by the sun, hence, unmelted; 2. 5. 13

UNTENDERED, unoffered, i.e. unpaid (second of two exx. in O.E.D.); 3. 1. 10

UNTIE, explain; 5. 4. 148

UP, roused; 3. 3. 107

UPCAST (see note); 2. 1. 2

UPON, supported by; 1. 6. 134

USE, (i) customary exercise; 3. 1. 54; (ii) need; 4. 4. 7

UTTERANCE, 'at utterance', to the last extremity; 3. 1. 71

VANTAGE, (i) opportunity; 1. 3. 24; 2. 3. 45; (ii) benefit; 5. 5. 198

VARIABLE, various; 1. 6. 133

VARLET, rascal; 4. 2. 83

VAULT, mount (fig.); 1. 6. 133

VENGE, avenge; 1. 6. 91

VENT, (i) emit; 1. 2. 4; (ii) make known; 5. 3. 56

VENTURE (see note); 1. 6. 122

VERBAL, verbose (see note); 2. 3. 106

VICIOUS, wrong; 5. 5. 65

VIEW (see note); 3. 4. 148

VIPEROUS, malignant; 3. 4. 39

VOUCH, affirm with certainty; 1. 4. 56

VOUCHER, guarantee; 2. 2. 39

VOYAGE, hostile expedition (fig.); 1. 4. 157

WAGE (vb.), wager; 1. 4. 131

WAGGISH, roguish; 3. 4. 158

WANTON, pampered child; 4. 2. 8

WARRANT, pledge; 1. 4. 57

WATCH (sb.), wakefulness; 3. 4. 41

WATCH (vb.), stay awake; 2. 4. 68

WEATHER, adverse weather (rain, wind, frost, etc.); 3. 3. 64

WEEDS, clothes; 5. 1. 23

WELL, (i) (expressing acquiescence), 'very well'; 1. 2. 39; (ii) almost fully; 5. 4. 104

WHAT HO!, form of call or summons; 1. 6. 138, 147, 154

WHEN AS, when; 5. 4. 138; 5. 5. 435

WHILES, while; 1. 6. 66

WHILST, until; 3. 6. 39

WHORESON, epithet of abuse; 2. 1. 3, 13

WILL, (i) desire; 1. 6. 46; (ii) command; 4. 2. 334

WIN OF, get the better of; 1. 1. 121

WINDOW, shutter (cf. *J.C.* G.) (fig.), eyelid; 2. 2. 22

WINGED, having flown; 4. 2. 348

WINK, shut the eyes; 5. 4. 186, 190

WINKING, with eyes closed; 2. 3. 23; 2. 4. 89

WINTER-GROUND (see note); 4. 2. 229

WINTERLY (fig.), harsh (here first fig.); 3. 4. 13

WITCH, wizard; 1. 6. 165

WIT, intelligence; 1. 2. 29; 2. 1. 8

WITHOUT, outside; 4. 2. 307

WITNESS, testify to; 3. 4. 66

WIVING, marriage; 5. 5. 167

WOODMAN, hunter; 3. 6. 28

WORD, (i) represent as in words (nonce-use); 1. 4. 15; (ii) speak the words of (a song); 4. 2. 240

WORM, serpent; 3. 4. 35

WOULD, wish; 1. 2. 20, 21, etc.

WRING, writhe; 3. 6. 78

WRIT, command; 3. 7. 1

WRY, go wrong; 5. 1. 5

YOKE, join; 4. 2. 19, 51

YOND, yonder; 3. 3. 10; 4. 2. 292

ZEPHYR, a mild, gentle breeze (prop. the W. wind); 4. 2. 172